T0224146

IFIP Advances in Information and Communication Technology   416

IFIP – The International Federation for Information Processing

IFIP was founded in 1960 under the auspices of UNESCO, following the First World Computer Congress held in Paris the previous year. An umbrella organization for societies working in information processing, IFIP's aim is two-fold: to support information processing within its member countries and to encourage technology transfer to developing nations. As its mission statement clearly states,

> IFIP's mission is to be the leading, truly international, apolitical organization which encourages and assists in the development, exploitation and application of information technology for the benefit of all people.

IFIP is a non-profitmaking organization, run almost solely by 2500 volunteers. It operates through a number of technical committees, which organize events and publications. IFIP's events range from an international congress to local seminars, but the most important are:

- The IFIP World Computer Congress, held every second year;
- Open conferences;
- Working conferences.

The flagship event is the IFIP World Computer Congress, at which both invited and contributed papers are presented. Contributed papers are rigorously refereed and the rejection rate is high.

As with the Congress, participation in the open conferences is open to all and papers may be invited or submitted. Again, submitted papers are stringently refereed.

The working conferences are structured differently. They are usually run by a working group and attendance is small and by invitation only. Their purpose is to create an atmosphere conducive to innovation and development. Refereeing is also rigorous and papers are subjected to extensive group discussion.

Publications arising from IFIP events vary. The papers presented at the IFIP World Computer Congress and at open conferences are published as conference proceedings, while the results of the working conferences are often published as collections of selected and edited papers.

Any national society whose primary activity is about information processing may apply to become a full member of IFIP, although full membership is restricted to one society per country. Full members are entitled to vote at the annual General Assembly, National societies preferring a less committed involvement may apply for associate or corresponding membership. Associate members enjoy the same benefits as full members, but without voting rights. Corresponding members are not represented in IFIP bodies. Affiliated membership is open to non-national societies, and individual and honorary membership schemes are also offered.

Arthur Tatnall Tilly Blyth Roger Johnson (Eds.)

Making the History of Computing Relevant

IFIP WG 9.7 International Conference, HC 2013
London, UK, June 17-18, 2013
Revised Selected Papers

 Springer

Volume Editors

Arthur Tatnall
Victoria University
City Flinders Campus, PO Box 14428, Melbourne, VIC 8001, Australia
E-mail: arthur.tatnall@vu.edu.au

Tilly Blyth
Science Museum
Exhibition Road, South Kensington, London SW7 2DD, UK
E-mail: tilly.blyth@sciencemuseum.ac.uk

Roger Johnson
Computer Conservation Society
24 Comet Close, Ash Vale, Aldershot, Hampshire, GU12 5SG, UK
E-mail: r.johnson@bcs.org.uk

ISSN 1868-4238   e-ISSN 1868-422X
ISBN 978-3-662-52521-0   e-ISBN 978-3-642-41650-7
DOI 10.1007/978-3-642-41650-7
Springer Heidelberg New York Dordrecht London

CR Subject Classification (1998): K.2, K.3, K.8.0, H.5, I.3.7, K.4

Typesetting: Camera-ready by author, data conversion by Scientific Publishing Services, Chennai, India

Printed on acid-free paper

Springer is part of Springer Science+Business Media (www.springer.com)

Preface

Why is a study of the history of computing important? Displaying and examining the remains of old mainframe and mini-computers is of considerable interest to those who were involved in building or using them, but for others, these displays or the descriptions of this technology are of little relevance and are difficult to engage with. Many people have a modest appreciation of how electronic digital computing has developed over the last 70 years, but they understand (or care) little about details of the configurations of these machines or how they differ from modern computers. How can we turn our histories into a form that people today can understand and appreciate?

The articles in this book have resulted from a conference – Making the History of Computing Relevant– held in the Science Museum, London, in June 2013. The conference costs were completely sponsored by Google. The aim of the conference was to discuss what needs to be done to make the history of computing relevant and interesting to the general public today: to discuss how we can display the *meaning* of computing and make it "real." Would shifting the emphasis from the technology itself to how it was used make a difference? How about stories of the designers, builders, and users of these computers? Would the use of replicas, re-builds, or simulations make this history more interesting? What lessons does history tell us about the possible future of the digital revolution? The conference was organized by IFIP WG 9.7, Science Museum, British Computer Conservation Society, and Google.

The articles in this book were selected from those presented at the conference, and the authors were given an opportunity to improve them, before publication, based on conference feedback. All have been peer reviewed. The book contains several sections to provide some coherence to the articles:

- The Importance of Storytelling in Museums
- Spotlight on Some Key Collections and Their Future Plans
- Thoughts on Expanding the Audience for Computing History
- Spotlight on some Research Projects
- Integrating History with Computer Science Education
- Putting the History of Computing into Different Contexts
- Celebrating Nostalgia for Games – And Its Potential as Trojan Horse
- The Importance and Challenges of Working Installations
- Reconstruction Stories

The chapters cover a wide range of topics related to the history of computing, and offer a number of different approaches to making this history relevant. These range from discussion of approaches to describing and analyzing the history through storytelling and education to description of various collections, working installations, and reconstruction projects.

June 2013   Arthur Tatnall
                                                              Tilly Blyth
                                                              Roger Johnson

Organization

Program Committee

Arthur Tatnall (Chair)	IFIP WG9.7, Australia
David Anderson	IFIP WG9.7, UK
Tilly Blyth	Science Museum, UK
Martin Campbell-Kelly	UK
John Impagliazzo	USA
Roger Johnson	CCS, UK
Lars Leide	IEEE Annals, Denmark
JochenViehoff	Heinz Nixdorf MuseumsForum, Germany
Lynette Webb	Google, UK

Local Organizing Committee

Tilly Blyth (Chair), Science Museum
Roger Johnson, CCS
Lynette Webb, Google
Selina Pang, Science Museum
Arthur Tatnall, IFIP WG9.7

Table of Contents

Integrating History with Computer Science Education

Putting the History of Computing into Different Contexts

Celebrating Nostalgia for Games – And Its Potential as Trojan Horse

The Importance and Challenges of Working Installations

Reconstruction Stories

Part I

The Importance of Storytelling in Museums

Exhibiting the Online World: A Case Study

Marc Weber

Internet History Program Founder and Curator, Computer History Museum, Mountain View, California, USA
marc@webhistory.org

Abstract. The online world and its origins is one of the most obviously relevant areas of computing history to the general public. It is also one of the hardest to effectively interpret and display. This paper discusses the challenges of exhibiting the complex and mostly intangible online world – sometimes called "cyberspace" – in a museum context. These include not just display challenges, but also the difficulties of framing this complex, wide ranging, and largely unknown history in an accessible way. It presents some of the techniques we've developed as solutions at the Computer History Museum, with the hope they may contribute to an exchange of ideas. These techniques are still evolving. The three relevant galleries in our permanent exhibition form the first comprehensive exhibit on the history of the online world. A current temporary exhibit and five small permanent ones in development focus on specific areas of cyberspace.

Keywords: Online, Web history, Internet history, networking history, cyberspace, computer history, exhibit, museum, social media, Computer History Museum, computer, telecommunications.

1   Introduction

> "Writing about music is like dancing about architecture"
> *- origin uncertain, often attributed to Martin Mull*

Of all the areas of computing and telecommunications history, the online world is perhaps the most obviously and personally relevant to a wide variety of audiences. Whether you're a Maasai tribesman buying and selling cattle on your mobile phone, or a Norwegian bride walking to the altar with the groom you met online, it is hard to think of an area of modern life that is *not* being radically changed by the Web, the Internet, and mobile data. It is also hard to think of a field where even the wilder hyperbole about its importance has a better chance of turning out true.

When it comes to making online history relevant, that's the good news. The bad news is that the mercurial, complex, immaterial reaches of cyberspace are some of the hardest subjects to pin down and effectively display.

There are two main problems. First, the online world is insubstantial and more of a process than a thing, offering few easily exhibitable forms. Second, it's complicated.

A. Tatnall, T. Blyth, and R. Johnson (Eds.): HC 2013, IFIP AICT 416, pp. 3–24, 2013.

The same wide-reaching impacts that make cyberspace important also mean that even its simplest stories quickly involve different technologies, and geographies, and politics. Telling them often requires a heavy burden of context and framing "backstories" just to make them intelligible.

A further wrinkle is that many people barely realize the online world has a history at all, or that its predecessors have potential lessons to teach us that go far beyond computing and touch on the most basic ways we share, navigate, and create knowledge.

At the Computer History Museum, we grappled with all of the issues above when we developed our permanent exhibition "Revolution: The First 2000 Years of Computing," which opened at the start of 2011. Taken together the "Networking and the Web" and "Mobile Computing" galleries, which I curated, form the first comprehensive exhibit on the origins of the online world. The parallel Web version of the exhibition[1] contains all of the same content plus more. We've continued to refine our palette of techniques with a temporary exhibit on the origins of "surrogate travel"

Fig. 1. A wearable costume of PegMan from Google Maps with Street View stands guard over the front desk

---

[1]   Revolution: The First 2000 Years of Computing," Web version. The Computer History Museum, 2011. http://www.computerhistory.org/revolution

and Google Maps with Street View[2], and with our current project, an upcoming exhibit on game-changing software[3] that will include in-depth case studies of Wikipedia, SMS text messaging, World of Warcraft, and iTunes. I'm the curator for all but the latter two.

We hope that by sharing these challenges and the solutions we chose, we may contribute to an exchange of ideas. A critical-long term goal of our Internet History Program is to make the history of the online world more accessible and useful, both to the public and to decision makers – who can draw from the lessons of its past in determining its future.

2   Exhibiting the Immaterial

The online world that increasingly absorbs our time and energy, fills the business pages of now-online newspapers, and makes or breaks regional economies is quite

Fig. 2. In the panel above the lighted screenshots are the dominant visual, with artifacts and text below as support

---

[2] "Going Places: A History of Google Maps with Street View." @CHM blog, the Computer History Museum, 2012. http://www.computerhistory.org/atchm/going-places-a-history-of-google-maps-with-street-view

[3] "Make Software, Change the World!" @CHM blog, the Computer History Museum, 2012. http://www.computerhistory.org/atchm/make-software-change-the-world/

insubstantial. If an observer from the past were to land in our time, he or she would be struck by how many people were staring into glowing, flickering, ever-changing rectangles. Some of the rectangles are hand-sized, like your smartphone. Others sit on desks or stands. The biggest cover walls. In the future, personal ones may be constantly suspended on the edge of our vision in heads-up displays like Google Glass. *The Onion* satirized this modern reality with "Report: 90% Of Waking Hours Spent Staring At Glowing Rectangles."[4]

An obvious technique for physical exhibits, then, is to pin and display some of the fleeting images on those glowing rectangles onto yet more special rectangles within the gallery, in the form of screenshots. We do exactly that, as you can see in these pictures from the "Web" gallery of our permanent "Revolution" exhibition (Figs. 2 and 3).

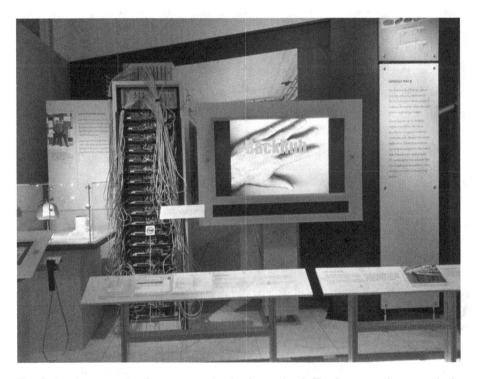

Fig. 3. Another example of a screen as the dominant visual. The image on the screen is the original logo for what became Google, called "BackRub." That's Larry Page's hand.

---

4   "Report: 90% Of Waking Hours Spent Staring At Glowing Rectangles." *The Onion*, 2009. 15 June 2009. http://www.theonion.com/articles/report-90-of-waking-hours-spent-staring-at-glowing,2747/

The Museum's VP of Collections and Exhibitions, Kirsten Tashev, intentionally took this a step further when she reversed the usual order of exhibits and put the screenshots up high as the star attractions, with a few intriguing objects in cases below to add texture. With the vivid lighted images and jewel-like detail of the objects, it is a powerful, sometimes beautiful technique.

But of course the online world is not just static images. It is more like an ongoing conversation, or a literature; an interactive experience that unfolds over months and years of practice and immersion. How can a visitor break into such an extended conversation in just a few minutes?

An obvious answer is to provide re-creations of the live online system itself. Simply let the visitor login to Minitel, the French online system that was a 1980s dress rehearsal for the Web, or browse early Web sites on original browsers, or surf the rich online discussions on the PLATO educational system. After all, the four playable games in our "Games" gallery – Pong, Adventure, PacMan, and Spacewar! – are extremely popular interactives (Figure 4).

Fig. 4. These playable games from the 1960s, '70s, and '80s are a popular interactive

Alas, it's not always so straightforward when it comes to complex online systems, whether Gopher or Minitel. Even if the original software exists and can be run reliably, there's a big potential obstacle: Learning! Games are literally *designed* to be fun. They're also designed to be quick and easy to get started, however hard to master.

Online systems are different. You may remember your early ventures into cyberspace through the glow of nostalgia. Or perhaps with mild disdain for what now seems like rudimentary technology. But either way, it's easy to forget the hours and the false steps it took your newbie self to get comfortable on the Web, or CompuServe, or whatever.

Three years ago the Museum helped host a spectacular multi-day commemoration of the 50th anniversary of the PLATO online system. As part of it the people at the PLATO History Foundation lovingly assembled a collection of PLATO terminals from several eras, connected to a working re-enactment of the system. For original members of this close-knit community it was clearly an important, even moving experience to login once again to the familiar orange screens. But I noticed that my feet weren't pulling me toward the re-enactment area where the terminals sat in front of low, comfortable chairs.

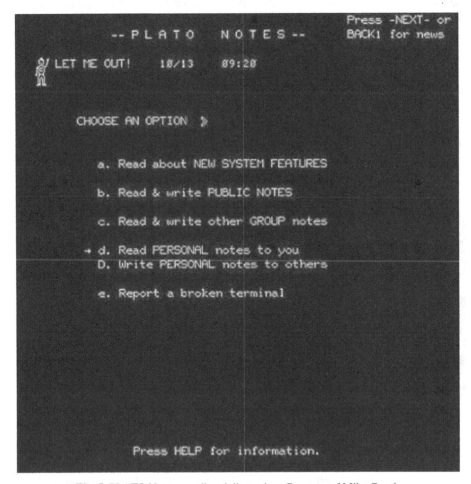

Fig. 5. PLATO Notes, email and discussion. Courtesy of Mike Capek

I'd never used PLATO and I was curious to know what it looked and felt like. But I realized I wasn't looking forward to the actual experience of getting started. It felt like work, like a tutorial in an unfamiliar piece of software, which is precisely what it was. It seemed like the kind of task to do at home or at my desk rather than in the middle of a conference. Now there were pioneers to meet, pictures to take, tasks waiting in my inbox. I eventually pushed myself, and spent quite a while playing with PLATO Notes and various educational modules. It was easy to use, and just as innovative as the old-timers said, and I'm glad I did it. But I've been studying the online world for nearly two decades. If a Web historian has to push himself to play with a historic system at an event, how much interest can you count on from the average casual museum visitor, pressed for time on a gallery floor?

It is also hard to say whether my session of mostly poking around and figuring out the lay of the land gave me any real sense of what an experienced PLATO user would actually do online. I imagine he or she would be more likely to jump straight into a rich conversation thread, for example, than spend time trying to figure out the commands that make PLATO Notes work. It can sometimes be more useful to look over the shoulder of an experienced guide than try to improvise a self-guided tour. Why not video where the expert goes, like a dashboard camera in cyberspace?

That's what we did in the Web gallery of "Revolution", where visitors can watch Web pioneer Kevin Hughes demo and explain a variety of key sites in "Surfing the Web in the Early 1990s" (Figure 6). It's also how we show the pioneering 1978 Aspen Movie Map in our temporary exhibit on the history of "surrogate travel" and Google Maps with Street View.

Fig. 6. At this personal video station, Web and graphics pioneer Kevin Hughes takes visitors on a guided tour of key early Web sites

A common rule of thumb with museum interactives is that they have less than 30 seconds to "hook" the visitor with some rewarding experience before the visitor loses interest, and *if* the hook works, perhaps another three to four minutes for the whole interaction. When it comes to raw, live content, many video games can and do make the cut. Surfing simple and appealing historic Web sites should also work well – at least as long as Web-surfing remains a familiar act for most visitors!

Fig. 7. This original early 1980s videotape shows a narrated demo of the pioneering Aspen Movie Map, which offered many of the features of Google Maps with Street View

But just as in the physical world, when it comes to more complex online tasks or environments visitors often benefit from a guided tour. These can range from simple video clips of online systems (Figure 7), narrated or not, up to various kinds of structured interactives. For instance, our upcoming Wikipedia exhibit may include an interactive that guides visitors through the basic process of editing Wiki articles. The structured portion of our Google Earth interactive let's users choose guided tours of historic Silicon Valley sites from the Hewlett-Packard garage to Netscape (Figure 8). But once at those sites, they are free to browse independently.

The rules change for the Web version of exhibits. Here the visitor is often comfortably seated somewhere quiet, rather than slogging through a gallery with finite energy and time. As we discover stable, permanent emulations of past online systems we hope to link to them from the Web version of "Revolution," [5] which includes all the content in the physical exhibition plus more. In my view, online is the right place to freely explore ancient online environments. This is where interested visitors, researchers, and students may truly get to know the many "webs" that came before the Web at their own pace.

Fig. 8. This giant Google Earth station lets visitors take a guided tour of Silicon Valley, or explore Earth, Mars, and the Moon on their own

Of course, only a few historic online systems are available in emulated form. Of those that still exist at all, a number require original hardware, which has its own issues; old computer equipment is mostly fragile, sometimes rare, and requires ongoing investments of time and money for maintenance and training. The result is that such setups are easiest to use occasionally or intermittently. Examples include special events, such as the PLATO commemoration, and scheduled demonstrations.

For instance, the Museum does scheduled demos of restored or historic machines including an early 1960s DEC minicomputer (where visitors can play the first shoot-em-up game against its creator), a medium-sized 1960s IBM business computer, and a mechanical Babbage Difference Engine. The PC "Explainer Stations" in development will give visitors hands-on experience with classic Macs and IBM PCs with a docent available to assist. A very early Galaxy arcade game is on temporary exhibit and fully playable. Similar models could be extended to classic online systems.

---

[5] "Revolution: The First 2000 Years of Computing," Web version. The Computer History Museum, 2011. http://www.computerhistory.org/revolution

Fig. 9. These early 1970s Galaxy arcade game consoles are on temporary exhibit and fully playable

In general, one of the biggest obstacle to direct re-creations of online systems is social interaction. A standalone early Web site or 1980s Minitel site is still quite meaningful without other live users. But a 1980s CompuServe chat room, a virtual world from the 1970s on, or a modern Twitter feed is far less so. To re-create such systems is like trying to freeze and reproduce the back and forth of a live, group conversation.

For highly social online systems like virtual worlds, some researchers have essentially had to give up on trying to meaningfully preserve the system itself. For them, video has become a standard way to capture the look and feel of the online experience *not* just for exhibits, but for preservation purposes. As the Web returns to the more social models and user-generated content that marked many early systems, the preservation of ordinary Web sites may face similar issues.

3   Audience Appeal

Objects vary a great deal in their natural "exhibitability," to use an awkward-sounding term. The spectrum can resemble Maslow's hierarchy of needs[6] in reverse, running from the personal and visual down to the dry and abstract. At the top might be

---

[6]   Maslow, A.H. (1943). A theory of human motivation. *Psychological Review, 50*(4), 370–96.

paintings and sculpture, since like most art they are purposely made to be interesting. High up, too, are small personal objects, jewelry and watches and such. Such items are carefully designed and easy for a visitor to "read." Their use is usually clear, as is their connection with the lives of their one-time owners.

Objects linked to taboo subjects like sex and violence score high, of course, from flint daggers to lingerie. Then there's nearly anything connected with vehicles, old or new, which perpetually fascinate, and all manner of machines with shiny moving parts. Then come the rest, wending their way down to things like ordinary documents and the sorts of anonymous enclosures that house much "back end" computer equipment.

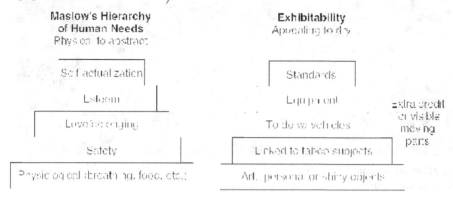

Fig. 10. Hierarchy of "exhibitability," at right

A number of computers and peripherals themselves can push one or another of the hot buttons above, from those in vehicles (Lunar Lander computer), to weapons (fire control computers), to clothing (wearable computing), and more. Some manage to tick multiple boxes, like the guidance computers for intercontinental ballistic missiles.

As we move closer to the online world, the easy pickings get scarcer. But there's still one relatively rich vein of "exhibitability": mobile computing, whose later history veers almost completely online. The little computers are a relative snap to display, since they're small and intimate enough to get much of the same design treatment, and human connection, as other poignant personal objects. Though in one sense they are just more life support systems for "glowing rectangles", mobile computers are far more different from each other – and thus intriguing – than their full-sized desktop cousins.

But the problem of how to show off *their* little rectangles remains. The thorniest question with the Mobile Computing gallery in "Revolution" was whether and how to show the actual contents of the screens, the software that makes them go. No option is perfect. To not show the screens at all would be like showing half of the device, especially with smartphones and handhelds where the software is often completely integrated. Trying to mock up the screen in place would look fake, the way smartphones are displayed today at stores that lack the budget for live demo models. The compromise we settled on is to show screenshots in a rotating picture frame positioned behind a cluster of machines. When we can find contemporary ads that clearly show the screen, we use those.

Fig. 11. In the section shown above, screenshots of the software from the physical objects on display is shown on the video screens

Fig. 12. A related example, where the large screen handles the task of showing the Palm software in action, through old TV advertisements as well as static screenshots

4   Exhibiting the Invisible

There is a final frontier, a place where the last crutch of easily exhibitable items gets kicked away. Behind the glowing screens that while away our hours lies an enormous infrastructure, one that runs out from our home Ethernet routers and spans the globe with wires, and server farms, and undersea cables, and satellites, and radio towers. The recent book *Tubes* by Andrew Blum[7] explores this physical structure of the online world.

But even though there's so much physical stuff, millions of tons of equipment power-hungry enough to suck down over two percent of the world's total production of electricity, there's a big problem when it comes to putting it on display. Much of it looks the same, and has for decades. Even removing a front panel often just reveals standardized circuit boards and power supplies with few obvious differences to the layperson's eye. In fact, it can be hard to tell from just looking whether, say, a given set of featureless cabinets in a windowless back room are for computer networking or telephone systems.

So how *do* you exhibit these underpinnings of the online world, explain the origins of the "plumbing" layers like the Internet where bits get moved around – but there may not even be any friendly screens or human interface of any kind? In developing the "Networking" gallery of "Revolution," this was precisely the challenge.

You can see gears move on a steam engine, or a Babbage engine. Even the old electromechanical telephone switches are impressively intricate and physical. But you can't see electrons move over a network. The action, the variety, the magic that eventually brings our screens to life is all on the inside, invisible. Also barely visible are the marks of the bitter, decades-long standards wars that form much of the history of networking.

Had ARCNET won the battle to wire the office instead of Ethernet, the only obvious difference might be a slightly different shape of connector to plug into the back of your machine. Had the French CYCLADES network become the standard for connecting networks to each other, instead of the now-familiar Internet protocols, there might be no physically visible difference at all. The equipment could look just the same. But the economics of the online world, the balance of power over standards, and in some cases what you can and cannot do on your glowing screens would be quite different.

So what do we do in the "Networking" gallery? Of course we show particularly meaningful or representative examples of the sorts of often "faceless" behind-the-scenes equipment that makes the online world run: a refrigerator-sized hardened IMP from the original ARPAnet; a Cisco router; a dish antenna; a Google server rack, and so on. But one or two of each major class of equipment is usually enough.

---

[7]   Blum, Andrew. *Tubes: A Journey to the Center of the Internet*. Ecco, 2012.

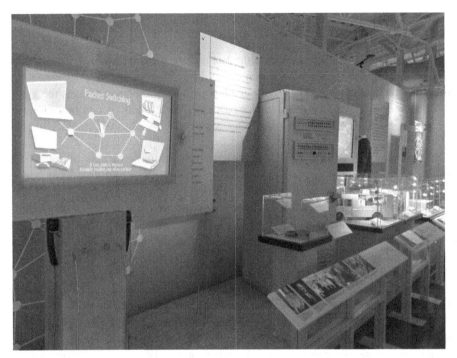

Fig. 13. A portion of the "Networking" gallery in "Revolution." An animated video explaining packet switching is in the foreground. A refrigerator-sized IMP (Interface Message Processor) from the ARPANET, which led to the Internet, is behind.

Beyond that, exhibiting a networking design like packet switching or a standard like Ethernet is rather like displaying the wind. Invisible itself, it can still be seen by its effects. This is where you enter the same rarified realm as exhibits on other abstract topics, from math to the hard sciences, or on processes like cellular respiration. The solution is to sharply outline the impact of the law, or concept, or other insubstantial thing on the tangible world around it. You show its effect through people, objects, interactives, and other things that *do* have a clear exhibitability – and become a kind of bait. It's like boldly outlining the visible arc of grass and trees as they bow to the unseen wind.

When creating an exhibit you have the luxury of hindsight. So those visible effects don't necessarily have to follow chronology. For instance, we start the "Networking" gallery with a common grounding theme throughout the exhibition; tracing the old roots of the subject to be explored. Here this takes the form of an interactive telegraph key. Visitors can tap out their initials, and feel under their fingers the staccato manifestation of the 200 year old "big idea" that underpins nearly everything in the gallery and the Museum: Transporting information over electrified wires. Over the centuries the wires have shrunk too small to see, and the switches have gone from something that filled your hand to millions per square inch. But the principle is the same, from Morse keys to ENIAC to the iPhone.

Fig. 14. Photogenic 19th century telecommunications equipment

The gallery briefly luxuriates in the gorgeous polished brass and delicate visible gears of the ultra "exhibitable" equipment from the first wired world, that of 19th century telecommunication. It shows early modems and a teletype. But then it tells the rest of the story with an increasing palette of indirect techniques. The principles of packet switching get covered in an animated movie. Pictures and stories about people – from the colorful networking and personal computing legend Bob Taylor, to Al Gore – literally flesh out the conflicts and ideas that drove the effort to tie computers together into a world-spanning net. Internet protocols get represented by a lovely scale model of the research van where they were first fully tested; The real van is in the Museum's collection. Books, t-shirts, and reprints of newspaper articles come in to illustrate particular points. A variety of network connectors show some of the few visible manifestations of the bitter and costly standards wars that raged through the 1970s and '80s.

More than half of the stories in our upcoming exhibit on game-changing software are about the online world. They will draw on and extend the full palette of techniques we've used to tell online stories in "Revolution." But the structure of this exhibit, "Make Software, Change the World," highlights another technique in itself: the case study. By going in-depth with real-world examples, from Wikipedia to iTunes to World of Warcraft, the exhibit will anchor the sometimes insubstantial tendrils of cyberspace with specific people, and places, and uses.

Fig. 15. Scale model of the SRI packet radio van, where the Internet, mobile data networks, and voice over IP (think Skype) were prototyped

5   Between Telecommunications, Literature, and Computers

Computers started as calculating machines made from spare parts of the then-century-old telecommunications industry. They were later converted into communications and knowledge devices. A century from now, they may be seen as part of a larger stream of the history of technology for dealing with information. But today they still straddle worlds. This creates tensions when it comes to practical exhibits. Is the online world part of computing, or of the history of books and sharing information, or of telecommunication? All solutions are compromises.

The online world doesn't appear out of thin air. Its glowing rectangles are attached to computers, and those computers to networking equipment. But how much to exhibit these physical "support systems" for cyberspace within an exhibit on the online world can depend on context. Is the online exhibit standalone, or is it part of a bigger exhibit on computers, or communications, or something else?

As I've mentioned, much networking equipment is short on exhibitability. Computers themselves, though, can push some hot buttons. Yet the stories that make these computers interesting often have little to do with any online roles. For instance, the story of early Apples is animated by the rivalry between Jobs and Gates and the funkily home-built nature of early PCs. The SAGE system was a milestone for networking with 23 centers connected in the 1950s. But it was equally important

Fig. 16. Just a support system for going online? SAGE terminal, Real Time Computing gallery, "Revolution."

for interactive computing, and use of a pointing device, and military computing, and more. Using such computers in a pure cyberspace exhibit can potentially shortchange their other roles. But putting them in other galleries reduces the stock of interesting online objects.

We put SAGE in the "Real-Time Computing" gallery, and the Apples are with PCs. Both are referred to in Networking and the Web. But it's an imperfect compromise, especially in the physical exhibit where there's no convenient way to cross-link.

6   Framing Complexity

Historical common knowledge is dramatically uneven. Most people have some idea of where the airplane came from, or the printing press, or spaceflight. But only a very few can tell you much about the origins of television or broadcast radio. Unfortunately for exhibit purposes, the online world falls into one of these societal blind spots.

The fact that most people are quite ignorant about the real origins of the online world is a double-edged sword. It makes it easy to offer enticing revelations as "hooks"; for instance that the Web was originally meant to be as participatory as a giant Wikipedia, or that social networking features go back to the 1960s. But it also means that exhibits need huge amounts of backstory and framing context for each section, adding to both the size of any display and to potential information overload for visitors.

Both of these effects are intensified by another factor. While most visitors have no preconceptions at all about, say, the origins of analog computers or disk drives, the Web and Internet are so much a part of modern life that nearly everybody seems to recall a few bits and pieces about how they got started, often wrong.

Fig. 17. "Who was online?" panel conceptually groups a number of disparate systems and explores who used them. Networking and the Web, "Revolution" exhibition.

6.1   Paradigm-Shifting Facts

Below are examples of key facts that stretch or challenge common knowledge, requiring a great deal of context and emphasis to get across. They thus presented both problems and opportunities when designing "Revolution."

6.1.1   The Web Is not the Internet!

The Web and Internet represent two completely different *levels* of the online world. They are as different from each other as TV sets from the shows that play on them, or programs from operating systems.

To many people, the Web and the Internet blend together in a kind of cyber mush; they have no idea where one starts and the other ends, and no practical reason to care. The fact that the Web is an online information system running over the basic "plumbing" provided by the underlying network – in this case the Internet – is extremely abstract to many visitors. But making this distinction is key to the narrative arc of the gallery, since each level has its own quite distinct history.

We went back and forth with possible solutions. Should we try to tell both stories in a single gallery – or have two completely separate galleries, "Networking" and "The Web"? Or compromise, and have two separate "tracks" within a single gallery?

In the end we used the two-track approach for the physical exhibition, where visitors turn left for networking ("Connecting Computers") and right for the Web ("Connecting People") and follow their chosen track along the wall. Local Area Networking like Ethernet is a semi-separate branch off of the main networking track. But we created two completely separate galleries for the Web version of the exhibition, partly because there's no clear online analog to separate but associated "tracks." Both the physical and online versions have an introductory panel called "What's the Difference Between the Web and the Internet?"

6.1.2   No Immaculate Conception
The Web and the Internet did not spring up out of nowhere. They each had predecessors and competitors, and are the survivors of fierce competitions for the system that would dominate their respective levels. The same is true of Ethernet in the realm of local networks.

Most visitors – including some computing professionals – have little idea that there were Web-like systems before the Web, or other ways of connecting computers (and computer networks) to each other than the Internet. Without this key fact, tracing the origins of cyberspace is a bit like trying to present the history of World War I to an audience that doesn't realize there was more than one side.

The cycle of invention, competition, and winnowing is a repeating theme in the history of computing and other technologies. Throughout the museum's exhibits we present not only the winning standard or company, but also explore at least a representative sampling of the losers and minor players. This structure makes immediate sense to visitors in areas where historic competition is well known, for instance "Personal Computers." But it requires more explanation for the galleries covering cyberspace.

In "Networking and the Web" and "Mobile Computing," we call out the centrality of competition in the panel text, titles, and graphics, and show at least one object to represent each major competitor. But to avoid overwhelming visitors with too many individual stories, we present the competitors as bundles. For instance, the section discussing Ethernet's fight with standards like ARCNET and Token Ring is called "Local Area Warfare". The section covering the Internet's surprise triumph over rival standards including OSI, SNA and PUP is titled "Protocol Wars"; the label for an image of Al Gore explains how his support helped the Internet beat far bigger rivals. A large lighted panel shows screenshots of a number of the Web's 1980s predecessors and competitors, titled "Walled Gardens," and the text emphasizes the "triumph of the underdog" nature of the Web's eventual victory.

6.1.3   It's Older Than You Think

From e-commerce to chat to social networking and user-generated content, most of the features we use on the Web today were already being used by tens of millions in the '80s on earlier online systems. But those systems weren't connected to each other.

Many visitors don't realize that the Web had any predecessors at all, as discussed in item two above. But in fact, starting in the early 1960s it was pre-Web online systems that pioneered most of the features we think of as "modern." The catch is that most of these earlier systems were isolated "walled gardens", available only to certain kinds of users or in certain geographic regions. Online systems in the 1960s through the '80s were a great example of William Gibson's observation that: "The future is already here; it's just not very evenly distributed."

A major focus of the "Web" sub-gallery overall is showing the surprisingly early origins of familiar features. It opens with a clay tablet to illustrate the 4500 year old roots of cross-references, now familiar as the clickable hyperlink. The "e-Commerce" section traces its roots to 19th century telegraph days. When it comes to specific aspects of online systems, say chat or virtual worlds, the gallery discusses or shows the pre-Web systems where they began.

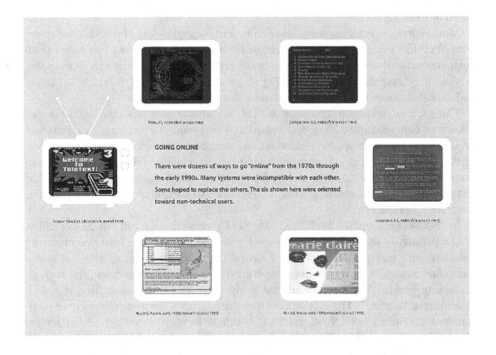

Fig. 18. "Walled Gardens" panel conceptually groups a number of 1970s and '80s online systems. Networking and the Web, "Revolution" exhibition.

6.2   Fun Facts

But not all these "revelations" require heavy lifting. A number are easily digested, gee-whiz facts that can surprise and occasionally delight visitors. For instance:

- Social and collaborative features are some of the original uses of online systems; the Web is now catching up.
- The globe was wired by the 1870s. The multinational communications industry was 100 years old when the digital computer was invented in the 1940s
- E-commerce, including spam, dates to the Victorian era
- Most early Web pioneers thought we would use directories, like Yahoo!, not search engines like Google
- Information overload is an old problem, and in the early 20th century inspired several Web-like systems based on microfilm, telegraphy, early television, etc.
- The origins of the clickable hyperlink can be traced back to cross-references between clay tablets

7   Conclusion

Showing online systems in a museum context may be as paradoxical as music criticism or dancing about architecture, as I hinted with the quote at the start of this paper. But that doesn't prevent us from trying to do it well.

The palette of techniques described in this paper represent one set of solutions to the difficulties of representing the complex, immaterial, and dynamic online world in a static gallery. We can bring the look and feel of cyberspace into that gallery with dramatic screenshots, video snippets of forays online, structured interactives, and live emulations of some simpler online environments.

When it comes to networking standards and other unseen underpinnings of cyberspace that lack a human interface, we can address the scarcity of naturally "exhibitable" objects by emphasizing related items that are more so, from iconic hardware to portraits of the personalities involved. These indirect techniques are similar to those used in other kinds of museum exhibits that deal with abstract concepts.

The huge gap between common knowledge about the origins of cyberspace and the reality is both a problem and an opportunity. The sheer amount of background information required could be overwhelming to visitors. But by choosing simple but powerful themes, like competition, and then emphasizing them repeatedly where appropriate, we can bundle a large number of separate stories into manageable frames. If this framing is done properly, the "revelations" that follow can be a fun rather than disorienting, and an important part of the visitor experience.

A problem that no single gallery or exhibit can address is the societal "blind spot" about the very existence, and importance, of the long and rich history that produced the online world. Only time, and continued efforts to both popularize that history and to integrate it into relevant academic disciplines from Internet Studies, to Computer Science, to Sociology can gradually change the common knowledge and assumptions with which visitors approach the subject.

Acknowledgements. The author thanks Kirsten Tashev, Dag Spicer, Alex Bochannek, and Emily Routman for help and advice in the preparation of this paper, and especially for all I've learned from creating exhibits together. I also thank Lynette Webb and Google for sponsoring travel to present the paper in person at the "Making the History of Computing Relevant" conference in London in June of this year.

References

1. Revolution: The First 2000 Years of Computing, Web version. The Computer History Museum (2011), `http://www.computerhistory.org/revolution`
2. Going Places: A History of Google Maps with Street View. @CHM blog, the Computer History Museum (2012), `http://www.computerhistory.org/atchm/going-places-a-history-of-google-maps-with-street-view`
3. Make Software, Change the World! @CHM blog, the Computer History Museum (2012), `http://www.computerhistory.org/atchm/make-software-change-the-world/`
4. Report: 90% of Waking Hours Spent Staring at Glowing Rectangles. The Onion (June 15, 2009), `http://www.theonion.com/articles/report-90-of-waking-hours-spent-staring-at-glowing,2747/`
5. Maslow, A.H.: A theory of human motivation. Psychological Review 50(4), 370–396 (1943)
6. Blum, A.: Tubes: A Journey to the Center of the Internet. Ecco (2012)

Narratives in the History of Computing: Constructing the *Information Age* Gallery at the Science Museum

Tilly Blyth

Keeper of Technology and Engineering, Science Museum, UK
Tilly.Blyth@sciencemuseum.ac.uk

Abstract. One of the challenges of exhibiting the complex, and mostly intangible, world of computing in a museum context is how you bring together the technology with the people involved and the information shared. The history of computing is not just a neat history of devices. Analogue, digital, mini, personal and supercomputers all reflect the material culture of information and communication technologies, but the story of information machines is a much more complex story of the interrelationship between networks of people, societal and cultural influences. This paper reflects on approaches to the display of the history of computing and suggests that a shift to narrative and users, rather than chronology and technological progress, invites a more engaging experience for the majority of visitors. It also suggests that there is an inherent value in the display of computing artefacts that goes far beyond that of working machines. Some machines can work on a profound level, not just a utilitarian one. The paper discusses the approach taken in the Science Museum's Information Age gallery, opening in September 2014.

Keywords: Museums, displays, history of computing.

1   Displaying the History of Computing

Texts on the history of computing tend to follow a standard sequential narrative - from calculating aids to mechanical, digital, and then electronic devices - the expected approach to history favours an understanding that is technologically driven. Exhibition displays of the history of computing have also tended to reflect as technocentric, chronological approach. Timelines offer a clear way in for the visitor, providing a strong structure and a clear sense of the development of a technology.

A beautiful historical example is IBM's exhibition *A Computer Perspective*, which opened in 1973 at their Corporate Exhibit Center in New York (Eames, 1973). Developed by the designers Charles and Ray Eames, the exhibit explored the history of computing though key objects in the centre of the space and a "History Wall" along the back that acted as a multi-layered timeline (1890-1950) documenting key events in the development of the computer.

Despite following a strictly linear structure that placed the technology at the heart, the "History Wall" played with ideas and people, alongside the technology, through its dense layering of labels and facts. Following an approach that can be best described as

A. Tatnall, T. Blyth, and R. Johnson (Eds.): HC 2013, IFIP AICT 416, pp. 25–34, 2013.
© IFIP International Federation for Information Processing 2013

visual hypertext, the display created connections through the careful placing of imagery, text and objects, to show a network of ideas, people and events that led to the development of calculation, automation, computation and artificial intelligence.

The Science Museum's own computing gallery, *Computing Then and Now*, which opened just a few years later in 1975, is another interesting example of how contemporary ideas about computing were mapped onto a gallery space.

Fig. 1. Science Museum's gallery *Computing Then and Now*, 1975, showing the computer terminal that allowed visitors to interact with the Imperial College computer

The gallery had analogue representations of computing on the North side and Digital on the South. It provided a progression from early aids to calculation, to a 1930s punched card office, to the development of electronic digital machines, elements of a contemporary computer (input/outputs, storage and processors), ending in state-of-the-art minicomputers. Although thematic as well as chronological, the gallery clearly provides a sequence through which visitors can build their understanding of the development of computing.

Despite the obvious benefits for audiences in terms of clarity about where they are in their gallery experience, critics of a chronological approach argue that such displays provide an interpretation of history that presents the past as an inevitable progression towards the present. This Whig historiography leads to technological determinism, where the development of technology follows a predictable and predestined path, rather than reflecting and developing according to our social structures and cultural values. Technology is thought to have an effect on society, rather than being part of a network of actors working together to create meaning and use through technological development. Clearly, if we subscribe to a social constructivist approach (Bijker, Hughes and Pinch, 1987) to the history of technology, we need to present a display with a more nuanced historical understanding, which places people and their context alongside the development of technology. We need to show how many of the routes of technological change were not pre-determined, but the result of parallel developments, or social, cultural and economic forces.

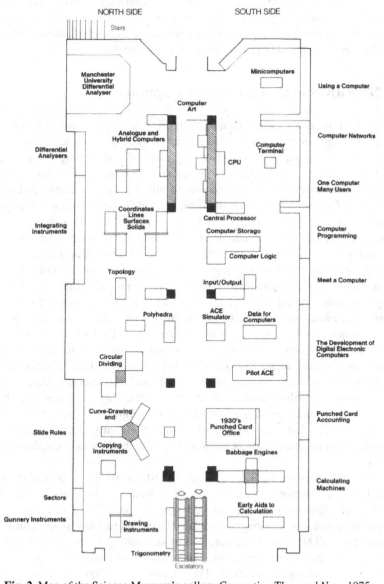

Fig. 2. Map of the Science Museum's gallery *Computing Then and Now*, 1975

This potentially shifts the display from a predictable and linear history, to view the development of computing in terms of ideas, personal motivations, or broader social and economic forces. It invites a more active relationship to our past, asking audiences to consider the social structure and knowledge frameworks in which our ancestors existed, and to consider individuals as actors in the history of technology that go far beyond the initial inventors and innovators, to those that used, developed and gave meaning to 'new' technologies .

Importantly, it also begins to bring the history of computing closer to a history of information, breaking the linear development of technology to invite visitors to see people, ideas and technology as relating and interlinking with each other. It suggests that linear and chronological displays limit the complexity of ideas we can present and limit the connections that visitors themselves may make.

2   Narratives in the History of Computing

In his book *Beyond the Glass Case* (2000) Nick Merriman suggests that people consume the past in two ways: through a personal past (a sense of the past experienced in personal terms) and through impersonal heritage (e.g. regional, national, international histories). This implies that museum curators not only have a responsibility to present the history of computing in a more dynamic and personal way because of a sense of 'good' historiography, but because of their public purpose to enthuse people in their own sense of heritage. Purely appealing to an impersonal heritage, such as the development of computing as an innovation driven story of monocausal progression, may do wonders for those who are already interested in the technology or the importance of changes in the computing industry, but it is unlikely to enthuse those who perceive themselves to have no immediate personal link to the development of computing (even though they may 'use' computers every day).

Rather than presenting the history of information as an inevitable consequence of past developments, museums can provide audiences with the tools for questioning the role and form of information technology in society. By viewing technology as a historical and cultural form, disseminated and appropriated by different users in different ways at different times, audiences are invited to orientate themselves within a broad history of information technology. In this way museums can become "enablers where people can harness their creative energies to construct a meaningful past of their own" (Merriman, 2000, p.95). Most importantly, it invites audiences to think, make leaps of imagination or comparisons with their ancestors, rather than read and learn.

So what techniques are open to museums in order to do this in an engaging way? Story telling is a common language for all of us from a young age. Through books, television and radio we have all enjoyed stories, but it is a form that has been relatively neglected in museology, particular science and technology museums. A few academics have highlighted the importance of storytelling for engaging people with science (Linett, 2013) and developing enthusiasm for technical subjects such as computer science (Impagliazzo, 2012). The museum professional Leslie Bedford

(2001) noted that 'Stories are the most fundamental way we learn. They have a beginning, a middle, and an end. They teach without preaching, encouraging both personal reflection and public discussion. Stories inspire wonder and awe; they allow a listener to imagine another time and place, to find the universal in the particular, and to feel empathy for others. They preserve individual and collective memory and speak to both the adult and the child' (p.33).

A strong story provides a great way of connecting visitors, enabling them to imagine the motivations of individuals and the constraints they were under. Each story has a linear structure, so the visitor is clear where they are in the story and how much longer they are required to focus. Importantly, if it is effective it can connect the visitor to history at an emotional level, so that they might invest more time to build a framework for understand broader historical events or connect with a scientific understanding. If the development of technology shifts from being an impersonal act that follows a predetermined route, to multiple stories that are defined by human values and beliefs, then visitors are more able to project their own thoughts, feelings and memories onto the story.

3   Shifting Technological History to the User

As historians and sociologists of technology and media began to question the role of the user as agents for social change in the 1980s and 90s (Bijker, Hughes and Pinch, 1987; Cowan, 1987; Silverstone, Hirsch and Morley, 1992), they illustrated the need to breakdown the linear model of technological innovation and diffusion, to show that users of technology are not passive consumers, but actively involved in the creation and domestication of technology. More recently Oudshoorn and Pinch (2003) stressed the importance of the representation of users in the co-construction of technology, whilst the historian David Edgerton (2006) suggested that we should refocus the history of technology on apparently 'old' technologies that are commonly used, as the majority of our world is reliant on the technologies we utilize, rediscover and redevelop, rather than on discoveries made at key moments of invention.

Such approaches invite technology, and in particular computing curators, to refocus the stories they tell in museums, and place users rather than innovators at the heart of the story. But what does this mean for visitors, who expect to hear about the firsts, the Eureka moment, lone engineer who invented a new approach?

I would argue that if done well, such an exhibition can be more engaging, telling stories of users as active co-producer, showing how the technology of computing is enmeshed in the culture through which it was produced and used. Rather than one significant individual, we begin to learn about teams of people working together to define a technology. The marketing materials that illuminate how the user and the non-user of new technologies were defined become vital, rather than relegated to the depths of 'trade literature'. And oral histories, that present an unofficial and often undocumented history – a 'history from below' – give a voice to many of those developers and users whose tales of technology are otherwise unheard. These can provide a rich resource for a deeper, more personal connection with technological histories and in particular with specific objects whose relevance and use might be lost.

Of course there are negative implications to a story telling approach. By their very nature, stories aren't always true and can often heighten the sense of adventure, tragedy or comedy in order to play on the audiences' emotional engagement. A story telling approach suggests a shift away from museums presenting 'factually correct' history, to the presentation of history that plays on audience feelings, presenting real historical figures as merely characters in a plot. It also presents the question; if a museum is about stories, can it also be about ideas? If the craft of a curator is to play with the experience of visitors, orchestrating moments of calm and reflection with moments of excitement and emotion, can it still invite visitors to make connections between objects and absorb ideas?

4   The Role of Objects

It is often said that for information technology, working machines are key to a museum display. Many believe that there is nothing less interesting than a dead computer, as the information and the interface are all lost from the machine. Some visitors want to look at a machine and understand 'how it works', others want to hear the noise and see how the machine was run. But technological objects can offer different types of museum experience to audiences. An object (even an apparently historically banal object) can have a power for visitors just in themselves. To focus on working machines only is to disregard the different type of experiences that an object can provide. It also disregards the craft of the curator in layering and texturing the experiences across the gallery.

In his essay 'Resonance and Wonder', the literary historian Stephen Greenblatt analyses the museum experience in terms of two types of audience response. "Resonance" is *"the power of the displayed object to reach out beyond its formal boundaries to a larger world, to evoke in the viewer the complex, dynamic cultural forces from which it has emerged"*. For Greenblatt this is essentially the knowledge and understanding provided by that object, if viewed through a cultural or historical lens. This could be the object as a working machine, or it could be the object with merely a label, inviting it to be considered in its wider context. It is about understanding the uses and instances which have created a meaningful frame for the historical artefact. In Greenblatt's words, it is "the power of the displayed object to reach out beyond its formal boundaries to a larger world".

In contrast Greenblatt's term "Wonder" refers to the object's aesthetic and poetic dimension, the power of the object "to stop the viewer in his or her tracks, to convey an arresting sense of uniqueness, to evoke an exalted attention". Greenblatt was originally referring to the arts and visual artefacts and some struggle to see how this sense of "Wonder" applies to scientific and technological artefacts. But computer and other information technologies have the power to command visitors' attention, even when their meaning or use is not commonly understood. The scale of a supercomputer computer, such as the Cray 1 from 1976, can provide visitors with a sense of awe from the bold theatrical design, or the magic of seeing "the real thing", achieved by icons such as the Apple 1 from 1976, can give visitors and exceptional sense of history.

Icons such as Charles Babbage's Difference Engine 1, with its intricate cogs and wheels, bring amazement that one individual could make such a leap of imagination.

It is the curator's role to amplify the experience of "Resonance and Wonder" through the stories that they choose to tell, the objects they display and the way the gallery is designed. Some significant objects might be presented as "design pieces" without any context or story, but purely to invite audiences to relish in the real or the beauty of the object. Others might be part of a narrative that engages the visitor emotionally in a story. A working object might focus the experience on to one type of understanding, "what did it do and how?", whereas carefully crafted locations of objects can allow visitors to make serendipitous connections, inviting the audience to think for themselves and construct their own meaning between objects.

5   Narrative in the Information Age Gallery

Opening in autumn 2014, Information Age will be based on the second floor of the museum, in what was the old shipping gallery, which is a vast $2500m^2$. The gallery tells the story of the transformations that have taken place in human communication in the last 200 years. Blending historic, iconic objects with up-to-the-minute technology and interactive media, it will expose, examine and celebrate the technology that has changed the way we share information and connect with one another.

Starting with the development of the electric telegraph in the 1830s, the gallery will tell stories through the eyes of those that invented, operated, and were affected by each new wave of technology. It is not a uniquely technological story, but a social story of the successes and failures, the brave new ideas and ambitious schemes, and of human nature and our universal need to connect with each other.

The gallery is constructed around six zones that reflect networks of people, technology and organisations: The Cable, looks at telegraphy, The Broadcast looks at radio and television; The Exchange focuses on telephony, The Constellation looks at Satellite communications, The Web looks at computing networks, and The Cell focuses on cellular mobile networks.

Each zone, or network, highlights 3 or 4 "transforming events" that are significant stories that enable visitors to experience a key moment of change through technology. A total of 21 transforming events across the gallery place the stories of users equally with those of the inventors of technology. Some present a key innovation e.g. Alexander Graham Bell's development of the telephone, but in this case the story of invention is contrasted with Bell's love story and through his competition with Elisha Gray.

In the section on computer networks, The Web, there are four stories. One story looks at the development of the world's first computer for commercial applications, the Lyons Electronic Office (LEO 1) in 1951. This doesn't just focus on the story of those who created the machine, but will highlight the importance of research and influences from a range of actors across Britain and America as knowledge about digital electronic machines is shared and developed. The teashop manageresses will also play a central role, showing how they became as much part of the 'information system' by calling in their weekly orders, as the LEO computer itself.

The other stories look at the Birth of Computer Networks: How the world's first international computer network – ARPANET – developed out of Cold War tensions in

1969; A Global Information Space: The creation of a new age by Tim Berners-Lee in 1990, where anyone can find and access information through the World Wide Web; and Computers for Users: The transformation of computers into intuitive and affordable devices in 1983 through the development of the Graphic User Interface and the launch of the Apple Lisa computer. In each story the users are actively involved in defining the meaning of the technology and the way it fits into existing social structures.

Gallery Architectural Strategy

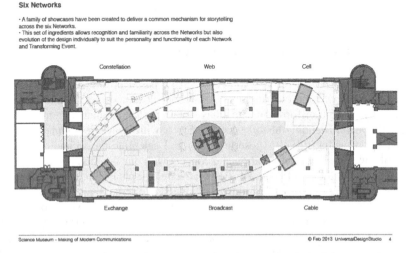

Fig. 3. Universal Design Studio (the gallery designer's) representation of the network structure across the *Information Age* gallery, 2013

Fig. 4. Representation from *Universal Design Studio* of one part of the Lyons Electronic Office (LEO 1) story on the *Information Age* gallery, 2013

We hope that this type of story and user-centric approach will create personal links for visitors and enable a dialogue with a broader audience than those already engaged with the history of computing. It should enable visitors to reflect on what the technology meant to our predecessors, and how these meanings are not given and defined by the technology, but are co-constructed with users in the way that they are consumed, marketed, used and re-appropriated.

The approach has radically altered the way the team is working on this project. It has meant that oral history and in some cases video, has become both a central tool for the research process. These multiple types of interpretation will form a very important part of the engagement of visitors on gallery, giving personality and historical context to the story, and in the longer term much of the material we collect will become a long-term digital asset within the museum's collections.

We also aim to play with Greeblatt's concepts of resonance and wonder through significant gateway objects. We have chosen particular objects for the awe and spectacle they provide to visitors. These will not be heavily interpreted through the stories, but we believe they will give a meaningful context, provide a visual pleasure and a historical anchor that can only be achieved by museum artefacts.

An example of this is the vast Russian supercomputer that will be placed in dialogue with a comparable machine from the USA, the CDC 6600. Although we only have space to display the main operating console, the scale of this machine and surprise of seeing the only Russian supercomputer from the Cold War in a Western museum collection should provide visitors with a real sense of astonishment.

6   Conclusion

The craft of the curator is in layering and texturing different types of experience across the gallery. Scientific and technical museums have tended to focus on one approach to history - chronological accounts that tell familiar technical stories of invention and progress. These appeal to a core audience who are already engaged with the history of computing, but provide few ways in to those who do not think computer history has relevance or interest for them.

The display of the history of computing, and more specifically the history of information machines, as a series of narratives that focus on the use of the machines, as much as the invention, provides museums with a real opportunity to broaden the audience for the history of computing. A people-centric approach, that sees the history of computing as a lens on society and humanity, helps to connect visitors with this technical history at a more personal level.

But where does this leave the artefacts of computing ; the historical evidence of the material culture of information processing and storage? Working machines can play an important role in helping visitors to understand the experience and environments of computing, but they should not only be considered as working tools. Greenblatt's appeal to the Resonance and Wonder of objects can be equally true for scientific and technological artefacts. If given the platform to perform, objects not only enable us to reflect on social and cultural forces, but to see the poetic and aesthetic dimensions of the machine and its design. All of these devices – our stories, users and objects – are the tools we are working with in the development of *Information Age* gallery.

References

Bedford, L.: Storytelling: The Real Work of Museums. Curator 44(1), 27–34 (2001)

Bijker, W., Hughes, T., Pinch, T. (eds.): The Social Construction of Technological Systems: New Directions in the Sociology and History of Technology. MIT Press, Cambridge (1987)

Cowan, R.S.: The Consumption Junction: A proposal for research strategies in the sociology of technology. In: Bijker, et al. (eds.) The Social Construction of Technological Systems. MIT (1987)

Eames, C., Eames, R.: A Computer Perspective. Harvard University Press (1973)

Edgerton, D.: The Shock of the Old: Technology in Global History Since 1900. Profile Books (2006)

Greenblatt, S.: Exhibition Cultures: The Poetics and Politics of Museum Display. In: Karp, I., Lavine, S. (eds.) Resonance and Wonder, ch. 3, p. 42 (1991)

Impagliazzo, J.: My Fascination with Computing History. In: Tatnall, A. (ed.) Reflections on the History of Computing. IFIP AICT, vol. 387, pp. 385–395. Springer, Heidelberg (2012)

Linett, P.: Interview: Ben Lillie on Science and the Storytelling Revival. Curator: The Museum Journal 56(1), 15–19 (2013)

Merriman, N.: Beyond the Glass Case: The Past, the Heritage and the Public, UCL Institute of Archaeology (2000)

Oudshoorn, N., Pinch, T.: Introduction: How Users and Non-Users Matter. In: Oudshoorn, N., Pinch, T. (eds.) How Users Matter: The CoConstruction of Users and Technology, pp. 1–25 (2003)

Silverstone, R., Hirsch, E., Morley, D.: Information and communication technologies and the moral economy of the household. In: Silverstone, Hirsch (eds.) Consuming Technologies, Routledge (1992)

Making History Relevant through the Provision of Education, Stories and Interactive Experiences

Arthur Tatnall[1] and Bill Davey[2]

[1] Victoria University, Melbourne, Australia
Athur.Tatnall@vu.edu.au
[2] RMIT University, Melbourne, Australia
Bill.Davey@rmit.edu.au

Abstract. What makes the history of something real and relevant to people? In this paper we suggest that people find artefacts and ideas more relevant when they can see where they fit into their own world – how they relate to their own society. The world has entered a time when Information and Communication Technologies (ICT) are becoming increasingly embedded in the way we live. ICT has become something we just take for granted. On the other hand, its history is often not seen as relevant. The mature ubiquity of ICT points to the importance of understanding its story. The history of computing should be presented in a way that opens the pathway to understanding the future. In this paper we examine some of the issues of presenting such an historical perspective, through the provision of education, stories and interactive experiences.

Keywords: History, computing, museums, exhibits, mainframes, dinosaurs, steam trains, real, relevant, education, experiences.

1   Introduction

'What is Real?' is a question addressed of one toy by another in the children's book: 'The Velveteen Rabbit'.

> *"What is REAL?" asked the Velveteen Rabbit one day, when they were lying side by side near the nursery fender, before Nana came to tidy the room. "Does it mean having things that buzz inside you and a stick-out handle?" [1 :14]*

When we encounter something new we often ask ourselves if it is 'real', by which we mean is it something that is relevant to us? Is it important enough to us to find out more about it and to get involved with it? In this paper we will address the question of what can make the history of computing relevant, or real, to people. 'Is it a real?' or 'Is it relevant?' tend to be questions asked by humans of artefacts such as old computers in an attempt to decide

Fig. 1. 'Velveteen Rabbit'

A. Tatnall, T. Blyth, and R. Johnson (Eds.): HC 2013, IFIP AICT 416, pp. 35–44, 2013.

how seriously to take them; to decide whether they are worth further investigation and could possibly be of some interest to them [2].

People only find out about something when they have some reason to do so or want to learn more about it. Some people are naturally interested in a given topic but others are not and need to be introduced to it. This has implications for the presentation of history. A person with no prior interest is unlikely to suddenly become interested. The old saying: *You can lead a horse to water, but you cannot make it drink* comes to mind. It is difficult to understand something that is outside your experience and First Generation mainframe computers are completely outside the experience of most people. Those who have lived through the computer generations certainly have experience of the history of computing, and this history is very real and relevant to them. On the other hand, anyone brought up to see a computer as a box, keyboard and screen on your desk finds mainframes completely foreign – 'are they computers?' Sixty years ago, to use a computer you needed to have a good understanding of what was going on inside it. Even thirty years ago it was desirable to have some idea of how a computer worked, but today this is not the case and so speaking about the memory, storage space or operations per second of these old machines does not necessarily mean much to most people.

Although old mainframe computers are outside the experience of most people, this is also true of dinosaurs and steam trains and almost all children find them interesting and can tell you quite a lot about them. What is the difference? Why is the history of dinosaurs innately interesting to many people but the history of computing not so? In this paper we will argue that for those who have not lived through the history of modern computing as a participant and so do not find this a fascinating topic, it is necessary to find something to attract or interest them. We suggest that this can be achieved through the provision of a combination of education, storytelling and interactive experiences related to computing to make history real and relevant to them. Sometimes, however, the history of technology makes little mention of computers where it could do so. Films and books about Enigma have made Bletchley Park and cryptology relevant to many people, but the re-built Colossus is hardly ever mentioned.

One way people can gain interest is to have learned, or been taught something about the history of computing, or to have watched a relevant film or video – to have received some education on this topic. Another way to experience this history is through simulations and interacting with re-builds of technological artefacts, but this does not necessarily mean much to most people unless they can see where it all fits in with their lives. For this, education is necessary to introduce cultural relevance to viewing the history. When looking at the display of a 1950s mainframe, for example, we can ask questions such as:

- 'Who were the people who built it?'
- 'For what purpose did they build it?'
- 'Did it follow from what was learned in earlier inventions?'
- 'Where did this lead to?'
- 'What difference did it make to lives of people at the time?' and
- 'How has it led to today's technology?'

These questions can then pave the way to putting this history into a cultural context and making it culturally relevant. Providing some of the background about the inventors, technicians, programmers and users would help here.

2   How the History of Other Topics Is Made Relevant

It may be possible to use methods and approaches from other historical areas and cultures to suggest ways of improving interest in computing history. In this section a few examples are examined.

2.1   American History

Their history is relevant to most Americans partly due to a number of national holidays representing real events in American history: Columbus Day (remembers Christopher Columbus' arrival to the Americas on October 12, 1492), Martin Luther King Day (celebrates the life and achievements of an influential American civil rights leader), Independence Day (commemorating the adoption of the Declaration of Independence on July 4, 1776), Presidents' Day (Washington's Birthday, Feb 18), Memorial Day (commemorates all men and women, who have died in military service for the US) and Veterans Day (November 11). US children also are taught a lot about their past Presidents (and can probably recite the list), their origins, their history, their independence, the civil war and about many other aspects of their country. Their history has been made very real and relevant to them because of formal education and of listening to interesting stories as well as being able to visit historic sites and make use of interactive displays and simulation games. This is in addition to their being reminded of this history by the names of US public holidays.

Fig. 2. USS Constitution

2.2   Dinosaurs

To many children, Palaeontology (the scientific study of prehistoric life) is real and relevant because of the romance of the dinosaur. The film 'Jurassic Park' was a good start and David Attenborough's 'Walking with Dinosaurs' TV program and exhibition did much to popularise the dinosaur. Watching children move through the Walking with Dinosaurs exhibition and observing the model dinosaurs moving, the relevant of dinosaurs to them can readily be seen. Added to this the sheer size of dinosaur skeleton bones, like the one in the entrance to the Natural History Museum in London, make it hard not to develop some

Fig. 3. Dinosaur skeleton in a museum

interest. Many children have also been given a dinosaur toy at some stage or have seen the Flintstones or Dorothy the Dinosaur on television. For children, dinosaurs have become very real and relevant mainly through storytelling. In many cases this interest remains through life.

2.3   Machines

At Museum Victoria in the 1950s and 1960s there was a gallery with lots of model mechanical devices that could be operated by pressing a button. These devices included mining machinery, farm machinery, factory machinery and various types of mechanical engines. The first thing that most children (especially boys) wanted to do when they went to the museum was to visit this gallery and start pressing buttons. Whether they learned much about the devices themselves from this, or just enjoyed pressing buttons to make them work is an open question. These machines became very real and relevant though offering the children an interactive experience.

Fig. 4. Machine in a museum

2.4   Steam Engines and Vintage Cars

Although there are few places in the world where steam trains still operate there is a certain romance about them that many people find attractive and interesting. They find displays and even trips in these stream trains act to make them very relevant. This relevance is due mainly to the provision of an interesting experience but perhaps also to their size and to the noise and steam they emit. Likewise displays and processions of vintage cars have a natural romance that many people find attractive and that make these machines something that is relevant to them.

Fig. 5. Puffing Billy, Melbourne

3   Museums and Computers

The purpose of collecting computing artefacts in a museum can be for all or for some of the following:

- for their preservation
- for research purposes and
- for display to the public to encourage an understanding of the place played by this technology in leading to the ICT of today.

Kreps [3] notes that museum curators are now responsible for researching, interpreting and presenting collections that can be displayed in exhibitions and in publications as well as other media. Not all museums see their role in covering each of these areas. In the late 1980s the Museum of Vertebrate Zoology at the University of California, Berkeley, for instance considered their role to be in scientific research and not in public instruction with a sign at the front door stating: 'NO PUBLIC EXHIBITS' [4]. In relation to museum displays, Cameron [5] argues that *"Many visitors still long for a tangible, factual and validated scholarly narrative they can rely on"* but also for a range of differing opinions. It has also been argued that the museum collection is *"vital to the understanding of heritage"* [6]. There seems to be a general consensus that an important role of museums is vested in the displays of artefacts around which visitors can build on their previous experience.

We would argue that to make the history of computing relevant, significant artefacts should be on display with the purpose of facilitating learning, but not just formal learning through lectures, books and notes but also by discovery learning. Visitors to displays bring their own "historical experience, knowledge and beliefs" [7] and there is little likelihood of complete audience control in a display. An interesting idea is that of "chances" afforded by the display of artefacts. In education it is often the creation of an opportunity for students to discover a concept that has the most impact on the student. In the museum context the idea of creating "chances" has been postulated to have the characteristics of:

> *"Chances should not be explicitly displayed to users. However, such chances should rather easily be discovered and arranged according to the user's interests and situations. There should be a certain freedom for user to arrange chances."* [8]

The convergence of the idea of chances and discovery learning comes from the intrinsic detail of a real artefact. Real artefacts contain so much detail that it allows for a wide variety of visitor experience [9]. One visitor can see the teeth of the dinosaur and be amazed when comparing this to the baby tooth she just lost, the next can see the punch-card used to make music and compare it with the guitar strings they learnt to use that afternoon. The details of a real artefact matter when people attempt to make the connections that embody meaning. Moser expresses this as follows:

> *"Displays create new worlds for objects to inhabit and these worlds are full of "devilish details" that really matter when it comes to creating a system of meaning relating to the subject being represented."* [10]

4   Streams in Computing History

To think, as many people do, that computing began with the machines built in the 1940s is clearly erroneous as the history of computing goes back much further than this and can be traced back to earlier technologies that performed (although perhaps much more slowly) many of the tasks now performed by computers. In the popular imagination, however, the computer's ancestry is often related only to the history of calculating machines, but this is just one strand in the history of technology leading to what we now call a computer. We will argue that to concentrates only on this is to do an injustice to the history of computing. Tatnall [11] suggests that developments in four broad sets of technologies, often overlapping, paved the way for the development of today's ICT.

4.1 Technologies to Aid Calculation

We have needed to perform calculations since time immemorial and especially since people began trading with each other. Two types of calculation had to be handled: one involved counting and the other measuring, as people needed to count livestock and measure cloth. Following the calculating devices that nature provided: figures for counting and the forearm for measuring, a whole range of mechanical, and later electrical and electronic machines were developed to aid us to perform calculations, leading to the use of today's supercomputers.

4.2 Technologies for Automation and Control

One of the things that distinguish us from other animals is the use of tools. Humans are not especially good at any particular physical task but we can think creatively and so produce machines to assist us [12]. Apart from the power and action aspects of mechanisation, control is of great importance and it is this that forms part of the history of computing. Techniques for control are based on programming in all its forms from mechanical sequencing to the machine code operation of early computers, programming of more recent computers and to use of integrated circuit technologies in automatic machines.

4.3 Technologies for Information Processing and Information Management

Information arises out of human actions [12] and non-human things become information only after a human has interpreted them. An important consideration is how people generated information as part of the process of building up a complex social structure and the technologies they used to assist in doing this from library records and collections to computer databases.

4.4 Communication Technologies

Communication, probably beginning with sign language, is another of the attributes that characterise humans. Communication involves passing some form of message from one person to another. The communications technologies that have been used over the years include use of symbols, cave paintings, petro glyphs, writing, paintings, photography, radio, semaphore, telephone, telegraph, newspapers, television and the Internet. This progression is an important aspect of the history of computing.

But communication could also be seen in the result of many interactive human activities such going to the theatre or playing a card game.

4.5   Other Cross-Stream Influences

In addition to these four steams, other influences on the history of computing cross each stream, in many cases since their beginnings. These influences include military involvement, business and commercial use, medical applications, scientific research, entertainment and personal use of various forms of information technology. We believe that any discussion of the history of computing must consider these and how they interacted with each other to produce what we now know as Information and Communication Technology (ICT) in order to make this real and to achieve relevance.

5   Education: Learning by Discovery and Chance

Techniques of discovery learning originated in the 1960s through the work of Jerome Bruner who suggested that "*Practice in discovering for oneself teaches one to acquire information in a way that makes that information more readily viable in problem solving*" [13 :26]. This approach is supported by the work of learning theorists such as Seymour Papert and Jean Piaget and relates to the concept of learning by doing, following from the words often attributed to Confucius: "*What I hear I forget, what I see I remember, what I do I understand*". Abe [8] suggests that people should be given the opportunity to learn and discover through chances, that these should not be explicitly displayed but rather arranged to aid discovery and that they should be related to the person's interests and background. In the constructivist view of how students learn, teachers are often encouraged to focus on discovery learning. At one extreme this can mean that students are free to work with little or no guidance, but Mayer [14] suggests that *guided* discovery is a more effective approach than pure discovery.

In making the history of computing real and relevant to people we suggest that discovery learning has an important role to play and can be introduced through the use of interactive exhibits and displays that, after being given some idea of what to look for, encourages the user to try to find out for themselves. This is much more likely to make the history of computing more relevant that static exhibits, whether of the original artefact or of re-builds.

5.1   The Lego Approach to Discovery Learning

As is well known, one of the big advantages of Lego is that a given set of building blocks can be used to make a variety of models, and even in the case of specific purpose Lego kits many different variations on the basic model can be built [15, 16]. The construction guide for a Lego model [17] often follows the approach of:

1. Firstly providing detailed schematic instructions for building the first model
2. Followed by outline details of the construction of a similar model and

3. Finally provision of a photograph of the real object is used to suggest other construction possibilities that are left up to the builders' imagination.

Many museums offer education programs to school children on topics including the history of computing and these are certainly worthwhile. Unless they are backed up with other education or experiences, however, in most cases they are soon forgotten. One way around this is for schools to run special programs over several weeks leading up to the museum visit to interest students in the history of computing and also to follow up experiences and education. Following the Lego Approach it might also be useful to provide students with part of an idea relating to computing history and so lead them to self-discovery of what follows. Another approach is to encourage students to look for historic computers in old films or TV programs such as Star Trek and compare the flashing lights and spinning tape wheels to computers of today. The value of TV programs showing aspects of the history of computing also should not be underestimated.

6   In the History of Computing, What Is Real?

This paper addresses the question of what people find real and relevant in the history of computing, why this is so, and how to increase this relevance. Do we need them to have *"things that buzz inside ... and a stick-out handle"* [1 :14] or is there something else that makes things real and relevant?

When it was first introduced in the late 1970s many people saw the Apple // as a toy and not a 'real computer'. It was not until VisiCalc software appeared on the Apple // that people started to consider it to be real and relevant for more than game playing. Victor Frankenstein's creation [18] never became real in his novel. But if Frankenstein's monster never succeeded in becoming real in this way, in many ways it has become real, even if only as a concept, in our world as we have found a use for the analogy of Frankenstein's monster to describe any 'unnatural creation' of modern technology [2]. Returning to the Velveteen Rabbit:

Fig. 6. A toy that has become very 'real'

> *"Real isn't how you are made," said the Skin Horse. "It's a thing that happens to you. When a child loves you for a long, long time, not just to play with, but REALLY loves you, then you become Real." [1 :14]*

Does the history of computing become real and relevant when people really 'love' it? Perhaps it becomes real when they find what they see as a significant place for it that fits into their own world.

7   Conclusion

We have argued that the history of computing will become relevant to people when they see how it can fit into their own lives and how it relates to their own society and culture. For some people this history is immediately of interest and is very relevant. For others some work is required to make it relevant. We suggest that this can be achieved through the provision of education, stories and interactive experiences. The display of artefacts is an important cog in the job of making computer history real, but prior educational experiences will allow people to experience rich 'chances' with these artefacts. Artefacts accompanied by stories allow a visitor to a museum to become more involved and educational experiences within the environment of the artefacts are likely to increase involvement. Brabazon [19] speaks of this interaction between history, artefacts and education as *"a reflexive loop between teaching, learning, display and visitors"*. The current view of the education community of a developing individual who creates their own conceptual framework from their experiences reinforces this view of the way forward in making computer history real and relevant.

References

1. Williams, M.: The Velveteen Rabbit, or How Toys Become Real, p. 35. Heinemann, London (1922)
2. Tatnall, A.: In Real-Life Learning, What is Meant by 'Real'? In: van Weert, T., Tatnall, A. (eds.) Information and Communication Technologies and Real-Life Learning - New Education for the Knowledge Society. IFIP, vol. 182, pp. 143–150. Springer, New York (2005)
3. Kreps, C.: Curatorship as Social Practice. Curator 46(3), 311–323 (2003)
4. Leigh Star, S., Griesemer, J.R.: Institutional Ecology, 'Translations' and Boundary Objects: Amateurs and Professionals in Berkeley's Museum of Vertebrate Zoology, 1907-39. Social Studies of Science 19(3), 387–420 (1989)
5. Cameron, F.: Contentiousness and shifting knowledge paradigms: The roles of history and science museums in contemporary societies. Museum Management and Curatorship 20(3), 213–233 (2005)
6. Ames, M.M.: Counterfeit Museology. Museum Management and Curatorship 21(3), 171–186 (2006)
7. Boon, T.M.: A Walk in the Museum with Michel de Certeau: A Conceptual Helping Hand for Museum Practitioners. Curator, the Museum Journal 54(4) (2011)
8. Abe, A.: Curation in Chance Discovery. In: Ohsawa, Y., Abe, A. (eds.) Advances in Chance Discovery. SCI, vol. 423, pp. 1–18. Springer, Heidelberg (2013)
9. Demant, D.: Why the Real Thing Is Essential for Telling Our Stories. In: Tatnall, A. (ed.) HC 2010. IFIP AICT, vol. 325, pp. 13–15. Springer, Heidelberg (2010)
10. Moser, S.: The devil is in the detail: museum displays and the creation of knowledge. Museum Anthropology 33(1), 22–32 (2010)
11. Tatnall, A.: History of Computers: Hardware and Software Development. In: Encyclopedia of Life Support Systems. UNESCO - Eolss Publishers Co Ltd: Ramsey, Isle of Man (2012)
12. Tatnall, A., Davey, W.: Information Technology Studies. Jacaranda Press, Brisbane (1990)

13. Bruner, J.S.: The Act of Discovery. Harvard Educational Review 31(1), 21–32 (1961)
14. Mayer, R.E.: Should There Be a Three-Strikes Rule Against Pure Discovery Learning? The Case for Guided Methods of Instruction. American Psychologist 1994, 14–19 (2004)
15. Davey, W., Tatnall, A.: Problem Solving and Management Information Systems. In: Research and Development in Problem Based Learning. The Australian Problem Based Learning Network, Newcastle (1994)
16. Tatnall, A., Davey, W.: Conceptual Development in an Object Environment. In: Selwood, I., Fox, P., Tebbutt, M. (eds.) World Conference on Computers in Education VI (WCCE 1995), Liberating the Learner - Conference Abstracts Proceedings, p. 322. Aston University, Birmingham (1995)
17. Anov, A.: Programmable Systems: Teacher's Materials. Lego Group, UK (1986)
18. Shelley, M.: Frankenstein, or the Modern Prometheus, 261 This edition published by Penguin Classics, London (1818)
19. Brabazon, T.: Museums and popular culture revisited: Kevin Moore and the politics of pop. Museum Management and Curatorship 21(4), 283–301 (2006)

Part II

Spotlight on Some Key Collections and Their Future Plans

The Heinz Nixdorf Museums Forum, Central Venue for the "History of Computing"

Norbert Ryska and Jochen Viehoff

Heinz Nixdorf Museum, Paderborn, Germany
jviehoff@hnf.de

Abstract. In the late 1970s Heinz Nixdorf began to collect historical calculating devices and early computers to serve as the basic exhibits of a computer museum. After Nixdorf's death, the Nixdorf Foundation was set up to develop the museum. To see the different ways of looking at computer history, a pluralistic approach was chosen, with the focus on the history of objects, ideas, people or societies. This paper tells something of the development, goals and purpose of the museum.

Keywords: Computer museum, Nixdorf, Nixdorf Computer AG, simulations, replicas, designers, builders, education.

1   Prologue: 1975 – 1992

It was in the late 1970s that German computer entrepreneur Heinz Nixdorf began to collect historical calculating devices and early computers. These objects were to serve as the basic exhibits of a computer museum which he intended to establish on his Paderborn premises. Not only had Nixdorf collected some 1,500 objects by the time of his sudden death in 1986, but he had also been presented with an initial exhibition scenario by the Berlin exhibition architects.

2   Development Phase: 1992 – 1996

Following a six-year hiatus, the idea of the museum was revived by the Nixdorf Foundation and a ten-strong working group comprising technology historians, exhibition architects and one of the authors (Ryska) was established with a view to performing a feasibility study. The contextual framework stipulated by the Nixdorf Foundation was initially restricted to the history of office computing in the light of the product range manufactured by Nixdorf Computer AG. However the working group opted to dispense with this narrow outlook, instead developing an extensive tour through the 5,000-year history of arithmetic, writing and communication. This idea, which ultimately cost DM 120 million, was finally sanctioned by the Nixdorf Foundation. The concept was absolutely unique.

A. Tatnall, T. Blyth, and R. Johnson (Eds.): HC 2013, IFIP AICT 416, pp. 47–52, 2013.

The following objectives were pursued and achieved in planning the permanent exhibition on the "History of Computing" which was to be set up over 6,000 square metres of floor space in the former headquarters of Nixdorf Computer AG:

3   Concept and Goals

The working group identified 60 topics to be elaborated by technology historians from around the globe and local curators before being implemented across two 3,000-square-metre storeys.

- 1st floor: From the abacus to the computer (3000 BC – 1950)
- 2nd floor: Computers conquer the world (1950 – present)

A chronological presentation of the "History of Computing" was preferred to a diachronic approach, i.e. a "back to the roots" or "from the roots onwards" perspective.

In a bid to get to grips with the different ways of looking at computer history, a pluralistic approach was chosen, with the focus on the history of objects, ideas, people or societies, depending on the topic in question.

To avoid having to forgo more complex yet important issues, it was decided that the individual topics could certainly call for different levels of understanding, in line with the principle that not everyone is interested in everything in any case.

The objects, contents and presentations should be "unique", i.e. not be available in the same form anywhere else in the world.

In a bid to render the museum experience more memorable for visitors, exhibits should, where possible, have a "back story", whether this be the curious tale of the Chess Turk, Hollerith's use of the punched card for data processing, the fact that Friedrich Nietzsche typed on a Malling Hansen, Zuse's construction of the Z1 in his living room, how Curt Herzstark's Curta calculator was developed in a concentration camp, the cracking of the ENIGMA code at Bletchley Park and Moore's Law as the only "law" in IT history.

An important objective for a public simply wallowing in superlatives was of course to procure "exhibits with cult status" (firsts, rarities, exotic models) such as the Apple I, Altair, CRAY 2, Enigma, computers used in space and Heinz Nixdorf's first computer, to name just a few examples. In the case of IT products such as calculators and mobile phones, their range and diversity was also to be demonstrated.

The successful procurement of significant loans such as components of the ENIAC (NMAH), the Typex encryption machine (Science Museum London) , the Geheimschreiber machine (Siemens AG), the D11 tabulator (IBM), the on-board computer of the Gemini Space Capsule (Air & Space Museum) and encryption devices (NSA) is evidence of the importance attached by international lenders to computer history.

4   What about Stories about the Designers and Builders of these Computers?

A central "Hall of Fame" (15 people) and an electronic "Wall of Fame" (152 people) expressed the concept that man was to serve as the focal point in the contemplation of his dealings with technology – in his role as a scientist, inventor or entrepreneur.

5   Using Simulations and Replicas to Illustrate the History of Computing

From the outset, content planners endeavoured to create an even balance between hands-on functional models (some 30 in number) and multimedia methods of communicating information on technology (around 30 multimedia presentations). For the first time, the computer became an instrument used to impart information on its own history.

The idea was to demonstrate the inventive spirit and technological competence of earlier ages by means of numerous replicas of historical calculators and machines.

6   Problem Areas

In researching historical computers, we came across surprisingly little awareness of tradition, particularly in the IT industry itself. Even "classic devices" were often no longer available (in sufficient quantities) at their manufacturers. The "last of the Mohicans" included Digital Equipment, IBM, Siemens, Bull and Ericsson. Philips, for example, closed its spectacular company museum Evoluon in Eindhoven in 1989 in the midst of a financial crisis.

The central exhibition area "How does a computer work?" was implemented for the first time in 1996 and completely revised in 2003. Both approaches fell short of our own and visitors' expectations. It is still difficult to illustrate clearly how a computer works by means of analogies or modelling – especially, of course, in the case of software. The HNF nevertheless created an exhibition section entitled "Software and computer science" in 2007 in an attempt to remedy these deficits. The HNF is the first museum ever to address this topic and has now been presenting it for ten years in a variety of ways.

As of 2014, it is planning an IT_Lab to impart the basics of computer technology in interactive fashion in the style of science centre exhibits.

7   Motivation

In the future, the museum both can and should play an important role as an extra-curricular educational resource for the imparting of core skills in areas such as the natural sciences and technology and in the provision of experience-oriented learning environments. In this context, the successful special exhibitions at the HNF demonstrate clearly the value of interactive and multimedia exhibits in the modern-day transfer of knowledge.

The objectives in updating the permanent exhibition are to preserve the fundamental character of the venue as a museum for information and communication technologies, while meeting the new expectations of future generations of visitors.

8   Concept

As part of the planned renovation and updating of the permanent exhibition (Update 3), the "exit area" on the second floor is to be extended as a laboratory for scientific experiments in the field of information technologies. To supplement the sections "How does a computer work?" und "Digital workbench", clusters of hands-on exhibits will enable visitors to work on basic scientific aspects from the fields of electronics, computers and the media interactively in a "laboratory situation".

Unlike "conventional" science centres, the Laboratory for Information Technologies has a clearly defined contextual focus on topics relevant to the HNF. In-depth levels of information as well as the reference to objects that is so characteristic of the HNF are also planned for each individual section.

The modular topic islands allow the integration of current technology trends almost as they happen. Moreover, the focus on the scientific and technical basics will considerably extend the duration of the cycle – and thus the topical reference – vis-à-vis device developments and application ideas.

The new laboratory unit geared to basic aspects can be advertised in targeted fashion as part of marketing measures with a view to attracting more groups from schools. A "science centre" in the museum context oriented clearly towards the information technologies in terms of topics would furthermore constitute another unique feature of the HNF.

9   Planning Stages

- Stage I: Five stations with basic scientific aspects of information technologies
- Stage II: Five stations with other topics relevant to the HNF

Completed project: 10 stations each with 3-4 laboratory workplaces for scientific hands-on experiments oriented towards basic aspects

10   Main Topics

Bits and bytes, electricity, microelectronics, calculation and logic, peripherals, semiconductors, data storage, GPS, networks, nanoelectronics, computers of the future, energy, green computing, digital media, mobile communications, robotics

We have discovered over time that current IT devices which are generally already in private use attract relatively little attention in the museum. Due to the extremely rapid pace of development in the industry, many of these devices become "obsolete" within a few years, if not months in some cases. A period of at least 40 years then elapses before these devices are once again looked upon with some degree of curiosity by visitors from the younger generations. In the meantime they are largely regarded as nothing more than electronic junk.

A museum is also no longer capable of reproducing the vast variety of products available in today's ICT industry. What's more, a serious evaluation of technologies and products can only take place once several years have elapsed.

The maintenance of early computers in particular (1950s-1980s) has proved and continues to prove impossible or unfeasible on conservational grounds in many cases, due to the frequent difficulty of obtaining spare parts, a lack of software and insufficient know-how.

Fortunately, the number of simulations of historical computers – of particular interest to fans of retro computers – is rising steadily. Some of the historical operating systems of home computers implemented by the HNF in its PC gallery and elsewhere via emulators include the Apple II, C64, CPM, MS-DOS 1.x, 2.x, 3.x, 5.x, 6.x, Windows 1, Windows 2, Windows 3.11 and Windows 9.x. Retro computing can be traced back to a longing to return to the origins of information technology; it also offers the opportunity to work with hardware at close quarters and to "have a say" at systems level. It is easiest to explain the basic principles of technology with reference to historical systems, as the latter are not overly complex.

11   The Importance of Education in Making History of Computing Relevant

HNF has compiled a varied educational museum programme to motivate children and young people to take an active approach to the exhibits and their history. At workshops children can, for example, build robots, encrypt messages or learn how to 'make' paper. Teachers and pupils are given numerous ideas for study content. Besides a guided tour of the permanent exhibition, special tours can be booked on such topics as arithmetic, writing, inventors and entrepreneurs, women's work in information technology, cryptology and the history of communications.

12   Trial Phase (1996 – present day)

Numerous activities have taken place in a bid to further popularise the "History of Computing" since the HNF first opened in October 1996. Only the biggest projects are named here.

In 1998, 1999 and 2001, the HNF joined forces with Westdeutscher Rundfunk 3 to stage the "WDR Computer Nights", a 7-hour live TV marathon attracting 3,000 visitors to the HNF as well as hundreds of thousands of television viewers.

The permanent exhibition was updated in 2004 with the addition of new themes such as robotics and artificial intelligence, mobile communications and digitization. The new galleries present the latest information technology themes in an interactive, multimedia exhibit. Visitors can try their skills at old and new computer games, test advanced man-machine interfaces and experiment with the latest applications and products from research and industry in the showroom

In 2004, the big special exhibition "Computer.Brain" offered a comparative presentation of these two thinking tools. Significant fields of application of the computer were subsequently also presented in the form of "Computer.Medicine" in 2007 and "Computer.Sport" in 2009.

The relevance of the "History of Computing" for the public is ultimately also clear from the HNF visitor figures: over 16 years, the museum has registered some 1.9 million visitors, 36,000 guided tours and 13,000 events, as well as generating a huge media response (400 million readers and viewers/listeners ??) and a consistently high level of appreciation from within the computer industry.

The Computers' Collection at the Polytechnic Museum

Marina Smolevitskaya

Scientific Researcher, Computer Collection Curator, Polytechnic Museum, Moscow, Russia
`smol@polymus.ru`, `msmolevitskaya@yandex.ru`

Abstract. The Polytechnic Museum has the Fund Collection "Electronic Digital Computing Machines". There are more than seven hundred objects and over two thousands documentary, printed and graphic items today. All four generations of electronic digital computing machines are presented in the Museum. Some of the EDCM are working. In addition, the Museum created fourteen personal funds of Russian scientists who devoted their activity to computer science. This computers' collection is the only one of such variety and size in Russia.

Keywords: Polytechnic Museum, collection, personal funds, electronic digital computing machines, using simulations and replicas to illustrate the computing history.

The fund collection of "Electronic Digital Computing Machines" (EDCM) was formed in the 1960s. There are more than seven hundred objects and two thousand documentary, printed, and graphical items today. The Museum created thirteen personal funds of Russian scientists who devoted their activity to computer science: S. Lebedev, I. Bruk, B. Rameev, V. Glushkov, A. Lyapunov, U. Bazilevskiy, N. Matjukhin, M. Kartsev, A. Kitov, N. Brousentsov, V. Petrov, V. Burtsev, S. Mergelyan. It is very important to point out that this fund collection is the only one of such variety and size in Russia.

The first electronic digital computing machines appeared in the USSR in 1951 and allowed scientists to solve difficult scientific and technical tasks. They were the Small Electronic Calculating Machine (MESM), developed under the leadership of academician Sergei Lebedev, and the Automatic Digital Computer (M-1), developed under the leadership of Isaak Bruk. N. Matjukhin and M. Kartsev were among the developers of the M-1 computer and later, they created their own computer engineering schools. The documentary materials about these machines and their developers were demonstrated in the Museum halls of datamation. The original report of the M-1 Automatic Digital Computer, developed in the Laboratory of Electro-systems at the Institute of Energy of the USSR Academy of Sciences, is one of the most interesting documents in our department.

In 1948, Isaak Bruk together with Bashir Rameev received the first author's certificate of the Automatic Digital Computing Machine in Russia. The Museum is the keeper of this certificate. Later, B. Rameev created the "Ural" family of computers. One could see the Small Automatic Electronic Digital Computing Machine "Ural-1" (Fig. 1) in the Polytechnic Museum exhibition.

A. Tatnall, T. Blyth, and R. Johnson (Eds.): HC 2013, IFIP AICT 416, pp. 53–63, 2013.
© IFIP International Federation for Information Processing 2013

Fig. 1. The Small Automatic Electronic Digital Computing Machine "Ural-1" at the Polytechnic Museum

Some Museum objects of computer science have obtained the status of "Relic of science and technology"; as such, they are under the protection of the Museum and the state. The Small Automatic Electronic Digital Computing Machine "Ural-1", some units of the first Soviet serial computer "Strela" and other Museum objects have such designated status. There are several units of the first Soviet serial computer "Strela", developed in 1952 by the Special Design Bureau SDB-245 in the EDCM Fund collection of Polytechnic Museum. These are the fragments of the Control Panel (Fig.2), several processor blocks realized on the vacuum-valves (Fig. 3), six cathode-ray tubes (elements of quick-access storage) and wide ferromagnetic tape used as an external information carrier (Fig.4).

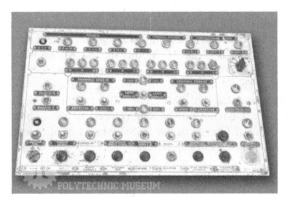

Fig. 2. The Control Panel fragment of the first Soviet serial computer "Strela"

Fig. 3. Several processor blocks of the first Soviet serial computer "Strela"

Fig. 4. The cathode-ray tube and the wide ferromagnetic tape the first Soviet serial computer "Strela"

Usually all electronic digital computing machines are divided into four generations. The Small Automatic Electronic Digital Computing Machine "Ural-1"and the first Soviet serial computer "Strela" present the first generation of machines in the Museum. The processor of these machines was realized on electronic tubes, and the operative memory was realized on magnetic drum or cathode-ray tubes.

Then the second generation of machines is represented by the electronic digital computing machine "Razdan-3" (Fig. 5) and others soviet mainframes. The processor was built by using semiconductors and operative memory was built of ferrite cores. There were several ferrite cubes in one machine. There are many matrixes of ferrite cores inside such cube. We can see how these devices worked on the demonstration model.

The Museum collects and keeps the various types of memory on ferrite cores. For example, it contains the Ferrite Cube of the Operative Memory of the Electronic Computing Machine (ECM) M-4 (Fig. 6), developed under the leadership of M. Kartsev. The capacitor-type ROM block of the ECM M10 (Fig. 7) is a very interesting object, which was designed in the Scientific Research Institute of Computing Complexes also under the leadership of M. Kartsev.

Fig. 5. The electronic digital computing machine "Razdan-3"

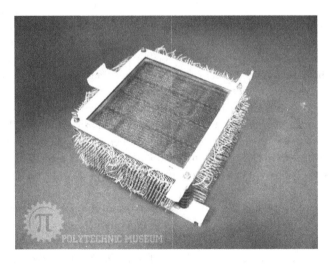

Fig. 6. The Ferrite Cube of the Operative Memory of the Electronic Computing Machine M-4

Fig. 7. The capacitor-type ROM block of the ECM M10

The unified system of electronic computing machines on integrated circuits represents the third generation, developed in the USSR at the beginning of the 1970s in cooperation with the socialist countries. It represents a family of software compatible machines with different productivities that build on the unified elemental and constructive base with a unified structure and a unified set of peripheral units. The processor and the operative memory were mounted on integrated circuits.

A remarkable exclusion is the experience of creating the ternary computers "Setun" (Fig. 8) and "Setun-70" at Moscow State University. The experience convincingly confirms practical preferences of ternary digital techniques. N. Brousentsov initiated the design of small digital computing machine "Setun" in 1956. (Note that Setun is the little river that flows into the river "Moscow" near the University.) The Setun was a small, inexpensive computer that was simple to use and to service for schools, research laboratories, offices, and manufacture control. Fast miniature ferrite cores and semiconductor diodes were used as the element base for this machine. Simplicity, economy, and elegance of computer architecture are the direct and practically very important consequences of ternary machines. The computer "Setun" has the status of "Relic of science and technology".

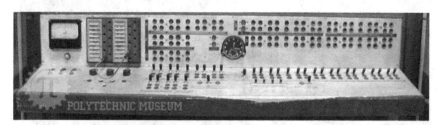

Fig. 8. The Control Panel of the ternary computer "Setun"

The Computing Center with the third generation machine is showed through the scale model of the Electronic Computing Machine US-1050 (Fig. 9) and some original units of this machine (Fig. 10). Visitors can see integrated circuits, which made the peculiar revolution in computing science, on the boards of the operative memory of the ES-3222. Plotters were used widely with these machines for the first time.

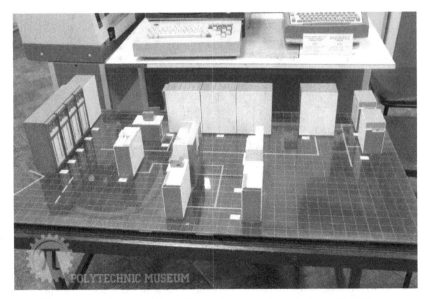

Fig. 9. The scale model of the Electronic Computing Machine US-1050

Fig. 10. Some original units of the Electronic Computing Machine US-1050

The processor and operative memory of the fourth generation of electronic computing machines appeared on very large-scale integrated circuits. We demonstrate the functioning of one of the first such Soviet computers – the Microprocessor Laboratory "MikroLab КР580ИК80" in the Museum.

There is a unique computer for spaceship use called the "Argon-16" (Fig. 11), that can be seen only in this Museum. It contained a synchronous computer system with triple redundancy and majorization carried out on per unit base with eight levels. It consists of three computers with data channels and a set of interfaces to the control system. The instruction set is specially designed for control tasks. I/O operations combine with the calculation process.

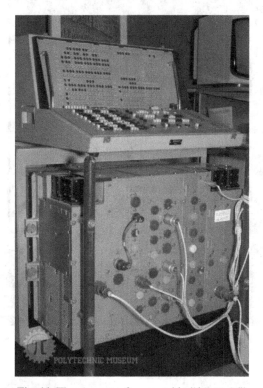

Fig. 11. The computer for spaceship "Argon-16"

Since 1975, the "Argon-16" computer became the basic component of control systems of "Soyuz" spaceship, the "Progress" transport ships, and orbital space stations "Salute", "Almaz", and "Mir". Exclusive reliability had provided long usage for it. The total output for these machines is 380. No failure of the system was noted during its twenty-five years of operation when working in control systems. It is unrivalled among space computers by production volume. The specialized computers for aviation are presented in the Museum exposition.

In 2005, the Museum received the "El'brus 3.1" super computer system (Fig. 12), developed at the Institute of Precision Mechanics and Computer Technology. It also received one processor block and one operative memory block of the "Electronica SS BIS-1" super computer (Fig. 13), created under the leadership of academician V. Mel'nikov at the Cybernetics Problems Institute and the "Del'ta" Scientific Research Institute. In addition, the Museum actively collects Russian and foreign personal computers.

Fig. 12. The "El'brus 3.1" super computer system

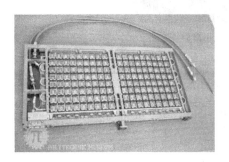

Fig. 13. The processor block and the operative memory block of the "Electronica SS BIS-1" super computer

Up to the end of the last year we had the Museum's halls devoted to Soviet scientists and engineers who worked in computing science. The visitors could see documentary, printings, and graphic materials of scientific, official, and biographic activity. Also there are materials about international recognition of Russian scientists in computer science. The International Computer Society of the Institute of Electrical and Electronic Engineers awards scientists of different countries the title "Computer Pioneer". Russian scientists S. Lebedev, A. Lyapunov, and V.Glushkov received this title in 1996. The children of these scientists presented the diplomas and large bronze medals to the Museum.

Since 1994, the Department of Computer Engineering and the Automatics Department of the Russian Academy of Science awards a premium, named after S. Lebedev, for successes in the area of computing systems development. This Museum keeps copies of the diplomas awarded by the Russian Academy of Sciences to Russian scientists.

Unfortunately, it is practically impossible to restore the first electronic digital machines for demonstration of their work. However, with the aid of modern computers it is possible to show the operation of the separate devices. One of such complex demonstration was created on the base of plotter "US-7051M" and the personal computer, which works in the DOS medium. This plotter worked under the control of a special block in composition of United System computers. We didn't have such a control block, but a student of Moscow Institute of Electronic and Mathematics, Dmitry Schepovalin developed a new interface between this plotter and personal computer on modern microchips (integrated circuits). The control programs, written in the algorithmic language C++, and the demonstration programs allowed drawings of images chosen by the user from the computer library, for example, the logo of the Polytechnic Museum. It is important to note that in the created demonstration complex in the base of plotter US-7051 and personal computer partially the history of appearance and development of the algorithmic languages is reflected and remains the same.

With the aid of a modern multimedia computer, it was possible to listen to computer music: from the first solo-voice melodies "Uralskie napevy" of R. Zaripov, to the polyphonic compositions of A. Stepanov (played on the first computing machines in the 1960s). They were rewritten from old recording tapes.

In 2005, the Museum began to carry out work according to digitization of video films from the scientific-auxiliary fund of the Museum. Five films are already in digital format. For example, the Museum digitized "Academician Lebedev", "Machine Geometry and Graphics" and "Curved Surfaces in Automatization System". The Museum plans to continue this work.

At this time the Polytechnic Museum has entered a period of global modernization. The Board of Trustees of the Museum adopted a new scientific concept of exposition of the Museum, the proposed "Event Communication". The Museum staffs are working on the creation of new expositions together with colleagues from the "Event Communication". The Duffel Fund of the Museum will be transported to the Territory of Techno Park of one of the former car factories. Temporary exhibition will be created in the Pavilion «Transport» on the territory of the all-Russia Exhibition Center. The Museum must vacate the building fully by July 2013. Then its reconstruction will begin.

The updated exposition on the history of electronic computing machinery is intended to make this more understandable and accessible for all categories of visitors. Today many people are active users of personal computers and know that their main devices are CPU, memory, external devices for changing information, but they are hidden from our eyes. All these devices are in the computers of all generations, but in the first three generations of computer we can see these directly and observe the evolution of the element's base. Now many of the students who will be specialists in information technologies don't know about the first computers and don't know about the existence of supercomputers. Frequently we can hear from visitors: «I thought that computers are only desktop!». For many, the history of computers consists of a maximum of the last 2 decades. An understanding of the history of computing needs to show all computer generations and compare the characteristics of these devices.

As is well known, the operating exhibits caused the greatest interest among the visitors. In the Polytechnic Museum Small automatic electronic computing machine «Ural-1» was exhibited, which was released by the Penza computing-analytical machines plant in 1959. It is the tubes computer extant in Russia fully. Of course more visitors would be interesting to see how this machine works. This complex problem was decided by two Moscow students Mixail Glyanenko and Dmitry Solov'ev. They developed and implemented a demonstration complex on the basis of a Small automatic computer «Ural-1». The students used modern integrated circuits instead of the processor based on electronic lamps and memory on a magnetic drum. For demonstration of the functioning of the machine a very simple task was selected: addition in binary code. The solution of this task can be observed on the indication panel. At the same time the electronic lamps of the processor glow. Thus, visitors get a full idea about how worked the very first computers.

Fig. 14. The working BESM-6

In 2012, the Museum got working the BESM-6 (High-speed Electronic Counting Machine) (Fig. 14), the best semiconductor computer, which was created in the USSR. Now this Machine is in the Museum's Depository. After the reconstruction of the Museum's building BESM-6 will be exhibited and I hope that we will be able to show visitors its work. There are more specialists who were involved in building or using this machine and I am sure of their support.

Many visitors do not know about the most important task of computers: to compute, and solve the most complicated scientific-technical and engineering tasks. Many of our contemporaries think that computers are designed for office work and games. It is therefore important to show clearly what problems were solved on the first computers and on the most modern powerful super-computers.

Also the preservation of the past years' software is very difficult, and especially its demonstration in the Museum space. The corresponding working equipment is required to demonstrate such programs. It's possible for personal computers, but for the old mainframe it's a practically impossible task.

Part III

Thoughts on Expanding the Audience for Computing History

Making History Relevant: The Case of Computing

Gauthier van den Hove

CWI, Amsterdam, Netherlands
`G.van.den.Hove@cwi.nl`

Abstract. We investigate the motives to practice history, and the role that history could play for a scientific discipline. We consider these questions successively from three interrelated points of view: "history: why?" (§ 1), "history: for whom?" (§ 2), and "history: how?" (§ 3). Only the second of these sections is specific to the field of computing; the two other ones are more general, and could probably be applied to other fields as well. Needless to say, the responses that we propose are elements rather than definitive answers; the author also apologizes in advance if these reflections turn out to be nothing but platitudes: he was not trained as a historian, and it is very well possible that these three questions have already received more convincing answers elsewhere.

Keywords: History, computing, historical and ahistorical disciplines.

1 History: Why?

If one considers the relation that the fields of human knowledge maintain with their own history, there seems to exist a dichotomy between two kinds of disciplines. In philosophy or in arts for example, the detailed study of the history of the field is seen as something of great importance. It is even a prerequisite to be competent in these fields, and students typically spend hours and days studying the achievements of the masters of the past, for example Plato's *Meno* or Beethoven's *Symphonies*. On the contrary, in mathematics or in the field of computing, history is most often seen as something of little or no importance: a student in mathematics for instance will not spend a single minute reading Euclid's *Elements*, even if he uses the results discovered by Euclid daily, and likewise a student in a computer science program will not study the details of, say, the Multics operating system, even if some of the ideas and techniques introduced in Multics are widely used nowadays. All fields of human knowledge can, apparently, be separated in two according to that criterion: is the study of the field's history seen, by the participants of that field, as something essential or not?

This distinction between "historical" and "ahistorical" disciplines is of course not our own discovery: it corresponds for example to the opposition between the "two cultures," literary and scientific, described by C. P. Snow in his famous article and lecture.[1] However, while the lack of interest for history is clearly a distinctive trait of

---

[1] Snow, C. P., *The Two Cultures, The Two Cultures and The Scientific Revolution.*

A. Tatnall, T. Blyth, and R. Johnson (Eds.): HC 2013, IFIP AICT 416, pp. 67–78, 2013.

the vast majority of contemporary scientists, one could argue that there are exceptions to this rule, for instance A. Weil in mathematics. This single example suffices to demonstrate that it is not clear that sciences are, by nature, ahistorical disciplines. In other words, it shows that it is necessary to question our distinction and its validity (§ 1.1) before trying to derive a few conclusions (§ 1.2 and § 1.3).

1.1   On the Difference between Historical and Ahistorical Disciplines

It is immediately evident that what happened in the past is not less important for ahistorical disciplines than for historical ones: scientists build upon what has already been achieved by their predecessors, and do not start over again as if nothing had been done before them. This was already clear in the two examples above: the results discovered by Euclid and the techniques introduced in Multics are still used today. What makes the difference between a historical and an ahistorical discipline is thus not that what is dated is considered as outdated for the latter and not for the former. The difference is, rather, that they bear a different relation to the documents in which the results have first been expounded or realized. In philosophy or in arts for example it is necessary to study Kant's *Critique of Pure Reason* to understand it or Bach's *Goldberg Variations* to understand them, and teachers will advise students to distrust textbooks and to read the original documents as much as possible. On the contrary, in mathematics or in the field of computing, the older results have been absorbed in later works, and teachers will not advise students to read to original documents, but instead to rely on textbooks in which all the important results are presented synthetically. Even more so, should a student try to read Euler's *Introduction to Analysis of the Infinite* or to study the details of the ITS operating system for instance, most if not all teachers would urge her not to do so, explaining that it would be a terrible waste of time, or that it is worthless to know the details of these works, or even that studying them could cause confusion.

The difference in the relations with the original documents is more precise than the still vague opposition between historical and ahistorical disciplines with which we started. In turn, it leads us to try to understand its cause.

A first reason that could be proposed is that literary disciplines do not aim, contrary to scientific disciplines, at understanding reality, but only at understanding and commenting these documents. It is easy to see that this reason is not a good one: there is, at the very least, no general agreement in literary disciplines that their only aim is to understand documents from the past, independently of their relation to reality. One would not study Hegel's *Elements of the Philosophy of Right*, for example, only to understand what a particular man thought in 1820, but to understand modern political systems better.

A second possible reason is that it seems that there is no unity in literary disciplines, contrary to scientific ones. A sign of this is that it is common, in literary disciplines, to describe oneself as a "Heideggerian" or as an "Aristotelian" for instance, that is to say, to make oneself a disciple of a certain master, whereas in sciences no one would claim to be a "Newtonian" or an "Einsteinian." This division of literary disciplines in particular schools of thought, each of them being in a close relation with a given master which it considers as a reference, could explain that these founder's creations are studied in detail, because each participant of the field has to situate himself within the various traditions and to justify his choice. This reason seems a bit more convincing than the previous one, but it is, again, not a good one. There are schools of thought in sciences as well: for example, logicism, intuitionism and formalism are three different ways of founding mathematics. More generally, even if the different traditions are not as apparent in sciences as they are in literary disciplines, because they are not named after their founders, it is clear that they exist; their existence becomes the most apparent, as has been shown by T. S. Kuhn, when they enter in conflict with each other.[2]

A third possible reason to explain the different relationships with original documents is that literary works seem to be more personal than scientific contributions: Schubert's music for example could not have been written by anyone else than Schubert himself, whereas Heisenberg's contributions to physics could in principle have been discovered by someone else. This could explain that it is important to study the original documents in literary disciplines, both because they contain something unique that cannot be synthesized, and because one should learn to create something that is original, contrary to scientific disciplines in which one should contribute something to a larger edifice. This argument seems again better than the previous one, but it is still not a good one. Many literary works would not be described by their author as a creation, but rather as something they have discovered or received. Moreover, sciences are also a creative endeavour in which the scientist's personality plays a role. A. M. Turing gave for instance the first convincing definition of computability in 1936; given that a number of other scientists had attempted to define it earlier without success, it is very unlikely that his contribution could have been made by someone else.

The three arguments we have examined have shown to be unconvincing to justify the difference between disciplines in which studying the original documents is considered important and those in which it is not. Discussing every possible argument would of course be an endless task. We therefore have to reconsider the same question from another point of view, by looking at the inverse question, namely: are literary disciplines historical by nature, that is, is the study of original documents something essential in these disciplines? It turns out that the answer to that question is negative: the study of original documents was not always seen as something important in these disciplines, which means that they have become historical at some point. Descartes or Kant, for example, were apparently very mildly interested in referring to original documents. It is thus not only incorrect that sciences are by nature ahistorical; it is also incorrect that literary disciplines are by nature historical.

This conclusion leads us to a new question: why did literary disciplines became historical, that is, why did the study of original documents became one of their important traits? The main motivations behind this change seem to be a consciousness that studying the past is a source of inspiration (§ 1.2) and a condition of progress (§ 1.3).

---

[2]   Kuhn, T. S., *The Structure of Scientific Revolutions.*

1.2   History as a Source of Inspiration

Stating that history is a source of inspiration seems a rather vague idea, particularly for scientific disciplines; it is thus necessary to explain in more detail what it means. Thucydides, who is considered as the first historian, already explained that history is useful for *"those who want to have a clear view of what happened in the past and what — the human condition being what it is — can be expected to happen again some time in the future in similar or much the same ways."*[3] This makes it clear that the aim of history was, right from the start, to shed some clarity not only on past events, but also on current and future ones. What Thucydides had in mind are politics: his detailed study of a specific political event was therefore not meant to satisfy a mere curiosity, but he conceived it as a contribution to the culture of those who are involved in politics, to serve as an inspiration for their choices and acts, by making them aware of a number of constant laws of the "human condition." These laws are not explicitly stated, because it is a part of the reader's task to understand them; they are only illustrated by concrete examples. In other words, his *History of the Peloponnesian War* is a case study in politics.

Thucydides' approach is applicable, *mutatis mutandis*, to scientific disciplines. One could try to use it to identify the qualities that make a good mathematician or a good physicist for instance; however, such questions are not, strictly speaking, scientific ones, and are subject to too much uncertainty to constitute a significant contribution to the culture of mathematicians or physicists. Of more interest for scientists are detailed studies of specific scientific achievements, in which they could observe concrete ways of doing successful science, and that could become a kind of model for their own research. It is well-known that the hypothetico-deductive method in mathematics for instance is a way of presenting results, but not a way to discover new results; the elements of method to discover new results can only be found by looking at concrete scientific works. To this, one could object that there are no such constant laws in the scientific method, as has been shown for example by P. Feyerabend.[4] This is true, in a way, but only if one understands that these laws should be, like scientific laws, applicable everywhere in the exact same way. On the contrary, the laws of method are, like the laws of human condition that Thucydides wanted to illustrate, much closer to civil laws: they have to be adapted to the case at hand. It is precisely because such laws cannot be stated universally that scientists have to invent them, and it is precisely because they are hard to invent that one should better, whenever possible, adapt them from a solution to a similar problem.

Declaring that history is a source of inspiration is thus very similar to G. Pólya's advice to students to look back when they have found a solution to a problem: *"By looking back at the completed solution, by reconsidering and reexamining the results and the path that led to it, they could consolidate their knowledge and develop their ability to solve problems."*[5] If this kind of reflexivity is beneficial for a student, then there are no reasons to believe that it is not, on a larger scale, also helpful for advanced scientists.

---

[3]   Thucydides, *History of the Peloponnesian War*, I, 22, 4.

[4]   Feyerabend, P., *Against Method*.

[5]   Pólya, G., *How To Solve It*, I, § 13, pp. 14–15.

1.3   History as a Condition of Progress

The perhaps most used quotation to justify the need of history is G. Santayana's aphorism: *"those who cannot remember the past are condemned to repeat it."*[6] It is, however, often given a different meaning than the one Santayana had in mind when he wrote it down. Because it uses the verb "condemn," it is interpreted as referring to past errors only, and indeed it seems that their repetition is better prevented when they are known and documented. This interpretation would give a rather limited and negative role to history, namely, to record the wanderings of the past. Its original meaning becomes clear by looking at its immediate context: *"Progress, far from consisting in change, depends on retentiveness. When change is absolute there remains no being to improve and no direction is set for possible improvement; and when experience is not retained, as among savages, infancy is perpetual. Those who cannot remember the past are condemned to repeat it."* In other words, Santayana does not tell us that it is necessary to remember past mistakes to avoid falling in the same traps, but that it is necessary to retain experience in order to progress; if not, then knowledge or society stagnates.

The need of history does not, however, follow immediately from this observation: even in sciences, in which studying original documents is currently not seen as something important, experience is retained, but it is absorbed and synthesized in later works. There is thus no risk to "reinvent the wheel," at least for the most important results. However, something is lacking in such syntheses, namely what the now common interpretation of Santayana's aphorism designates: the ideas that seem good only for a while, the failed attempts to solve a problem, the methods that have proven to be wrong. The risk is thus, in trying to solve the problem of the motion of vehicles, to reinvent something that is not a wheel. This is the second role of history, complementary to the first one: it can help scientists to detect early on that a path they could be tempted to take is actually a dead alley. Put another way, history can help them to walk faster on the paths of science.

2   History: For Whom?

History has, unlike other disciplines, no specific subject to study, except history of history. All other subjects that it could study already belong to another field of human knowledge. The immediate consequence of this fact is that the primary audience of historical works are never other historians, with the exception of history of history. In disciplines in which history is currently not seen as something important, it is thus tempting to target the layman, because of the lack of interest of the participants of the field. However, as we have just seen, history is, at its best, a source of inspiration and a condition of progress. This implies that the history of a field should, on the contrary, as much as possible be targeted at the primary actors of that field. This can be seen in the fields in which history already plays an important role: studies on Hegel's philosophy are written primarily for philosophers, and studies on Le Corbusier's

---

[6]   Santayana, G., *The Life of Reason*, vol. I, ch. XII, p. 284.

architectural creations are written primarily for architects. Targeting the general public would inevitably imply to dumb the material down to reach the lowest common denominator of its interests, and therefore to lose the attention of those who are the main contributors to the field.

An additional difficulty, clearly not unique to the case of computing, arises at this point: the field of computing involves many different aspects, which are far apart from each other. Computer programmers, hardware designers, capital investors, computer scientists and computer users are all primary actors of the field, and yet their interests do not overlap and are even in conflict with each other. The kind of details and the kind of approach that will interest a computer scientist will probably not interest a computer user, and vice versa. History is, in that respect, very much like cartography: it is not possible to put every possibly relevant information on a single map; otherwise it becomes unreadable. Latitudes and longitudes, fauna and flora indications, roads and paths, buildings, geological or agricultural information, names, traffic density, altitudes, average temperature and precipitation, crime rates, population density and average wealth are for instance all relevant information, but only a few of these can be put on a given map, depending on its purpose. Even the scale of a map depends on its purpose: a too small one is impractical for car journeys, and a too large one useless for hiking. It would obviously be absurd to try to argue that one of these maps is better than the others: it all depends, again, on their aim. What is clear however is that its purpose should be explicit, and likewise that the target audience of a historical work should be clearly identified. Put another way, it is thus necessary to make a distinction between the different audiences, because it is impossible to address all of them simultaneously. The resulting historical works will be very different depending on the chosen target audience, and will probably be mostly useless, except occasionally, to other audiences.

We will therefore briefly consider three possible audiences for history of computing: computer scientists (§ 2.1), computer programmers (§ 2.2), and teachers (§ 2.3). Other possible audiences could, and certainly should, be considered, but they fall outside of our area of least incompetence.

2.1   History for a Computer Scientist

Confronted with the idea that studying history could perhaps be useful for him, a computer scientist would probably immediately object that his science, and for that matter any other science, is concerned with truths that are independent of time and place, and not by the particularities of this or that specific past event. The four-square theorem for example was first stated by Diophantus during the third century, and was first proven by Lagrange in 1770, but it would not change anything to mathematics if it was suddenly discovered that this theorem was already stated by Archimedes, or that Lagrange actually copied his demonstration from a not yet known manuscript of Fermat.

This radical opposition between the scientist's and the historian's approaches seems irreconcilable: the main task of a scientist is to establish general laws, whereas a historian should, on the contrary, refrain as much as possible from doing so.

This opposition is so strong that Aristotle considered that even poetry is more universal than history.[7] This binary view is not incorrect, but it misses something important, namely that science is a human activity, and that its results are thus discovered over time. This does not mean, obviously, that scientific laws are relative, but only that the order in which the different elements of a science are discovered is not without importance and without meaning. New concepts and theories are always introduced in presence of a difficulty: this implies that one cannot correctly understand the nature of a scientific concept if one does not see how it was born, that is, for what problem it was a solution, and what was the difficulty that it allowed to overcome. There is always a part of arbitrariness in scientific concepts, and understanding why and how they were created is necessary to understand them better, very much like understanding the motives of someone's choices is necessary to understand them. Such studies are thus necessary to become conscious of their arbitrariness: scientists are often so accustomed to them that they could tend to forget that they could have been different, very much like one tends to forget that counting in base ten or having weeks of seven days is arbitrary. Historical works written for computer scientists should therefore try to give an insight into the core concepts of the discipline, by trying to identify the origin of the difficulties that led to the creation of these concepts, and by comparing them with the other options that were rejected.[8]

Another argument that a computer scientist could object to the need of history is that the aim of science is to advance, and that history, looking essentially backwards, cannot, by its very approach, help a science to do so. This is, again, correct, but it relies on a too narrow understanding of what science is. Doing science does not only consist in piling new discoveries on top of an existing knowledge; it is also a matter of organizing this knowledge and these discoveries as a coherent whole. There are thus at least two different ways to contribute to the progress of a science: either by discovering a new result, or by putting order in it; history can help a scientist at least for the latter task. More generally, historical works can help scientists to put the latest discoveries in perspective, to determine to what degree a claimed novelty is actually novel, and to become more conscious that their discipline evolves slowly. In other words, it can help a discipline to constitute itself as a coherent body of timeless truths.

Finally, for a young discipline such as computer science, in which the fact that the underlying hardware changes so fast gives the inevitable impression that it is continuously evolving, history may also contribute to an increase of the perception of its stability over time, that is, to an increased consciousness of its scientificity.

2.2   History for a Computer Programmer

A programmer will probably be even less interested in historical studies than a scientist, at first sight. It is for example totally irrelevant, in the daily practice of a

---

[7] Aristotle, *Poetics*, 1051b6–7.

[8] An example of this kind of work, in a different field, is Bourbaki, N., *Éléments d'histoire des mathématiques*.

doctor, that the stethoscope she uses has been invented by a Breton called Laennec in 1816; she will certainly not be a better doctor if she knows this. Likewise, it is not important for a programmer to know who discovered the sorting algorithm he uses, what language was the first object-oriented one, or who invented the principles of database organization. If history consists in documenting who invented what and when, then it is indeed useless for an engineer. What could, on the contrary, be interesting for engineers is a precise exposition of the intellectual conditions under which the techniques he uses were invented. Studying the context of the discovery of these techniques will not only help him to grasp their precise meaning and purpose: it also illustrates a way of approaching new problems that has proven to be successful. Acquiring this way of thinking is perhaps even more important for programmers than mastering these particular techniques.

Concretely speaking, historical studies aimed at computer programmers should take the form of detailed expositions of the implementation of innovative computer programs. Such expositions can help him to understand the thought processes of those who created them, and to get a better problem solving mindset. These expositions should not only present the implementation itself, but, as far as possible, the alternative schemes that were not chosen, along with the reasons why they were not chosen. Finally, because computer programmers try to avoid introducing errors in their programs, and put lots of energy in correcting them, such studies should also present the errors that were discovered, how they were discovered, why they were introduced, and how they were solved.[9]

2.3   History for a Teacher

A teacher is in a very different perspective than a scientist or an engineer: her aim, as a teacher, is not to discover new results or to implement new computer programs, but to present the most important results and techniques as clearly as possible to her students. It seems that for doing this she does not need to study history, because she can use the work of experts who have already spent time to digest the literature and to present it in reference textbooks. Using primary sources instead of textbooks would be a waste of energy, because she would redo something that has already been done, and most probably not as well. Moreover, the original presentation of many important results or techniques is often obscured by an outdated vocabulary, or by obsolete notations.

All this is true, but it considers the problem of teaching only from the point of view of the teacher and of the results to be taught. Equally important are, however, the student and his difficulties, and it is there that history can play a role. Studying original papers can help the teacher to understand why something that she considers obvious or trivial is actually not obvious or trivial at all: not only did it take years or centuries to develop, but it was considered difficult at some point, it was not

---

[9]   An example of this kind of work is Organick, E. I., *The Multics System: An Examination of its Structure.*

immediately adopted, and it was perhaps even criticized when it was proposed. In short, there is no better way to become really conscious that something is not easy than to realize how much people have struggled with it.

However, such studies can only be profitable if one assumes that there is at least a similarity between the difficulties of the students and the difficulties experienced by those who discovered the results and techniques, or those who were first in contact with them. Such a similarity seems indeed to exist, and G. Pólya even draws a parallel between Haeckel's biogenetic law, which states that *"ontogeny recapitulates phylogeny,"* that is, that the development of an individual animal mimics the evolution history of its species, and mental development compared to the development of a discipline.[10] It is indeed clear that students will have, at the very least, the same difficulties as the thinkers of the past who had to discover the concepts and to master them: there is no reason to believe that a concept has become obvious simply because time has passed since it was discovered.

3   History: How?

Some elements about the kind of approaches that can be used in history of computing have already been given above, but it is now possible to characterize it more generally, albeit negatively, by pointing out three common temptations of historical research: focusing on "firsts" (§ 3.1), exhaustiveness (§ 3.2) and anachronism (§ 3.3).

3.1   The Temptation of "Firsts"

Chronologies are, admittedly, not much more interesting than listing the random draws of a lottery by date; they even put many schoolboys off history. The reason behind this fact is obviously not that establishing facts is not important for a historian, but that facts are a mere starting point of his work. What makes a historical work interesting and useful is not the collection of brute facts on which it relies, but the causal relations between these facts; the proper work of a historian is to uncover these relations.

One of the consequences of this rule is that history should not focus on the paternity of ideas (or, even worse, on the paternity of words), because determining who invented this or that or who deserves this or that title has little to do with the causal relations that should be sought. It is well known that results and ideas are often discovered independently by different people, sometimes after having been forgotten for some time, and that ideas rarely spring out of nowhere, but are often the result of a larger cooperation. It is thus far more enlightening to try to understand for what reasons someone became aware of an idea than to try to determine if nobody ever had that idea before him. For that matter, most debates on "firsts" are debates on definitions, which implies that they can have no conclusion.

---

[10]   Pólya, G., *The Teaching of Mathematics and the Biogenetic Law.*

3.2   The Temptation of Exhaustiveness

A possible difficulty of historical research, certainly present in history of computing, is the enormous amouht of material that has to be dealt with. One of the effects of this fact on historical works is that one could be tempted, in the name of accuracy, to give as many details as possible and to give as many references as possible, resulting in a gratuitous show of erudition.

The similarity between history and cartography, of which we made use above, can again be helpful here: it is never possible to put all the details on a map and, even if maps of a smaller scale will contain more information than others, they will never indicate every plant, every stone and every lump of dirt. Likewise, one of the main tasks of a historian is to make a selection among the facts of which he is aware, that is, to identify the facts and references that are relevant to his topic, as in museums for example, in which only a tiny fraction of the collections are on display. Otherwise historical accounts become noisy and, in the end, unreadable, because they add an unnecessary burden for the reader, namely to select the relevant information in the vast amount of details.

3.3   The Temptation of Anachronism

Anachronism consists, in its most common form, in reading the past through modern glasses, that is, in interpreting the events of the past from the standpoint of the present. The consequence of anachronism is not only that it does not do justice to the past, but mainly that it prevents us to learn something from it, because our ideas are often foreign to those of the past and will inevitably affect its interpretation. For example, interpreting Euclid's *Elements* with modern algebraic symbols would be anachronistic, because he is reasoning with magnitudes and not with quantities; likewise, translating Aristotle's *Analytics* into the symbolism of modern logic would be anachronistic, because he is reasoning about concepts and not about symbols. The correct historical attitude, on the contrary, bears some resemblance to the method used by Husserl for instance, namely *"to begin in absolute poverty, with an absolute lack of knowledge."*[11] This does not mean that the less the historian knows about the topic he studies, the better he will be, but that he should temporarily forget what he knows to enter the minds of the actors of the past without preconceived ideas.

An immediate consequence of this rule is that writing history by conducting interviews, which is especially tempting in history of computing because some of the main contributors to the field are still alive, should be avoided. It is certainly much easier to do than to dig patiently and attentively in the primary sources, and it will probably even be easier to read,[12] but it will always result in a very biased picture of the past, and most probably in a history focusing on anecdotal details and accidental circumstances. It is well-known that memory distorts the past, which means that an

---

[11] Husserl, E., *Cartesian Meditations*, § 1.
[12] See Thucydides, *History of the Peloponnesian War*, I, 22, 4.

actor of a past event will, many years later, explain it with what he now understands, and with what happened after it, whereas a historian should try to explain that event only with what was understood and what happened before it. Simply stated, interviews are not reliable sources, and using the best available sources has always been a necessary condition of historical research.[13] More generally, even carefully written recollections should be taken with an extreme care; it is only when the primary sources are not available anymore that it can be necessary, by lack of better information, to use secondary sources.

In the fields in which history already plays an important role, history is, by the way, never based on interviews or on recollections; these success cases should perhaps be taken as a model, before trying to invent a new way of doing history. One could of course object that the original documents are not free of errors, which is true. However, the fact that interviews are inherently unreliable sources does not imply that it is possible to rely on original documents without submitting them to a critical analysis; what is at least certain is that original documents are not affected by later ideas and facts. One could also object that the bias or the errors that can exist in a single interview could be compensated by working with collections of interviews from many different actors; alas, historical truth is not more democratic than scientific truth.[14]

Conclusion

Paraphrasing Santayana, we can conclude that "*those who can remember the past will repeat it.*" As we have seen, this does not mean that history seeks to resurrect the past, but that its main aim is to help the participants to a field to benefit from the experience of those who came before them. The best service that history can do for them is to provide them with detailed case studies, oriented towards their specific needs, that can become for them a source of inspiration. Following an old medieval saying, we could say that this can help them to become "dwarfs standing on the shoulders of giants." This saying has two complementary interpretations: its modern interpretation puts the emphasis on the fact that the dwarf can see a bit further than the giant, and its medieval interpretation on the fact that the dwarf is much smaller than the giant.[15] In other words, history can be helpful both to progress, and to remain modest.

Acknowledgments. The author thanks K. R. Apt, H. Cazes, M. van Emden, M. Laurent, B. Le Charlier and P. McJones for their comments, suggestions and support.

---

[13] See for example Thucydides, *History of the Peloponnesian War*, I, 21, 1, and I, 22, 2–3, and Ranke (von), L., *Deutsche Geschichte im Zeitalter der Reformation*, bd. I, p. ix.

[14] Ranke (von), L., *Deutsche Geschichte im Zeitalter der Reformation*, bd. I, p. x.

[15] Jeauneau, E., *"Nani gigantum humeris insidentes"* – *Essai d'interprétation de Bernard de Chartres*.

References

Aristotle: Poetics (ante 322 B. C.)

Bourbaki, N.: Éléments d'histoire des mathématiques, Hermann (1984)

Feyerabend, P.: Against Method. New Left Books (1975)

Husserl, E.: Cartesian Meditations (1929), Cairns, D. (tr.). Martinus Nijhoff (1950)

Jeauneau, E.: "Nani gigantum humeris insidentes" — Essai d'interprétation de Bernard de Chartres. Vivarium 5, 79–99 (1967)

Kuhn, T.S.: The Structure of Scientific Revolutions. University of Chicago Press (1962)

Organick, E.I.: The Multics System: An Examination of its Structure. MIT Press (1972)

Pólya, G.: How To Solve It. Princeton University Press (1945)

Pólya, G.: The Teaching of Mathematics and the Biogenetic Law. In: Good, I.J. (ed.) The Scientist Speculates, Heinemann, pp. 352–356 (1962)

Ranke (von), L.: Deutsche Geschichte im Zeitalter der Reformation, bd. I. Duncker und Humblot (1839)

Santayana, G.: The Life of Reason. Charles Scribner's Sons (1905)

Snow, C.P.: The Two Cultures. The New Statesman and Nation 52, 413–414 (1956)

Snow, C.P.: The Two Cultures and The Scientific Revolution, 1959 Rede Lecture. Cambridge University Press (1959)

Thucydides: History of the Peloponnesian War (ante 395 B. C.), Mynott, J. (tr.) (The War of the Peloponnesians and the Athenians). Cambridge University Press (2013)

"The Internet: A Belgian Story?"
The Mundaneum

Creating a New Forum to Debate the Internet Issue in the French-Speaking Part of Belgium

Delphine Jenart

Deputy Director of the Mundaneum, Belgium
delphine.jenart@mundaneum.be

Abstract. Today the Mundaneum in Belgium is an archives centre and a museum. But the origins of the Mundaneum go back to the late nineteenth century. Created in Brussels by two Belgian jurists, Paul Otlet (1868-1944), the father of documentation, and Henri La Fontaine (1854-1943), Nobel Peace Prize, the project aimed at gathering the entire world's knowledge to file it using the Universal Decimal Classification system that they had created. Today their work is interpreted as the first paper search engine in History. The cultural project of the institution is both aimed at highlighting the heritage and questioning the future of access to knowledge.

Keywords: Information science, heritage, Paul Otlet, Henri La Fontaine, Universal Decimal Classification, Universal Bibliographic Repertory, information technology, search engine, museum, archives, Belgium, Unesco.

Brussels, 1934. *"Here, the work desk is no longer loaded with books. Instead, there is a screen, and within easy reach, a telephone. All the books and all the information are somewhere else, far away, in a huge building. From there, the page that needs to be read is made to appear on the screen to find the answer to the question asked on the telephone."* Paul Otlet (1868-1944), Treaties on Documentation.

Without knowing that this was written in 1934 by a lawyer passionate about bibliography, these few sentences may seem somewhat insignificant. However, today they provide an insight into a work that was clearly ahead of its time.

Mons, 6 June 2012, 11:32 p.m. In the wake of the World Science Festival in New York[1], the story had just broken on Yahoo! News: *"The history of the Internet has been traced back even further into the past. The concept of the "web" in fact dates back to 1934..."*

At the time when we were celebrating the 20th anniversary of the World Wide Web (1989-2009) and the 30th anniversary of the Internet (1983-2013), the Mundaneum,

---

[1] World Science Festival, New York, June 2012 :
   http://worldsciencefestival.com/blog/
   alex_wright_premonitions_of_the_internet

A. Tatnall, T. Blyth, and R. Johnson (Eds.): HC 2013, IFIP AICT 416, pp. 79–85, 2013.

created at the beginning of the 20th century by Belgians Paul Otlet and Henri La Fontaine, invited us to discover a new perspective on the history of information and communication technologies.

Robert Cailliau, co-founder of the World Wide Web together with Tim Berners Lee (CERN, 1989), admitted[2]: *"The history of the Mundaneum confirms my beliefs with regards to the invention of the Web: it isn't an invention, but rather a convergence of elements and precursors which have more or less laid the foundations of what we know today; attempts which have been of huge importance. We were just in the right place at the right time to launch what we now call the Web..."*

1   A Little Bit of History

The Mundaneum is the work of two Belgian Lawyers, Paul Otlet (1868-1944) and Henri La Fontaine (1854-1943, winner of the Nobel Peace Prize in 1913). At the end of the 19th century, both men aspired to collect and index all knowledge in order to share it on a global scale and thereby promote the idea of peace between nations.

Fig. 1. Paul Otlet, father of Documentation, Brussels, 1934 (collections of the Mundaneum)

It was in Brussels in 1895 that the men laid the foundations of the *Office International de Bibliographie* (OIB). Otlet and La Fontaine drew upon the knowledge and techniques of their time to design and build the very first paper search engine, The "Universal Bibliographic Repertory", based on record cards indexed

---

[2]   October 2012, RTBF La Première (www.rtbf.be)

using the "Universal Decimal Classification" system (UDC), which they developed from American librarian Melvil Dewey's Decimal Classification. The UDC is still used in libraries today, but Paul Otlet and Henri La Fontaine's contribution to the science of modern information management is not limited to just this classification system.

Fig. 2. Henri La Fontaine, Nobel Prize for Peace in 1913 (collections of the Mundaneum)

Fig. 3. The Universal Bibliographic Repertory, Brussels, 1910

Paul Otlet, who is recognised as the father of documentation, was the first to conceptualise and devise a classification tool which digitised access to knowledge. Considering the notion of information as independent from its medium but also the need to come up with powerful means of transmitting this information, he created blueprints for many systems between 1900 and 1935, each more visionary than the next. As a result, Paul Otlet left us with many drawings and descriptive notes of what technology would become a century later: the video conference, the conference call, the mobile phone, cloud computing – in other words, the global communication network!

Fig. 4. Sketches by Paul Otlet, Brussels, between 1900 and 1934 (collections of the Mundaneum)

"It was a steampunk version of hypertext!" exclaimed the co-founder of Wired magazine (USA) and author of "What Technology Wants", Kevin Kelly, when he discovered Otlet's work.

"The Semantic Web is rather Otlet-ish", maintains Michael Buckland, professor at the School of Information at the University of California, Berkeley.

As a true data scientist, in 1934 Paul Otlet had already sized up the challenge of the years to come: "Mankind is at a turning point in its history. The mass of data acquired is astounding. We need new instruments to simplify it, to condense it, or intelligence will never be able to overcome the difficulties imposed upon it or achieve the progress that it foresees and to which it aspires." (Paul Otlet, Treaties on Documentation, 1934).

At the heart of their era, Paul Otlet and Henri La Fontaine were truly passionate about the culture of the network. As such, they set up a global intellectual cooperation network rallying together multiple institutions, such as universities, libraries and associations from around the world, to ensure their project's success. Thanks to their lobbying skills, they formed an international relations network which included personalities such as the Lumière brothers, Ernest Solvay and even the American industrialist and pacifist Andrew Carnegie.

Fig. 5. Andrew Carnegie's visit to the "Palais mondial", Cinquantenaire, Brussels, 1913 (collections of the Mundaneum)

The Mundaneum, birthplace of international institutions dedicated to knowledge and brotherhood, became a universal documentation centre over the course of the 20th century. Its collections, comprising thousands of books, newspapers, small documents, posters, glass plates, postcards, and bibliographic records were gathered and stored in different locations around Brussels, including the Palais du Cinquantenaire, built in 1880 to celebrate the 50th anniversary of Belgium's independence.

This gave rise to a much more grandiose project in the mind of Paul Otlet: that of the World City, for which the French architect Le Corbusier would create plans and models. The aim of the City was to bring together the major institutions of intellectual work, such as libraries, museums and universities, on a global scale. Unfortunately, this project would never actually come to fruition.

The Mundaneum project, deeply rooted in utopian ideals, was quickly confronted with the magnitude of the technical development of its era.

Now located in the French speaking part of Belgium in the city of Mons, just a few miles from Brussels, the Mundaneum has become an Archive Centre of the Wallonia-Brussels Federation (Belgian State) and a temporary exhibition space. Mons is preparing itself to turn into a European capital of Culture in 2015.

The documentary heritage that is currently archived there is made up of the personal archives of its founders, books, small documents, posters, post cards, glass plates, the Universal Bibliographic Repertory (UBR), the International Press Museum and archive collections relating to three main themes: pacifism, anarchism and feminism. In June 2013 the UBR was added to the Unesco's "Memory of the World" Register[3].

Since the publication of the first biography of Paul Otlet in 1974, "The Universe of Information: the Work of Paul Otlet for Documentation and international

---

[3] UNESCO Memory of the World :
   http://www.unesco.org/new/en/communication-and-information/flagship-project-activities/memory-of-the-world/register/full-list-of-registered-heritage/registered-heritage-page-9/universal-bibliographic-repertory/

Organization", by an Australian student named Boyd Rayward[4], a large international scientific community has developed around the legacy of the founders of the Mundaneum.

Today, thanks to an abundance of literature (MIT press, Harvard University, the University of Indiana, the University of Illinois, Ghent University, Cambridge, Paris Sorbonne, UCLA-Berkeley, the Universities of Hamburg, Bologna, Montreal, and so on), Paul Otlet's undeniable contribution to information science during the 20th century and to our understanding of information technologies is now recognised.

At the heart of our information society, the Mundaneum project keeps its purpose alive by constantly updating its message. Bringing the ideas, archives and collections bequeathed by its founders face to face with current and future social issues: this is the ambition of the Mundaneum, which is currently looking toward "Mons, European Capital of Culture 2015", whose leitmotiv is none other than *"Where technology meets culture"*!

2   Making the History of Computing Relevant

It took the digital revolution for us to recognise Paul Otlet as the visionary that he was... but also to realise that the origins of information and communication technologies are much more deeply rooted in the history of mankind, and came long before the appearance of the first calculators. Could it be, as suggested by Alex Wright, journalist at the New York Times who wrote this great article about the Mundaneum *"The web time forgot"* and author of "GLUT: Mastering information through the ages", that it is "the way the technology industry works which discourages perception of the historical context"?

French philosopher Michel Serres describes the advent of information technologies as *"a cultural and cognitive revolution"*. This relates to the very depths of our being: our language, our "existence in the world". The legitimacy of its history makes the Mundaneum a unique place which offers a critical reflection on the digital revolution, of which we are all witnesses and participants. It is a revolution that has resulted in an emergent culture which affects all generations. Today, the Mundaneum takes on meaning in this new cultural landscape. This is why, more than ever, the Mundaneum is turning towards the younger generation who were born into the "digital age".

As a place where history meets technology, the Mundaneum dares to be a space for the socio-cultural mediation of communication technologies.

Spurred on by the revolution, the scope for action and reflection is immense:

Identifying and promoting the understanding of the social impact of these technologies, bringing ICTs and people closer together and demystifying their use, helping people understand how they can be used as medium for building social ties, encouraging everyone to consider their own status as a digital citizen and not only as a consumer of technologies, making the public aware of the development of new knowledge as well as new identities in the web 2.0 era based on issues linked to data

---

[4]   University of Illinois, USA.

organisation and control (big data, open data, etc.), promoting the society of knowledge by highlighting strategies for sharing knowledge, discussing issues related to freedom of expression on the Internet but also respecting and protecting the privacy of others, highlighting the scientific developments that foretell of a near future where technology permeates all aspects of our everyday lives...

3   An Exhibition Space, a Forum for Discussions, a Mediation and Meeting Place for Groups, and a Virtual Platform for Celebrating a Unique Legacy

In light of this vision, in 2010 the Mundaneum started to offer a programme of events dedicated to these issues. The launch of the collaboration between the Mundaneum and Google in 2012 (formalised in 2013) was intended to give greater impetus to this socio-cultural mediation project – the only one of its kind in Belgium!

Among the events organised by the Mundaneum are:

- An exhibition on the organisation of knowledge ("Renaissance 2.0 : a journey through the origins of the web[5]")
- A series of conferences/debates based on "The impact of information and communication technologies on society", addressing many topics from the freedom of expression on the Internet, digital studies, the Internet and multilingualism to scientific mediation in the Web 2.0 era, to name a few
- A series of large conferences led by Google aiming to highlight the European pioneers of computing history, during which we had the opportunity of welcoming Frenchman Louis Pouzin, inventor of the datagram, the Belgian Robert Cailliau, co-founder of the WWW at CERN, and even the researchers Alex Wright (USA), journalist for the New York Times, and Boyd Rayward (Australia), biographer of Paul Otlet, on "The forgotten pioneers of the history of the Internet "
- Every exhibition at the Mundaneum becomes the subject of significant pedagogical mediation (50% of the Mundaneum's visitors are made up of school groups), including ICTs (development of a serious game to enhance the museum visit)
- The organisation of a 'web fair day' designed to bring together young businesses that are involved in the web and the digital domain and students who are in the process of choosing their career path
- The creation of a space[6] dedicated to the Mundaneum on the Google Cultural Institute international platform (digitalarchives.mundaneum.org), which enables the Mundaneum to share its archives on a global scale and also to publish them in an aesthetically pleasing format.

---

[5] Mundaneum : http://expositions.mundaneum.org/en/exhibitions/renaissance2.0-en
[6] Google cultural Institute : http://digitalarchives.mundaneum.org

Part IV

Spotlight on Some Research Projects

The Konrad Zuse Internet Archive Project

Julian Röder, Raúl Rojas, and Hai Nguyen

Freie Universität Berlin, Institute of Computer Science, Berlin, Germany
{julian.roeder,raul.rojas,hai.nguyen}@fu-berlin.de
http://zuse.zib.de

Abstract. This paper provides an overview of the Konrad Zuse Internet Archive project which has been conducted from 2010 until 2013 at Freie Universität Berlin in cooperation with Deutsches Museum in Munich[1]. The project has been mainly concerned with digitising and publication of previously unreleased private papers of Konrad Zuse. We want to make the history of computing relevant to the general public and the archive has been extended by creating a panorama, simulations, films and an introductory encyclopaedia.

Keywords: History of Computing, Konrad Zuse, Private Papers, Early Computers, Online Archive, Repository, Digitisation, Digital Humanities, Open Access.

1   The Project

In the Konrad Zuse Internet Archive Project the documents of Konrad Zuse's private papers are being digitised, analysed and published online.

Konrad Zuse (1910-1995) was a German computer pioneer born in Berlin. Between 1935 to 1945 he constructed several calculating machines that have been recognized to be among the first computers worldwide. He used mechanical components and telephone relays to build binary floating-point calculators. At the same time engineers in the UK and the US developed computers with their own technology and methods. In 1949, Zuse founded a company that was one of the first commercial computer production businesses in the world. Due to WWII, for a long time only a few people knew about Zuse's work.

In 2010 - the year of Zuse's 100th birthday - the Zuse Project was launched at Freie Universität Berlin. The project is built around a cooperation with Deutsches Museum, where the originals of the private papers have been stored. The original documents of Zuse's private papers include sketches, photographs, manuscripts, typescripts, prints, shorthand notes. Most of this material was unpublished and has been released successively on the internet in an open access online archive (see Fig. 1). The documents were digitised in high quality for long-term archiving and then the images were processed for the presentation in a web browser. With the publication of these documents the project contributes to the preservation of cultural heritage and provides

---

[1]   The project was supported by the German Research Foundation (DFG).

public access to it. The Konrad Zuse Internet Archive is the digital primary source in the world for those who want to become acquainted with Zuse's work and study it in detail.

Konrad Zuse Internet Archive

History: Home / Collections / Home /

Who was Konrad Zuse?

Konrad Zuse (1910-1995) was a computer pioneer who built one of the first program-controlled computing machines. Between 1936 and 1945 he built his first four computing machines - the Z1, Z2, Z3 and Z4. In 1945 he moved to Bavaria where he continued to construct computing machines with his new company. There he also designed one of the first high-level programming languages - the so-called Plankalkül. Learn more about Konrad Zuse and his machines in the Encyclopedia (please see menu above).

What is the Konrad Zuse Internet Archive?

This online archive offers access to the digitized original documents of the private papers of Konrad Zuse. These documents include technical drawings, photographs, and various documents, some of which are written in shorthand. The originals and the master copies of the digitized images are stored at the archives of Deutsches Museum. Learn more about the project.

How was the Konrad Zuse Internet Archive implemented?

The Konrad Zuse Internet Archive is based on the open source repository software imeji. Compared to a regular website a repository can also manage metadata in addition to the images. Metadata are information about the images describing them and their contents granting a better understanding of the presented object. imeji is developed by the Max Planck Digital Library and the Konrad Internet Archive Project is contributing to its development in order to create a general solution for projects that want to publish images online. Learn more about imeji.

Recent comments

Fig. 1. Screenshot of the project website

2   Making the History of Computing Relevant

The goal of the project in general was to encourage people to explore Konrad Zuse's work, to learn about it, and to understand the history of computing. In order to turn information about computer history into a form that people can understand and appreciate the project took several steps which shall be described below. For some of these actions, education experts were involved to ensure the comprehensibility of the presented subjects by non-experts.

2.1   Panorama

In order to understand old computing machines it is important to give interested persons the opportunity to get a picture of the object in question. The first step in approaching complex machinery such as a computer is to become acquainted visually by grasping its dimensions, structure, materials etc. Therefore the project created a sophisticated 360° object panorama of the Z1 calculating machine (Zuse's first computer, constructed in 1938[2]) consisting of over 1000 high-resolution images. The user can move around the machine, view it from different heights and zoom in to see the different elements of each functional unit (see Fig. 2). The whole machine is broken down into several functional units to illustrate the interplay of the different parts. Thus each functional unit is bordered by a white line to emphasize and separate it from the others. If a user hovers over a functional unit of the machine a description text is displayed to clarify its role. The panorama gives a good first impression of a historical computing machine and opens up the contextualizing and understanding of follow-up experiences in this field.

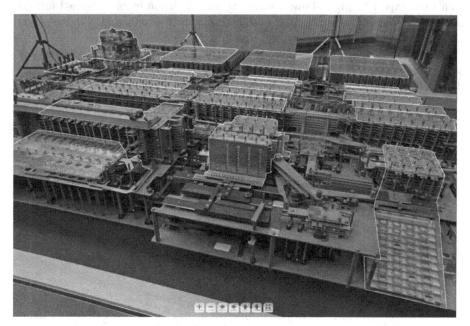

Fig. 2. Screenshot of the panorama

2.2   Simulations

To demonstrate the operational functionalities of Zuse's machines several simulations have been developed in the project. The interactive simulations encourage the users to explore the work of Konrad Zuse. Another crucial element is the flexible usability of the simulation. Giving the possibility to freely rotate, continuously zoom, adjust the transparency and toggle on and off the visibility of different layers of the machine at will, grants an interesting vein of discovering the key features

---

[2]   Since the original machine was destroyed during WWII, Zuse built a reconstruction in the 1980s of which the photos were taken.

and details of the machine. The operationality of the machine is made clear by the graphical representation of each construction element and their movements. Coloured highlighting indicates where elements have been activated and how they initiate movements of other elements to bring the machine into the next state.

Another significant construction requirement was the meaningful usability of the simulation. The user can input numbers into the simulation (see Fig. 3) and afterwards the detailed calculation is simulated step by step. This means that the users can really calculate with the simulated machine. For each instructional machine step the mathematical meaning, such as intermediate results and carry-overs in binary and decimal notation, are displayed. Thus the mathematical and the engineering aspects of the machine are connected and it is spelled out how they constrain each other. Buttons to start, stop, pause, reset and repeat the last computational step of the machine, along with some expert settings, allows controlling the simulation in an individual fashion and timing. In this manner the user interaction is directly connected with the object and thereby an intensive empowerment is achieved.

Since all these functionalities may confuse non-experts a help page and a step-by-step guiding system is integrated into the simulation to break complicated processes down and provide explanatory descriptions of each step.

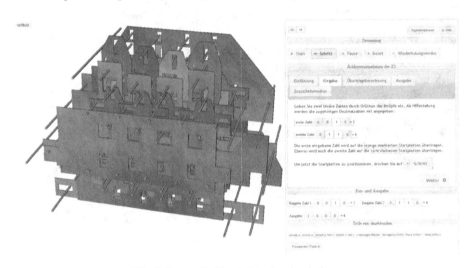

Fig. 3. Input of addends into the simulation

2.3   Films

Another way of presenting intricate machines is by descriptive films. On the project website two animated films about Zuse's Assembly Line Self-Replicating Systems and Helix-Tower are exhibited. These machines are not computers, but they underpin the style of engineering and way of constructional thinking of Konrad Zuse. Both machines are from the late work of Zuse and depict the continuation of his computational machine concepts to other fields of engineering.

2.4   Encyclopaedia

Since Zuse's work comprises many different machines and a broad variety of employed technologies it was important to offer means to familiarize the users with certain basic terms and concepts. The technical implementation of his diverse machines and their capabilities as well as the utilized terminology within Zuse's private papers is relevant in understanding his work. The machines were made up of thousands of pieces that work together like a clock – each piece has its function and is necessary for the overall working of the machine. However Zuse used a set of standard construction elements that were reused wherever it was possible. This concept reduced the complexity of the machines and the constructional effort needed.

On the project website an encyclopaedia with thematic subpages is provided. These subpages are concerned with Konrad Zuse, his machine, essential technologies, fundamental construction elements and important theoretical and mathematical concepts. The subpages are linked to each other as well as to appropriate objects in the online archive and thus the contents can easily be reached by the users. Since the subpages are mutually explanatory a consolidated knowledge on the topic is presented. Thereby the users are enabled to put a certain object into context and to understand the function of important construction elements within Zuse's machines.

2.5   Konrad Zuse as a Designer and Builder of Computers

Konrad Zuse's personal history is presented on the project website. His high school and student period, the building of his first computing machines between 1936 and 1945 and the formation of his company are portrayed. Various photos of Zuse and research essays about him are available as well.

Zuse's role as an inventor of computers was worked out in detail by our cooperation partner Deutsches Museum.

2.6   The Online Archive

There are a lot of different possible questions about Zuse's work and in comparison to related developments in the history of computing. For this reason the goal was to create a searchable database for the digital documents (e.g. in Fig. 4). The images and the information about them (so-called metadata) are managed by an online archive software that is co-developed in the project and is integrated in the project website[3].

The online archive software permits quick navigation, search and browsing and therewith easy access to the documents via (re-)entry points. Browsing through the contents is achieved by tabulated thumbnails which lead to the higher resolution images. For flexible viewing of the documents different tools for interactive viewing and scientific analysis such as zooming, rotating, panning as well as colour and brightness adjustments permits the user to examine a document in an individual manner. Thumbnail navigation, facet navigation and sortable lists grant a comfortable

---

[3] http://zuse.zib.de

overview over the available contents. The advanced search functionality includes logical AND, OR and NOT connectives and the possibility to specify a certain collection of images to search in. Furthermore the user can precisely define the search criteria and key words in order to obtain detailed results.

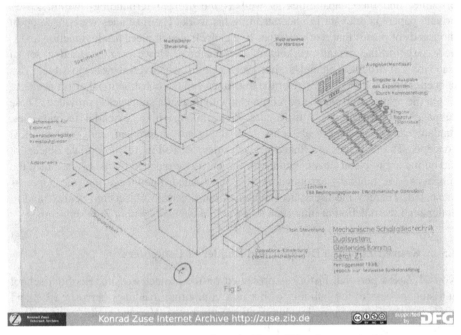

Fig. 4. Example of a document from the Konrad Zuse Internet Archive

2.7   Open Access

The Konrad Zuse Internet Archive is an online archive that complies with the open access paradigm. It is free of charge and all documents are published under an open license that allows reuse and sharing. No registration or login is required to view the contents. Using standard formats the stored data is compatible and interoperable with external services which can access the archive via an interface.

The online archive software is open source and is developed by a developer community in which different institutions participate.

2.8   Relation to Modern Computers

Computers became ubiquitous in the recent past on the one hand but opaque in their operational functionality to most users on the other. The early computers of Konrad Zuse worked with similar abstract concepts as modern computers but they are much easier to understand because they were bigger and slower. By presenting the above mentioned endeavours on the project website a better understanding of modern computers for non-experts shall be achieved as well. Creating a link between historical and modern computers is essential to make the history of computing interesting to the general public since it correlates history to modern everyday life.

Acknowledgements. The Konrad Zuse Internet Archive Project was supported by the German Research Foundation (DFG).

References

1. Rojas, R. (ed.): Encyclopedia of Computers and Computer History. Fitzroy Dearborn, Chicago (2001)
2. Rojas, R., Hashagen, U. (eds.): The First Computers - History and Architectures. MIT Press, Cambridge (2000)
3. Rojas, R. (ed.): Die Rechenmaschinen von Konrad Zuse. Springer, Berlin (1998)
4. Rojas, R.: How to make Konrad Zuse's Z3 a universal computer. IEEE Annals of the History of Computing 20(3), 51–54 (1998)
5. Rojas, R.: Konrad Zuse's Legacy: The Architecture of the Z1 and Z3. IEEE Annals of the History of Computing 19(2), 5–16 (1997)

Discovery of Two Historical Computers in Switzerland: Zuse Machine M9 and Contraves Cora and Discovery of Unknown Documents on the Early History of Computing at the ETH Archives

Herbert Bruderer

Swiss Federal Institute of Technology, Zurich
herbert.bruderer@inf.ethz.ch, herbert.bruderer@bluewin.ch

Abstract. Since 2009 we have been trying to find out more about the beginnings of computer science in Switzerland and abroad. Most eyewitnesses have already died or are over 80 years old. In general, early analog and digital computers have been dismantled long ago. Subject to exceptions, the few remaining devices are no longer functioning. Many documents have gone lost. Therefore investigations are difficult and very time-consuming. However, we were able to discover several unknown historical computers and hundreds of exciting documents of the 1950s. In 2012, the results have been published in a first book; a second volume will be forthcoming next year.

Keywords: Cora, ERMETH, ETH archives, Hasler AG, Heinz Rutishauser, Konrad Zuse, M9 (=Z9), Mithra AG, Paillard SA, Remington Rand AG, Unesco, Z4.

1   Introduction

My investigations into the history of computing started in 2009 in connection with the Zuse centenary (100th birthday of the German computer pioneer in 2010). The goal was to get a more comprehensive and deeper understanding of the events of the pioneering days. Coincidentally and to our surprise we discovered the program-controlled Zuse relay calculator M9 whose existence was unknown even to computer scientists. Shortly afterwards another machine emerged: the Swiss made transistor computer Cora. From 2010 to 2013 several contemporary eyewitness discussions concerning M9 and Cora took place. In addition to the oral history we attempted to find objects which may have been conserved. To our knowledge, in both cases only a single machine has survived. For the first time, the ETH archives in Zurich were systematically examined with regard to the early history of computing. We soon became aware of their rich cultural heritage. The archives are indeed a true treasure for the history of technology. Research is still ongoing.

A. Tatnall, T. Blyth, and R. Johnson (Eds.): HC 2013, IFIP AICT 416, pp. 96–104, 2013.

2   Discovery of Historical Computers

2.1   2010: Discovery of the Zuse Machine M9 (=Z9)

The M9 was the first program-controlled Zuse machine manufactured in series (25–30 copies). Remington Rand AG, Zurich, initiated the design and construction of the M9 by Zuse KG. M9 is equal to Z9. The name derives from Mithra AG, a Zurich based subsidiary of Remington Rand. It was chosen in order to avoid patent contests. In 2011, we found unique photographs and drawings of the M9 in the Swiss mountain valley of Toggenburg. These are the only existing high-quality pictures of the Zuse calculating punch. To our knowledge, a single copy of an M9 has been preserved. It is now at the main repository of the Museum für Kommunikation in Berne. The machine had been used by the government of the city of Winterthur. We conducted a video interview (DVD) with three eyewitnesses (technical staff) of the M9.

Fig. 1. The program-controlled decimal Zuse relay calculator M9 (=Z9) at Dietfurt (Switzerland), © Max Forrer, Oberhelfenschwil

2.2   2011: Discovery of the Contraves Computer Cora 1

Cora is the first Swiss transistor computer, designed and built by Contraves AG, Zurich. Chief engineer was Peter Toth from Hungary. Cora was operational in 1963 and controlled a high-precision plotter called Coragraph. It was demonstrated at the Swiss national exhibition in Lausanne in 1964. The plotter produced technical drawings such as the outline of the castle of Thun, however the computer was hidden behind a wall. The system was sold throughout the world. As far as we know, only one copy of the Cora 1 is still alive. It can be seen at the Bolo museum of the Swiss Federal Institute of Technology, Lausanne. The Swiss engineer Peter Blum was responsible for the Cora 2 which was available in 1969. The machine was primarily developed for military applications. Contraves also wrote a Fortran compiler.

Fig. 2. The first Swiss transistor computer Cora 1 and its Hungarian designer Peter Toth, ©Musée Bolo, EPFL Lausanne

3   Discovery of Historical Documents

3.1   2011 to 2013: Discovery of Unknown Documents on the Early History of Computing

We found very interesting documents in the archives of the Swiss Federal Institute of Technology, Zurich (ETH Zurich). Other findings relate to the Museum für Kommunikation. The documents mostly refer to the electromechanical digital Z4 and the electronic digital ERMETH. These letters, contracts, reports, and papers necessitate a (at least partial) rewriting of the early history of computing in Switzerland and elsewhere.

3.2   Zuse Machine Z4

In 1950, ETH was the only university in Continental Europe with a functioning computer. Zuse's digital relay calculator Z4 was in operation in Zurich from 1950 to

Fig. 3. The Zuse machine Z4 (with floating-point arithmetic) at Hopferau (Bavaria) was in a bad condition (1949), © ETH Zurich, Bildarchiv

Fig. 4. The program-controlled binary Zuse relay calculator Z4 in operation at the ETH Zurich (1950-1955), © ETH Zurich, Bildarchiv

Fig. 5. The world's highest massive dam (Swiss Alps). The Z4 calculated the tensions, ©Grande Dixence SA/essencedesgin.com

Fig. 6. The Swiss jet fighter P-16 on Lake Constance. The Z4 was used for the flutter calculations, © Staatsarchiv, St. Gallen

1955. ETH had rented the machine. In many respects, Z4 was more modern than its American counterparts because it was a program-controlled binary device using floating-point arithmetic. Overall cost: 50 000 Swiss francs. The Z4 solved some 100 numerical problems, for example calculations about the world's highest massive dam (Grande Dixence, Swiss Alps) and the Swiss jet fighter P-16. Wolfgang Pauli, Nobel prize laureate in physics, was probably the most famous user of the Z4. In 1951, Heinz Rutishauer independently invented the concept of a language compiler. At that time this method was called automatic programming. He was one of the principal creators of the programming language Algol. The experience gained with the Z4 facilitated the self-made construction ERMETH. Thanks to the rental of the Z4 by ETH and Remington Rand's order of a series of M9, the Zuse KG was able to survive.

3.3   ERMETH (Electronic Digital Computer of ETH)

ERMETH, the first Swiss-made computer, was designed and built from 1953 to 1956 by Eduard Stiefel, Heinz Rutishauser and Ambros Speiser. It was fully operational in 1957 with a magnetic drum (capacity 10 000 words). ETH designed a small experimental drum (eventually connected to the Z4 as replacement of the old mechanical memory that was error-prone) and a large definitive drum. Unlike the Z4, the ERMETH was a decimal stored-program computing machine. Rutishauser (a mathematician) and Speiser (an electrical engineer) spent a year of study (1948/1949) in the USA in order to learn the state of the art in computing. They worked at the Harvard University (with Howard Aiken) and the Institute for Advanced Study in Princeton (John von Neumann). Von Neumann had studied chemistry at the ETH. The original budget for the ERMETH (in 1953) was 800 000 Swiss francs, the final cost (in 1957) amounted to 1 000 000 Swiss francs. Swiss industry (Hasler, Gfeller, Wittwer) participated in constructing the ERMETH which was in operation until 1963. At first, ETH thought of a relay computer. As the relays were not reliable enough, they later changed their opinion in favour of vacuum tubes (valves).

Fig. 7. The first Swiss computer, the stored-program decimal electronic digital ERMETH, ETH Zurich (1956), © Museum für Kommunikation, Berne

Fig. 8: The Swiss-made magnetic drum of the ERMETH (capacity 10 000 words, 80 000 bit, 1957), © Museum für Kommunikation, Berne

3.4   A Selection of the New Documents Found in Switzerland

- Zuse's intention to flee (sic!) to Switzerland in 1949 with his principal engineers and their families. What was the reason for Zuse's anxiety?
- Several rather complex contracts between Zuse KG and ETH concerning the Z4 (1949). At last, we now know the exact cost of the Z4 (50 000 Swiss francs).
- Howard Aiken's favourable evaluation of the project ERMETH (1952).
- Answer to the question: Why did ETH prefer to design and build ERMETH instead of buying a computer such as Ferranti?
- Documents on the dramatic story of the construction of ERMETH: serious problems with the magnetic drum storage, the M10 disaster (failure of Remington Rand to produce a complex calculating punch), bankruptcy of the provider of the power supply, the insufficient air-conditioning plant from Sulzer, the premature departure of chief engineer Ambros Speiser to IBM at the end of 1955, the permanent shortage of money, etc. All this caused a delay of about two years.

- The licensing agreement between Hasler AG (now Ascom), Berne, and ETH concerning the magnetic drum of the ERMETH (1955).
- Letters confirming Hasler's intention to commercialize the ERMETH in Europe and USA (1954). This dream seems to have been spoilt by IBM and Speiser respectively.
- The competition arising from new US research laboratories (Battelle, Radio Corporation of America and IBM) challenging Swiss industry and science (headhunting of top scientists thanks to high salaries).
- A research contract between Paillard SA, Yverdon, and ETH regarding the design of a small digital electronic computer (1957–1960).
- Detailed correspondence mainly between Hans Pallmann (president of ETH council) and Eduard Stiefel (founder of the institute of applied mathematics at ETH) related with Z4 and ERMETH.
- Correspondence between ETH and Remington Rand/Mithra AG. Mithra was a subsidiary of Remington Rand (Switzerland), but was later directly governed by Remington Rand (USA). Mithra encountered insurmountable technical difficulties during the construction of M10 (successor to M9). ETH had ordered two machines. After a delay of three years they suddenly gave it up. Because of the problems, Presper Eckert, chief engineer of ENIAC, came to Zurich. In the end, the M10 was replaced by two Univac 120 machines. By the way, John Mauchly and Presper Eckert had Swiss ancestors.
- Establishment of an international computer laboratory by Unesco in Europe. In 1951, the University of Zurich and the Swiss Federal Institute of Technology (ETH) had applied for this center but later they cancelled the offer. In the end, the laboratory was established in Rome.

4   Additions

- **Mysterious meeting between the computer pioneers Alan Turing and Konrad Zuse.** Did Konrad Zuse meet Alan Turing in Göttingen in 1947? The German inventor Heinz Billing mentions an interrogation by British computer scientists in his memoirs. Unfortunately we did not find any further proofs.
- **Paul Bernays enforces a correction of Turing's paper "On computable numbers".** In 1936, Paul Bernays, a mathematician at ETH, detects some errors in Turing's famous paper. Turing therefore published a correction in 1937.
- **Later Swiss inventions.** Other significant Swiss achievements were the innovative work stations Lilith (1978, sold as Diser) and Ceres (1986) as well as influential programming languages like Pascal (1970), Modula, Oberon (by Turing award winner Niklaus Wirth and Jürg Gutknecht).
- **Falsification.** I received three detailed alleged eyewitness reports on Alan Turing, Contraves AG and Paillard SA. They were provided by the same author. The falsified adventurous paper on Turing is a product of fantasy, the text on Contraves is at least partially falsified. The articles on Contraves and Paillard have been published in a shortened version in "Ingenieure bauen die Schweiz" (NZZ publishers, Zurich 2013).

5   Conclusions

The history on the invention of the computer is full of controversy and often rather patriotic, biased or plainly wrong. Three nations – USA, England and Germany – claim to have invented the computer. Who is right? The answer is quite simple: The computer was independently born in these three countries. The actual response depends on the definition of the computer.

The archives of ETH Zurich are a very precious place for further research into the early history of computing. The newly found documents prove that the ETH president Hans Pallmann played a decisive role in renting the German Zuse relay computer Z4 and in building the Swiss electronic digital computer ERMETH. There are still many open questions: Where are the archives of Zuse KG? Who told Stiefel about the Z4? And we still miss the experimental magnetic drum fabricated by ETH and sold to Zuse. Did Contraves design another computer (C2000)?

The Z4 and the M9 (=Z9) are the only two early Zuse devices which were conserved. The original Z4 is exhibited at the Deutsches Museum, Munich. The M9 and the ERMETH are to be found at the Museum für Kommunikation in Berne.

Acknowledgements. The author is very thankful for the help of the ETH archives' staff.

References

1. Protocols of the ETH council, `http://www.sr.ethbib.ethz.ch/digbib/home`
2. Bruderer, H.: Konrad Zuse und die Schweiz. Wer hat den Computer erfunden (Konrad Zuse and Switzerland. Who invented the computer?), 250 p. Oldenbourg-Wissenschaftsverlag, Munich (2012) (with eyewitness reports and a worldwide bibliography of over 500 publications)
3. Bruderer, H.: Wer hat den Computer erfunden? Frühgeschichte der Informatik: USA, England, Deutschland, Österreich, Schweiz. Mit mehreren Zeitzeugenberichten. Bibliografie zur Informatikgeschichte mit über 1200 Einträgen, Munich/Berlin (2014) (Who invented the computer? Early history of computing: USA, England, Germany, Austria, Switzerland. With several eyewitness reports. Bibliography on the history of computing with over 1200 publications)

The Relevance of Computing Research History –
The Monads-PC: A Case Study

A. Barbara Ainsworth, C. Avram, and J. Sheard

Monash University, Melbourne, Australia
museum@infotech.monash.edu.au

Abstract. This chapter tells of the Monash Museum of Computing History, how it was started in 2001 and its purpose to preserve the computing history of Monash University and present this history to members of the University and the general public. It also describes Monash University's: MONADS research project.

Keywords: Monads, Monads-PC, Monash Museum of Computing History.

1   Introduction

The Monash Museum of Computing History (MMoCH) was started in 2001 to *preserve* the computing history of Monash University and *present* this history to members of the University and the general public. The Museum provides material for teaching staff on campus. To meet these objectives, the museum has been collecting computing material directly relating to Monash University including original hardware and software used on campus as well as biographical material relating to staff and students participating in IT related areas of study. To help with current teaching requirements, the museum is building a small computing reference collection to demonstrate key computing technologies. The museum has a research program directed towards the provenance of artefacts in the collection and also biographical material on people related to computing developments and use at Monash University.

In 2006 the MMoCH opened a new permanent exhibition. In view of our teaching commitments, the display has a mixture of typological approach and thematic ideas. During the design phase of the display, the staff felt it was important to show and important for students to see a multiplicity of objects because many computers and calculators appear to have similar functions but achieve this through different architecture.

To meet the design philosophy of the museum, the display is divided into four sections.

1. The role of calculating devices in the pre-development of computers
2. The development of computers within a chronological framework of photographic images of Australian society

A. Tatnall, T. Blyth, and R. Johnson (Eds.): HC 2013, IFIP AICT 416, pp. 105–117, 2013.

3. The Ferranti Sirius computer which was the first computer installed at Monash University
4. Monash computer legends (a select rotating biographical display on people connected with Monash University and computing)

Fig. 1. MMoCH Director, Ass. Professor Judy Sheard and Professor David Abramson with the MONADS-PC in the Museum exhibition space 2008.Source: Chris Avram, MMoCH (MONADS-PC, MMoCH collection item 2009.032)

As part of the Monash computer legends display, the original display was updated in 2008 with biographies on Professor David Abramson and Professor John Rosenberg who both studied and worked at Monash University during their careers. Research for this display highlighted a project, entitled the MONADS project that both professors had participated in during their studies. A custom-designed computer built during this project at Monash University, called the MONADS-PC, was located in 2008 at the University of Ulm, Germany. Through the efforts of Professor David Abramson and Jörg Siedenburg (Dipl.-Ing.), Faculty of Computer Science, Department SGI, University of Ulm, the MONADS-PC was shipped back to Australia and donated to the MMoCH.

The donation of the MONADS PC required some months of investigation into the provenance of the computer to establish the computer's date and history and then place its significance within the development of the whole MONADS project.

This work provides an interesting case study on the relevance of researching computer history and the lessons it can provide for approaches in modern research. The Monads project was an innovative project over more than 20 years, involving cross-institutional and international collaboration. Its work developed new approaches to both hardware and software. What were the successful features of the project? How can this be applied to modern research?

2   The Monads Project

In 1976 several staff and students in the Department of Computer Science, Monash University started a new research project called the MONADS project. It was initiated and directed by Professor J.L. Keedy. This was the start of more than twenty years of research under this umbrella project.

The MONADS Project had a number of different phases including software and hardware research. After the project was started at Monash University, research continued at different institutions including the University of Newcastle and later the University of Sydney as Monash staff and researchers took up positions at other institutions and worked with a number of researchers and students. Professor Keedy worked during the 1980s and 1990s in Germany as well as in Australia and moved aspects of the MONADS Project to the Technical University of Darmstadt and later to the University of Bremen and the University of Ulm. Over the life of the project, many different people have contributed to the various aspects of the project.

Of particular interest to the MMoCH is the development of the MONADS-PC in the 1980s. The MONADS-PC is a micro-programmed workstation designed to support a very large virtual memory, capability-based addressing and information hiding software modules. The MONADS-PC was designed in the mid 1980s at Clayton campus, Monash University by Professor David Abramson and Professor John Rosenberg. A number of MONADS-PC models were constructed at Monash University and the University of Newcastle during the 1980s. The computer donated to the MMoCH was sent to Germany from Australia in 1990.

For a project overview, Professor Keedy has created a detailed technical discussion of the project at http://www.monads-security.org/ with an interesting list of publications and thesis work associated with the project at different phases.

3   Background to Computer Research at Monash University and Start of MONADS Project

Monash University was established in 1958 and its first computer was installed in 1962. The Monash Computer Centre operated the computing equipment and also undertook some teaching. The University later developed an academic department in the Faculty of Science for teaching computer science at the Clayton campus during the 1960s. Professor Chris Wallace was appointed as Chair of Information Science in December 1967. The first subject was Information Science 303 for third year students. Seven honours students were enrolled in 1970. This was the beginning of a computer science research program. During 1972 the Department purchased its own HP2100A computer which was later modified for various research projects. In 1975 the Department's name was changed to Computer Science. This department grew to have a complete subject range through all levels of students and established a world-recognised research program. In 1990 the University created the Faculty of Computing and Information Technology which is now the Faculty of Information Technology[1].

It was during the developmental stage of teaching and research at Monash University that Dr. J.L. (Les) Keedy moved from England to become a Lecturer in the Department in 1974. He had previously worked with ICL (International Computers Ltd) in England[2]. In 1976 Keedy created the MONADS Project drawing on his experiences at ICL.

---

[1]   Rood, S. (2008). *From Ferranti to Faculty: Information Technology at Monash University, 1960 to 1990*. Monash University ePress, Melbourne. Australia.

[2]   J.L. Keedy biography http://www.jlkeedy.net/biography.html Accessed January 17, 2011.

Professor Keedy, in his notes regarding the development of the project, defines the original aims of the project as:

- *"To develop practical software engineering techniques for improving the specification, design, implementation and maintenance of large software systems, i.e. systems involving tens, hundreds and even thousands of man years of effort.*
- *To develop practical techniques for guaranteeing the security (i.e. the confidentiality, integrity and availability) of information held in large computer systems."* [3]

The name MONADS was taken from a word created by the philosopher Leibniz. Leibniz used the word to describe the basic elements that the world is constructed from. It was Leibniz's belief that these elements were unable to interact with each other but worked together in perfect harmony (in his view because they each had a spark of the deity!)[4]. The Monads program adopted this principal for software systems (*but without a spark of the deity* as John Rosenberg remarked[5]). As Keedy states,

"We believe that systems should be composed of stable and relatively independent components which have minimal interactions with each other. This can be achieved in practice by rigorously applying the information-hiding principle."[6]

The project was also focused on the security of the information held in a computer and this developed into work on producing hardware that would support a capability-based addressing system. Capability-based addressing is a method for a computer to have controlled access to 'capabilities'. The computer stores information in the memory but with capability addressing, these are protected objects and access to them is controlled by the kernel. This effectively allows for selective access to the memory by different users depending upon the software parameters.

In the project, the team developed hardware, languages, operating systems and software engineering techniques to meet its objectives. As such, it brought together specialists able to contribute to all of these areas.

In their 1985 article, Rosenberg and Abramson caution that the project appears to have a strong emphasis on hardware, computer architecture and operating systems as the main objectives. However they state,

---

[3]   See Keedy, J.L. The Monads Project http://www.monads-security.org/ Accessed January 17, 2011.

[4]   Monash Review (1986) "New Computer Helps Wipe Out Bugs" No. 1 – 86 p.1-2, http://www.adm.monash.edu.au/records_archives/assets/ docs/pdf/monash-review/1986-.pdf Accessed January 17, 2011.

[5]   Rosenberg, John in email to Dr Judy Sheard commenting on Monads draft paper November 17, 2012.

[6]   Keedy, J.L., Abramson, D., Rosenberg, J & Rowe, D.M. (1982) "The MONADS Project Stage 2: hardware Designed to Support Software Engineering techniques", Proc. 9th Australian Computer Conference, Hobart, August 1982, pp.575-580 p.576.

"The central theme of the project has always been and still is investigation of software engineering techniques for development of large 'real world' applications."[7]

The different phases of the project were given sub-names with MONADS as the common feature. The project can be divided into: Monads I, Monads II, Monads II/2, Monads III, MONADS-PC, Distributed MONADS-PC, Monads MM.

There was also considerable work made in the area of languages including: Leibniz, L1.

Later projects that have succeeded the MONADS Project include the SPEEDOS Project which was initiated by Prof. Keedy and his research group in 1998 at the University of Ulm, Germany. Another project called S-RISC was commenced after 1993[8].

4   MONADS Project Stages

4.1   MONADS I

The project commenced with the first stage that became known as MONADS I. Work was started by three Monash University PhD students – John Rosenberg, Ramamohanarao (Rao) Kotagiri and Ian Richards under the supervision of Professor J.L. Keedy. The Monads project team worked on both software and hardware developments to meet the needs of the project. The department's HP2100A minicomputer was modified to suit their requirements. It had already been modified by a postgraduate student, Rob Hagan, under the supervision of Professor Chris Wallace, in 1975 for their work on virtual memory. By 1976 the HP2100A memory hardware had been modified to support a demand-paged virtual memory. More adjustments were made in 1977 and laid the foundation for the hardware for the MONADS project[9].

John Rosenberg started work on creating the MONADS hardware kernel to be installed on the HP2100A. This Hardware Kernel was applied to four major areas: Memory Management, Process Management, I/O Management and Protection. This work was in part funded by a grant from the Australian Research Grants Committee (number F77/15337 I) and a Monash University Postgraduate Scholarship[10]. It is significant that this ARGC grant was probably the first one awarded by this Committee in the field of computer science research[11]. The MONADS I used the

[7]   Rosenberg, J. and Abramson, D.A. "The MONADS Architecture: Motivation and Implementation", Proceedings of First Pan Pacific Computer Conference, Melbourne, 1985, pp. 410-423. Invited Paper. p.411, http://messagelab.monash.edu.au/Publications/Publication?action=download&upname=monadsarch_motimp.pdf Accessed September 14, 2012.

[8]   See http://www.monads-security.org

[9]   Keedy, J.., Wallace, C.S., Rosenberg, J., Ramamohanarao, K., Richards, I., and Georgiades, A. *(1978)* A Collection of Papers on the Monads Operating System. Monads Report No. 1, Monash University - Department of Computer Science, February 1978: p.3-4.

[10]   Keedy, J.., Wallace, C.S., Rosenberg, J., Ramamohanarao, K., Richards, I., and Georgiades, A. (1978) P.25-26.

[11]   Email from Prof. J.L. Keedy to Ass. Prof Judy Sheard 14 November 2012.

modified hardware and the new software in a pilot version by 1978. However it did not meet the requirements of the project. To undertake the principle of information-hiding, the team worked on a software system that broke up information into small information hiding modules, these then performed specific tasks. At this stage of the project, the MONADS I hardware did not work effectively with the software modules and was inefficient[12].

Rosenberg, Kotagiri and Richards all completed their PhD thesis work on elements of the MONADS Project. John Rosenberg submitted in 1979, Rao Kotagiri completed his thesis in 1980 while Ian Richards finished in 1981[13].

4.2   MONADS II and II/2

Work commenced in 1980 on a new stage, a report in 1982 acknowledged the team working on the project. They were listed as: J.L. Keedy, J. Rosenberg, D. Abramson, David Rowe, Peter Dawson, Mark Evered, Mark Halpern, Ed Gehringer, Glenda Patterson, Kotagiri Ramamohanarao, Ian Richards, John Thomson, Brian Wallis, John Wells[14]. This group represented a mixture of PhD students and Honours students as well as staff.

In 1980 David Abramson, then a PhD student at Monash University, started work on MONADS II with funding from the Australian Research Grants Committee (ARGC Grant F80/15191), the Australian Computer Research Board and the Monash Special Research Fund (Grant no. SC18/79). This stage of the project also used the modified HP2100A computer. The processor in this model could develop 31-bit virtual addresses which were converted into physical memory addresses by the virtual memory manager. It had 400Kb of physical memory. The system also used 2 x 5Mb disk drives, 1 x 80Mb Winchester disk and a terminal multiplexor. The processor could also communicate with another unmodified HP2100A and a VAX 11/780 computer which they were using at the time for program compilation[15]. Abramson in his 1983 paper described the new hardware component of the project for the MONADS II as complete but noted several problems and described a new system called MONADS II/2. There was a move away from the HP2100A to using a Z8000 micro-computer with two Intel Multibuses. MONADS II/2 proposed a larger addressing range moving from 31-bit to 47-bit and a larger physical memory[16]. At this time, Professor J.L. Keedy completed his unsupervised staff PhD thesis in 1982, focusing on software engineering in the MONADS computer architecture[17].

---

[12] Abramson, D.A. 1983 "The MONADS II Computer System," Proc. 6th Australian Sciences Conference, Sydney, February 1983, pp1-10. p.2.

[13] Keedy, J.L. The Monads Project. p.8 list of PhD Theses,
http://www.monads-security.org/ Accessed January 17, 2011.

[14] Keedy, J.L. (1978) The MONADS Operating System p.5 in Keedy et al. (1978) A Collection of Papers on the MONADS Operating System. MONADS Report No.1 Monash University. - Department of Computer Science, February 1978.

[15] Abramson 1983 p.3.

[16] Abramson 1983 p.7.

[17] Keedy, J.L. The Monads Project. p.8 list of PhD Theses,
http://www.monads-security.org/ Accessed January 17, 2011.

4.3   MONADS III

The project continued to evolve and work started on MONADS III. However it was not completed due to the resignation of two main researchers from Monash University – Professor Keedy and Dr (later Professor) Rosenberg. Professor Keedy was appointed to the Chair in Operating Systems at the Technical University of Darmstadt in Germany in 1982[18]. He did not have the facilities to work on hardware developments but concentrated on software components of the project from 1982 to 1985. Dr Rosenberg also resigned from the project in 1982 and he left Monash University for two years, returning in 1984[19]. Work continued at Monash University on a scaled down version of MONADS III, called the MONADS II/2.

Fig. 2. Professor Les Keedy, Professor David Abramson and Professor John Rosenberg photographed in 1982 with the HP2100A and MONADS Series II hardware, Monash University. Source: David Abramson

---

[18]   Keedy, J.L. The Monads Project p.2, http://www.monads-security.org/ Accessed January 17, 2011.

[19]   Rosenberg J and Abramson D.A. (1985) "MONADS-PC - A Capability-Based Workstation to Support Software Engineering", Proceedings of Eighteenth Annual Hawaii International Conference on System Sciences, January 2-4, 1985 pp.222-230. p.230, http://messagelab.monash.edu.au/Publications/Publication?acti on=download&upname=monads_sesupport.pdf Accessed September 14, 2012.

Ed Gehringer, visiting Monash University as a Fulbright Fellow under the Australian-American Education Foundation from May 1981- January 1982 from Carnegie Mellon University, undertook to write a description of MONADS III system architecture. This became MONADS Report No. 12[20].

4.4   MONADS-PC

Professor John Rosenberg and Professor David Abramson started work on the MONADS-PC in 1984 at Monash University. They designed and built the first MONADS-PC, a single board computer. The MONADS-PC computer had 60-bit virtual addresses with capability registers and an efficient address translation unit. The project was a combination of hardware and software research to implement a paged virtual memory which was accessed by large addresses. There were several examples of the MONADS-PC built. The MONADS project continued using this hardware.

The MONADS-PC was designed to meet the need to limit the number of errors that occur when multiple programs interact within the computer and access the same data. Data can be stored permanently in the computer on the disc or temporarily in the memory while the computer is in active use. To meet the hardware requirements for this process, the hardware had to be modified and several new elements were added to allow the computer to map where all the addresses were located at the same time. The MONADS-PC was one of the first systems to place all storage in a single, distributed, virtual address space. The different programs and their specific use of the data are isolated into modules and they are controlled by software that only allows interaction by certain users. No module can change data in another module, so if an error occurs in one module, the error is not copied into another module. The MONADS-PC was a multi-user system and could support 5 or 6 terminals at the same time.

The project also developed a new computer language called Leibniz to provide the instructions for the control of the modules. This work was designed by Mark Evered who commenced at Monash University but transferred to Darmstadt under the supervision of Professor Keedy. He was awarded his PhD entitled "Leibniz A Language to Support Software engineering" in 1985 from the Technical University of Darmstadt.

David Abramson developed the circuit board for the first MONADS-PC. The prototype is currently on loan to MMoCH and on display in the Legends display section which features a brief biography on both Professor Abramson and Professor Rosenberg. The board has an unusual circuit-board construction method which employs insulated wires embedded in epoxy-resin that allowed very high-density circuit board layouts. Apart from the custom-designed board, the MONADS-PC was constructed from commercially available components[21].

---

[20] Gehringer, Edward F. (1982) MONADS: A Computer Architecture to Support Software Engineering. MONADS Report No. 12. Monash University – Department of Computer Science.

[21] The Age (1985) "*International spotlight on Monash pair*", The Age, Tuesday, February 5, 1985 p.30, Melbourne.

Work by Abramson and Rosenberg in the mid-1980s was largely carried out using resources from within Monash University's Department of Computer Science. In 1986 the project obtained funding from the Australian Research Grants Scheme as well as a collaborative research grant with the CSIRO Division of Information Technology[22].

Dr Rosenberg and Dr Abramson submitted a paper to the 18th Hawaii International Conference on System Sciences in 1985 on the MONADS-PC research. The paper was entitled "MONADS-PC - A Capability-Based Workstation to Support Software Engineering" and received the Best Paper Award in the Hardware Track. It was the only Australian paper presented at the conference[23].

Fig. 3. Photograph of Professor David Abramson and Professor John Rosenberg in 1985 with a version of the MONADS-PC, Monash University. Source: Monash University Archives MONPIX IN633.

There was some suggestion that the research could have some commercial future. Professor Rosenberg mentioned this idea in a 1985 article in The Age newspaper but cautioned that it would take two or three years to become a commercially viable product[24]. Commercial production of the MONADS-PC did not eventuate.

---

[22] Monash Review (1986) *"New Computer Helps Wipe Out Bugs"* No. 1 – 86 p.1-2; http://www.adm.monash.edu.au/records_archives/assets/docs/pdf/monash-review/1986-.pdf Accessed January 17, 2011.

[23] Williams, P. (1985) "Australian hardware impresses Hawaiian conference", Computer Weekly, January 25, 1985.

[24] The Age (1985) *"International spotlight on Monash pair"*, The Age, Tuesday, February 5, 1985 p.30, Melbourne.

Professor Keedy installed a MONADS-PC at the University of Bremen after he took up his position there in 1988 and then transferred it to the University of Ulm in 1993. This model of the MONADS-PC was built by David Koch at the University of Newcastle, New South Wales specifically for Professor Keedy using a custom circuit board. Some other units were partially built at the University of Sydney by David Koch while he was seconded to Sydney about 1991. Although these were not completed, the extra units (possibly one or two) and other custom circuits were sent to Germany as well[25]. David Koch's completed MONADS-PC was sent to Germany in 1990. Professor Rosenberg travelled to Germany and helped to install the computer with local research staff. This example of the MONADS-PC was donated back later to the Monash Museum of Computing History in 2008. Another MONADS-PC was built by Jörg Siedenburg at the University of Ulm[26].

4.5   Distributed MONADS-PC and MONADS MM

The MONADS Project was moved to the University of Newcastle, New South Wales in 1985. Professor Keedy had returned from Germany to establish the Department of Computer Science at the University of Newcastle[27]. He was later joined by John Rosenberg who moved to Newcastle as Senior Lecturer. They continued to work on the project and worked with research student Frans Henskens and also David Koch.

The MONADS-PC hardware could be connected to other computers and work on the system started to look at Local Area Networks. In 1985 David Abramson and Les Keedy published an early paper world-wide on distributed shared memory, which triggered further work at the University of Newcastle on local area networks. Much of the research on kernel software design and implementation was undertaken by Frans Henskens[28].

It was also proposed to develop a new computer, MONADS-MM, which would have 128-bit virtual addresses and a massive physical memory. Research continued in Germany when Professor Keedy moved to the University of Bremen and collaboration continued with Australian based members of the project. John Rosenberg moved to Sydney University to take up the position of Professor of Computer Science in 1988 but he maintained an interest in the MONADS Project. Work also continued at the University of Newcastle and research papers were published on aspects of the Project from the different institutions. Professor Keedy later undertook work at the University of Ulm in Germany as Director of the Department of Computer Structures. The 1995 website description of the Department of Computer Structures, University of Ulm notes that the department was begun in 1993 and its initial research focus was developed from the work of Professor Keedy

---

[25] Email from David Koch to Barbara Ainsworth December 17, 2012.

[26] Email from Professor Keedy to Ass. Prof Judy Sheard November 14, 2012.

[27] Keedy, J.L. Dr. (2011) The Monads Project, p.2.
   http://www.monads-security.org Accessed December 24, 2011.

[28] Keedy, J.L. Dr. (2011) The Monads Project. p.6.
   http://www.monads-security.org Accessed December 24, 2011.

and his assistants at the University of Bremen[29]. The MONADS Project was a key feature of their research programs. Work at Ulm has grown in new directions and they created a new project entitled SPEEDOS again focusing on security. Although now retired, Professor Keedy still maintains his research interest in SPEEDOS.

5   Summary

The MONADS project was a collaborative effort that spanned several academic institutions and combined the skills of both hardware and software specialists. The concepts developed by the team opened up development of hardware with new work in early networking, expanding hardware from 32-bit to 64-bit and major work on security software with information hiding, distributed virtual memory and capability addressing.

This research project represented the collaboration of computer departments from three Australian universities as well as three universities in Germany and a visiting scholar from the United States. Many of the key participants have continued to work in computer science research as well as take on academic roles. When Professor Keedy proposed the project in 1976, Monash University had only recently started to look at the possibilities of computer science research. It is an acknowledgment of Professor Keedy's perception of the possibilities of this research area in software engineering that the MONADS project continued for over twenty years and encouraged young computer scientists to undertake research.

Monash University played a key part in this significant research project providing both support through funding as well as encouraging research staff and students to participate as part of their academic development. The project led to new levels of research in computer science with researchers undertaking major developments in both the hardware and software components. The University encouraged this work and showed a continuous commitment to the concept of research from the beginning of the project.

The MONADS project had a long lasting influence on many of the researchers and many continued to work in the field of computer science with senior careers in academia. The project took on the name MONADS to define their approach to software being made of separate entities that work in harmony but do not interact. The actual process of the project itself proved to be the opposite of this concept with the concurrent work by different researchers in hardware and software continually interacting to create a functioning computer in the MONADS-PC.

The historical study of this project has provided a number of valuable insights into the role of different features contributing towards a successful computer project and the relevance of these insights for the modern researcher. It highlights several factors for a successful project.

---

[29] University of Ulm, Germany- Department of Computer Structures http://www.uni-ulm.de/uni/vereoff/fb/93-95/133.html.en   Accessed March 1, 2012.

1. The selection and definition of the scope of a new project, its relevance to computer development
2. The selection of personnel to undertake research and their long term commitment to developing new ideas and implementing them
3. The value of collaboration between different researchers; in this case, not just one field of computer study but also across several institutions
4. The support of the parent institution for the value of long term research as well as government financial support thought specific grants

For the Monash Museum of Computing History, this study was initiated by the acknowledgment of two successful Monash University graduates in the field of computing in our biographical display area. The subsequent donation of the MONADS-PC led to a greater understanding of the role of computer research both at Monash University and at other institutions. This historical study of a computer project has much wider implications and is relevant to our approach to modern computer research.

Acknowledgements. This research project was conducted at the Monash Museum of Computing History, Monash University, Australia. MMoCH would like to acknowledge the contributions of Professor David Abramson, Professor J.L. Keedy and Professor John Rosenberg for their time and valuable comments on the Museum's research for provenance details on the MONADS project and the MONADS-PC in the MMoCH collection.

References

Abramson, D.: The MONADS II Computer System. In: Proceedings of the 6th Australian Sciences Conference, Sydney, pp. 1–10 (February 1983)

Abramson, D., Rosenberg, J., Rowe, D.M.: The MONADS Project Stage 2: Hardware Designed to Support Software Engineering Techniques. In: Proceedings 9th Australian Computer Conference, Hobart, pp. 575–580 (August 1982)

The Age, "International spotlight on Monash pair", The Age, Melbourne, p. 30 (February 5, 1985)

Computer History Museum, Online exhibition "Computer History Timeline" (2012), http://www.computerhistory.org/timeline/?year=1981 (accessed September 9, 2012)

Gehringer, E.F.: MONADS: A Computer Architecture to Support Software Engineering. MONADS Report No. 12. Monash University – Department of Computer Science (1982)

Keedy, J.L.: The MONADS Operating System in Keedy et al. A Collection of Papers on the MONADS Operating System. MONADS Report No.1 Monash University. Department of Computer Science (February 1978)

Keedy, J.L.: Biography of Professor Keedy (1974-2011)JLKeedy.net: http://www.jlkeedy.net/biography.html (accessed January 17, 2011)

Keedy, J.L.: Department of Computer Structures. University of Ulm (1995), http://www.uni-ulm.de/uni/veroeff/fb/93-95/133.html.en (accessed March 1, 2012)

Keedy, J.L.: The Monads Project (2011), http://www.monads-security.org (accessed December 24, 2011)

Keedy, J., Wallace, C.S., Rosenberg, J., Ramamohanarao, K., Richards, I., Georgiades, A.: A Collection of Papers on the Monads Operating System. Monads Report No. 1, Monash University - Department of Computer Science (February 1978)

Keedy, J.L., Abramson, D., Rosenberg, J., Rowe, D.M.: The MONADS Project Stage 2: Hardware design to support software engineering techniques. In: Proceedings of Ninth Australian Computer Conference 1982, pp. 575–580 (1982)

Message Lab. Message Lab, Monash eScience and Grid Engineering Laboratory (December 22, 2008) (2012), http://messagelabe.monash.edu.au/News/MonadsandMuseum (accessed July 12, 2012)

Monash Review, New Computer Helps Wipe Out Bugs, No. 1–86, pp. 1–2 (1986), http://www.adm.monash.edu.au/records_archives/assets/docs/pdf/monash-review/1986-.pdf (accessed January 17, 2011)

Rood, S.: From Ferranti to Faculty: Information Technology at Monash University, 1960 to 1990. Monash University ePress, Melbourne (2008)

Rosenberg, J., Abramson, D.A.: The MONADS Architecture: Motivation and Implementation. In: Proceedings of First Pan Pacific Computer Conference, Melbourne (1985), http://messagelab.monash.edu.au/Publications/Publication?action=download (accessed September 14, 2012)

Rosenberg, J., Abramson, D.A.: MONADS-PC - A Capability-Based Workstation to Support Software Engineering. In: Proceedings of Eighteenth Annual Hawaii International Conference on System Sciences, January 2-4 (1985) http://messagelab.monash.edu.au/Publications/Publication?action=download&upname=monads_sesupport.pdf (accessed September 14, 2012)

Rosenberg, J., Keedy, J.L., Abramson, D.A.: Addressing Mechanisms for Large Virtual memories. The Computer Journal 35(4), 369–375 (1992), http://comjnl.oxfordjournals.org/content/35/4/369.full.pdf+html (accessed August 24, 2012)

Williams, P.: Australian hardware impresses Hawaiian conference, Computer Weekly (January 25, 1985)

Part V

Integrating History with Computer Science Education

Using Old Computers for Teaching Computer Science

Giovanni A. Cignoni and Fabio Gadducci

Department of Computer Science, University of Pisa, Italy
{cignoni,gadducci}@di.unipi.it

Abstract. Research on the history of computing often needs to adopt experimental archaeology methods: the rebuilding of old hardware and software requires us to proceed by hypothesis and experimentation. This is one of the key assets of the HMR project, whose main goal is the study of Italian computers from the Fifties and Sixties. The results obtained by the HMR research are made accessible to the public through exhibitions and workshops held at the Museum of Computing Tools of the University of Pisa. The visitors of the Museum, mainly students from middle and high schools, are introduced to the basic concepts of computer science through fascinating old machines. The paper reviews some of the results of the HMR project and presents how historical computers, either preserved at the Museum or rebuilt by HMR, are shown to the public to teach principles and mechanisms of computer science.

Keywords: computing history, computing museums, teaching.

1   Introduction

Computer science is a still young discipline. However, given the rapid evolution of technologies, it is already difficult to preserve the memory of its protagonists and of their results. In a few years, hardware and software become out-dated. Before they are recognized as relics of the past, they risk being forgotten and lost. The History of Computing thus needs commitment and resources.

Such a history, however, should not be just a celebration of the past. Among other things, the charm of vintage computers and their stories may be of help in order to make scientific and technological disciplines more appealing for students. Indeed, old machines are both odd and fascinating: they may stimulate young people to invest time in the study of computer science and electronics; or, at least, they may provide them with the basis to be informed users and consumers of technology.

The teaching of computer science requires a suitable array of examples. However, today hardware and software are often too complex to be properly dealt with. On the other hand, the computers of the past offer us real-life examples: they are intriguing because of their age or of their historical role, yet they are simpler, built on a human scale (often literally) and understandable in all their details.

The paper presents the experience of a fruitful interaction between historical research and scientific dissemination. The HMR project [1] at the Department of Computer Science of the University of Pisa investigates the history of Italian

A. Tatnall, T. Blyth, and R. Johnson (Eds.): HC 2013, IFIP AICT 416, pp. 121–131, 2013.

informatics by adopting methods and techniques that stress the technological aspects of the discipline. The Museum of Computing Tools [2] of the same University provides precious pieces of its collections.

Section 2 briefly describes the HMR project, its methodologies and main results. Section 3 is devoted to some of the machines in the collection of the Museum: it presents how, during the guided tours, they are narrated and illustrated in order to explain, in addition to their history, the underlying mechanisms by which they work. Section 4 describes the reconstructions made by HMR and in particular the simulator of the Macchina Ridotta, the very first Italian computer, designed and built in Pisa in 1957. The presentation is focused on the use of the simulator in the educational workshops offered to schools by the Museum.

2   The HMR Project

HMR is a research project focusing on the recovery of the history and the technology of old computers – with a special attention to Italian ones. HMR has historical and technological goals: on the one hand, HMR aims at recovering the facts concerning the development of those early machines; on the other hand, HMR plans to rebuild past computers through simulations and replicas. HMR is a project of the Department of Computer Science of the University of Pisa, ongoing since the beginning of 2006.

The project acronym stands for *Hacking the Macchina Ridotta*, with an explicit reference to the hacker culture [3]. In fact, in order to rebuild the computers of the past a full understanding of their technology is mandatory. A superficial knowledge does not suffice: all the details need to be explored and understood with curiosity and commitment. These same words are written in the definition of hacker which is given e.g. in the Internet Glossary RFC 1392 [4].

The *Macchina Ridotta* (MR, meaning Smaller Machine in Italian) was the very first computer designed and built in Italy: it made its début in Pisa in 1957. The MR was a result of the same project that in 1961 delivered the more famous *Calcolatrice Elettronica Pisana* (CEP, meaning Pisa Electronic Computer). The MR has been the first computer investigated by the HMR project. Today HMR has widened its research goals, but the MR still remains in the acronym in order to highlight the origins and the initial accomplishments of the project.

In fact, the MR almost completely disappeared from the history of Italian computer science [5]. It was the in-depth investigation of the recovered MR documentation that made possible to rediscover it and, by rebuilding its technology, to understand its achievements and its relevance. From an historical point of view, HMR added a new chapter to the annals of Italian computer science.

In March 2008, HMR celebrated the 50th anniversary of the MR with a lecture in the course on History of Computer Science. MR's birthday was chosen as the date written on the MR User Manual: March 1, 1958. Actually, the MR has been running since July 1957, but in early 1958 it started to deliver computing services to Italian research projects: a clear sign of its functionality and reliability. The Manual was concrete evidence and a valuable symbol of the presence of users external to the small group of computer pioneers that build the MR, such as the researchers of the Physical Chemistry Institute which programmed the MR for their purposes. A few months ago, the 55th anniversary of the MR was remembered by Google BlogSpot [6].

Information technologies developed quickly. The hardware was (and still is) superseded year after year. Old machines are forgotten, often scrapped. The other half of computer science, the software, was encoded in formats that rapidly become obsolete, the storage media degrade with time and today they are often unreadable. The same documentation is often lost, and maybe it was incomplete since the beginning – a long-standing bad habit of computer scientists. The protagonists of the events are often still with us, but their memories cannot keep track of the many details of such extremely complex systems. There is the need of digging in warehouses and archives as well as reassembling the pieces, in order to compare them with other contemporary computers and with the technological knowledge of the time. The gaps must be filled with assumptions and hypotheses which have to be checked and validated by experiments through simulations and replicas. The methodologies adopted by HMR [7] and other rebuilding projects in the world, like for instance [8] and [9], are thus reminiscent of those adopted in experimental archaeology.

The early Pisa computers are still the main objectives of HMR: there is still much to discover and rebuild. However, additional investigations focused on a range of topics, from the story of the first Olivetti machines, with their connections with industrial design and arts, to the evolution of personal computing from the early arithmometers of the XIX century to today portables. In all those cases, the results are also finalized to the dissemination and popularization of computer science.

3   The Computers at the Museum

Over the years, by rescues, recoveries, acquisitions, or donations, the Museum of Computing Tools of the University of Pisa gathered a relevant collection. Among the most valuable pieces, some of them are unique, such as the 1961 CEP and the Olivetti 9104, the latter explicitly designed for the Institute for Computing Applications in Rome. Other important artefacts are some early Sixties Olivetti products and a number of machines that, starting with the first arithmometers, made the history of personal computing.

HMR works with the Museum to narrate computers and their histories from both a scientific and a technological perspective. The computers of the past, explored as relics or rebuilt as actual or virtual replicas, are the protagonists of teaching and popularization initiatives that are unique in Italy. The following sections describe the most significant pieces that, in the activities performed at the Museum, have been used as examples to tell the stories and the technologies of computer science.

Historical data and technical information about the early Italian computers have been collected using as much as possible first-hand sources. For the CEP, the main reference is the original documentation in the Archives and Libraries of the University and the CNR. Useful sources are represented by foreign reports such as [10] and [11].

The literature on Olivetti computers mainly focuses on corporate events [12]. Reliable technical data are less documented, even if they can be found in foreign reports, as the files on ELEA 9003 [13] and 6001 [14] recorded by the U.S. Navy, or the correspondence between Canepa (head of the Olivetti Observatory of New Canaan) and Picone (director of INAC in Rome) in [15].

An overview of the evolution of those machines is out of the scope of our paper. For a recent summary in English of the main events concerning the CEP project, as well as the ELEA series, we refer the reader to [5] and the references therein.

3.1   Bull Gamma 3, 1953

The Gamma 3 Bull was built in 1952 [16]. It is one of the first European examples of commercial electronic machines, relevant to the history of French computing as well as to the Italian: Olivetti went into the computer business in 1949 by signing an agreement for the distribution in Italy of the Bull machines.

Since 1931 Bull started to produce electromechanical tabulators based on the patents of Norwegian Fredrick Rosing Bull. The Gamma 2 (1951) was the first one equipped with electronic circuits with diodes and vacuum tubes. The Gamma 3 was an immediate development and, in various versions, was produced in about 100 specimens until the early Sixties.

The Gamma 3 is proposed to visitors as an example of machine architecture with separate memories (in technical jargon, Harvard and not Von Neumann), thus, it is not in fact a modern computer. The specimen at the Museum is one of the first models, and the program memory was still made up of a massive plug-board and the software was actually hardware made of wires and pins inserted into the plug-board. Luckily, the complex operation of coding a program was not too frequent: several pre-coded programs were available and "loaded" into the machine directly by changing the plug-board. While showing the details, the most daring visitors are given the opportunity to test the weight of the programs of the Gamma 3!

The Gamma 3 is a witness of other facets of informatics. First of all, it uses punch cards. Second, it is a demonstration of how the market is sometimes independent of the technological level of the product. The Gamma 3 was a success even though it was an outdated product, for the aforementioned architectural characteristics and the odd mix of hardware technologies: alongside the digital electronic circuits, the Gamma 3 features a number of old electromechanical relays circuits.

3.2   Olivetti ELEA 6001, 1961

The ELEA 9003 was the first electronic computer produced by Olivetti. While a prototype of the ELEA series was presented at the Milan Fair in 1959, the first units were only delivered during 1960. ELEA 6001 followed a year later. Even if it is a follow-up product, a careful examination reveals a quite interesting machine.

In fact, the 6001 was an evolution of the 9003 designed to make the system more modular and versatile, thus able to satisfy different customers with respect to financial investment and application needs. It shared with the 9003 the general architecture and the set of peripherals, as well as the elegant exterior design by Ettore Sottsass. From a technological point of view, the 6001 introduced microprogrammed control and floating point arithmetic. It was a great market success (about 150 units sold, compared with about 40 of 9003), winning also scientific customers (it was e.g. purchased by the University of Padova, by the Politecnico of Turin and by the CNR of Rome).

In the Museum, the 6001 is proposed to the visitor as the final achievement of the series of wise R&D investments that, despite entering late in the market, led Olivetti to set-up a successful Electronics Division in just a few years.

3.3   Calcolatrice Elettronica Pisana, 1961

The 1961 CEP is showcased at the Museum. Apart from its historical value, its size and the (faithfully reconstructed) layout of its cabinets offer to visitors the unique experience of walking into a computer and discovering the components and their functions: the same, apart from the dimensions, of today computers.

The "walk" allows one to observe the input/output control board (actually, a 3 meters long rack), to appreciate the individual bits of the ferrite core memory, to recognize the registers of the processor, the read-only memory of the micro-programmed control, and the ALU components, up-to the individual stages of the parallel 36-bit adder.

Depending on the audience, a visit to the CEP may offer different levels of technicalities. The details offered by the Power Supply Unit range from the electrical representation of 0s and 1s to the trade-off between speed and energy consumption obtained by adjusting voltages. The matrix of the micro-programmed control allows the presentation of the mechanisms for decoding and executing machine instructions. The modular design of circuits together with the original instruments used for the construction and maintenance of the CEP provide an opportunity to actually understand what it meant to build a computer in the Fifties.

Due to the financial difficulties met by the project in its final years, the 1961 CEP was completed late and so it was, in some ways, already outdated. In particular, it was not possible to move toward a fully transistorized machine (thus reducing space, power consumption and heat dissipation issues), while this technological leap was taken by Olivetti with its ELEA series. This aspect of the CEP history let the visitors reflect on how risky can be for the technological future of a country to stop the research funding. The "walk" inside the CEP can also involve the visitors in a playful "transistors hunt" to find the few spots where, as a proof of their technological awareness, the Pisa researchers were able to introduce the new electronic components – thus discovering other traces of the participation of Olivetti to the CEP project.

3.4   Olivetti 9104 CINAC, 1966

In 1955 the CNR National Institute for Applied Computing (INAC) in Rome bought a Ferranti Mark I*. The Ferranti was one of the first European commercial computers, produced since 1951, and a direct descendant of the 1948 Manchester Baby Machine, the first modern computer. The Ferranti INAC was the second computer to operate in

Italy, a few months after the purchase by the Polytechnic of Milan of a CRC 102A, which had however less memory and worse performances.

In the early Sixties INAC decided to replace the Ferranti with a more modern machine by entering into an agreement with Olivetti. The new computer was eventually delivered in 1966, when the Olivetti Electronics Division had already been sold to General Electric. It was a one-of-a-kind specimen, identified as Olivetti Elea 9104 and renamed CINAC (for Computer INAC) by the CNR.

The 9104 was derivative of ELEA 4001, an average-size computer that was supposed to replace the ELEA 6001. The project was discontinued after the sale of the Olivetti Electronics Division to General Electric, but one of its variations, initially called ELEA 4-115, had great commercial success as GE-115.

The agreements between INAC and Olivetti established that the new machine had to be able to completely emulate the Ferranti. The request originated in the wealth of experience and, above all, of software libraries that the CNR Institute had developed in the long term adoption of Ferranti: a heritage that could not be lost and that can be interpreted today as a great attention to backward compatibility.

The emulation layer was extremely faithful: the Ferranti console and one of the typical viewers for the Williams memory banks were cannibalized and interfaced with the 9104, thus fully replicating the way programmers and operators were used to work. The presence of the original pieces of the Ferranti is thus another element contributing to the uniqueness and curiosity of the relic.

In addition, for the more technologically interested, the presence of the viewer of the memory banks is an opportunity to explore the theme of the storage technologies that preceded the ferrite cores, in this case the Williams Tubes adopted by Ferranti.

4   Vintage Computers That Work Again

A computer should always be shown in working conditions otherwise the exhibition is limited to the historical value of the relics, even if in some cases it is worth at least to appreciate the exterior design. An exhibition of switched off computers is, at best, only half of the story.

There are several ways to revive a vintage computer: restoration, rebuilding, simulation. Whatever the chosen way is, it is always a challenge in terms of time, efforts, and costs. Usually, the first difficulty is to obtain the technical information. As a consequence, the reviving process often needs to proceed by hypotheses and experiments. By applying these methods, HMR produced actual and virtual rebuilds of the MR.

- *Replica of the 6 bit adder.* Our research found a note reporting the activities of the early months of 1956. One of the achievements of those days was the building of a 6 bit adder. Likely, this was the first piece of digital hardware assembled in Italy. We built a replica according to the original blueprints, using components and tools of the period – a few of them recovered from the spare parts of the CEP project.
- *Educational 6 bit adder.* The 1956 adder has a modular structure that makes it suitable for explaining how binary arithmetic works. We thus built a version made by handy parts, which the students may play with. The logic and

modular architecture are the same as the original adder, but the electronic implementation today uses components to reduce the size and to work with low and safe voltage.

- *Simulator of the 1956 MR.* Our technological investigation was able to identify two versions of the MR. It was possible to retrieve almost all the documentation of the first design, dated July 1956, in particular a large collection of logical, electronic and mechanical blueprints. Due to the availability of its documentation, this version of the MR has been the first target of a virtual rebuild.

- *Simulator of the 1957 MR.* The 1956 design was heavily modified and the MR completed in 1957 was very different from its initial version. Unfortunately, little documentation remains of this MR version: a short user manual, a concise technical report and few photos. This second simulator fully emulates the machine core (CPU and memory) and the manual control panel. Work is in progress for the simulation of the I/O devices, including hardware errors and borderline situations.

A detailed discussion of the problems faced by HMR in the rebuilding of the MR is in [7], while in [17] the use of the simulator of the 1956 MR for the "restoration" of its system software is presented. In the following we focus on the use of the 1957 MR simulator in the teaching workshops held at the Museum. The virtual MR is used to revive the look and feel of an old computer and to show and discuss some of the principles and mechanisms according to which past and present computers work.

Fig. 1. The only surviving photo of the Manual Control Panel of the 1957 MR

4.1   The Control Panel Manual MR 1957

Fig. 1 reproduces the only surviving photo of the Quadro di Controllo Manuale (QCM, literally the Manual Control Panel), that is, the console of the 1957 MR. Fig. 2 presents the virtual QCM as it is reproduced by the simulator. The QCM was the main interaction interface with the MR. Among its main components there are:

- *Indicatore del Numeratore* (IN, literally numerator display, 10 lights, top right), displaying the binary value of the program counter;
- *Indicatore della Memoria* (IM, literally memory display, 18 lights, under IN), connected to the MR memory to display the binary value of the last written word; however, since the ferrite core memories have to be rewritten after each reading, IM shows also the last read word;
- *Tastiera della Memoria* (TM, literally memory keyboard, 18 vertical switches, under IM), used to bit-wise set a word to be written in memory;
- *Tastiera delle Istruzioni* (TI, literally instruction keyboard, 18 vertical switches, under TM), used to bit-wise set an instruction (for example, in Fig. 2 an unconditional jump instruction to the memory address 100 is set on TI);
- *Chiavi di Arresto Condizionato* (CAC1/2/3, literally keys for conditional stop, 3 vertical switches, bottom left), used to prepare the 3-bit codes that allow to stop the execution of the MR programs at defined breakpoints;
- *Commutatori dei Modi di Funzionamento* (literally switches for working modes, from left to right CNR, CRT, CEI, CAIM, 4 switches with 2 or 3 positions, bottom centre), used in combination to set the MR in different operating modes, such as the step by step execution of programs (by instructions or micro-instructions), the execution of instructions from memory or from TI, the loading of data or programs in memory by connecting I/O devices, in a way we may call direct memory access;
- *Pulsante di Avviamento* (PA, literally start button, bottom right), used to enable the clock pulse generator and to start the working cycle of the MR.

Understanding the role of all the QCM components is the result of a long process of analysis based on the recovered documents: scientific papers, project reports, internal notes and blueprints. The documentation collected in the Archives is fragmentary. Moreover, many documents are extremely concise. In a few cases we found only draft versions of documents and blueprints which still had errors, not to mention old fashioned terminology and notations.

Rebuilding the MR was like solving a big technological puzzle: putting pieces together, some recovered from the documents, other derived by assumptions made according to the knowledge of the time. The simulation, before becoming useful for dissemination, has been the key tool for testing the reconstruction hypotheses.

The methods and simulation tools used by the HMR project are actually a result of current research in modelling and simulation [18] and they are part of the teaching carried out at the Simulation Course held for the master degree in Applied Computer Science of the University of Pisa.

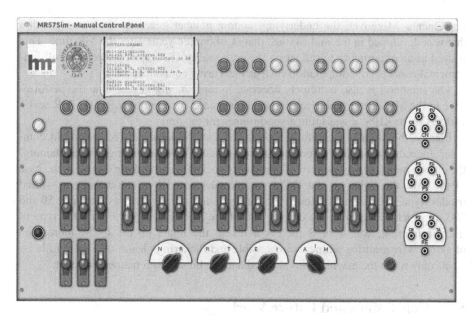

Fig. 2. The Manual Control Panel as reproduced by the simulator of the MR

4.2   The MR Simulator as a Teaching Workbench

The MR simulator is used in the workshops offered by the Museum to middle and high schools. The aim of the workshops is to introduce the concepts and the mechanisms of computer science by showing a fascinating device:

- most of the interaction with the MR is through the QCM, by reading the IN and IM displays and by setting data and instructions on TM and TI; everything is done bit-wise, a great exercise in binary arithmetic;
- the MR had a quite small set of instructions, all using the same format that is very simple and rational – today we would call the MR a RISC machine; this makes the MR easy to be presented, understood and used in a short time;
- the way the MR is operated exposes all the mechanisms that today remain hidden behind friendly user interfaces; from loading code into memory to starting it by manually executing unconditional jumps, all the events happening in a computer when a program is launched are fully disclosed;
- MR, as practically all computers of its time, was not conceived to interact with the user during program execution; however, by using the ability to set and activate breakpoints, it is possible to make pseudo-interactive programs useful to explain the basics of human-machine interfaces.

A typical demonstration session with the simulator starts by the execution of single instructions directly from TI, by setting the 5 bits (10 to 14) of the instruction code and the 10 bits (0 to 9) of the operand. A further step is to run simple programs that allow the use of the MR as a simple calculator – with display and keyboard in binary.

For a "gaming" experience, a program transforms the MR into a classical slot machine. Besides the fun, the example is interesting for the kind of user interaction that it implements. Moreover, the underlying random number generator uses an algorithm that was developed in the mid-Sixties, that is, about ten years after the MR time. This is used as an opportunity to reflect on the universality of computers and to recall fundamental concepts of computation such as the Turing equivalence.

The simulator is also extremely accurate in reproducing in real-time the performance of the MR. It is possible to run benchmarks and measure how fast the MR was – with about 70 KIPS, it was quite a good runner for the time.

Finally, the simulator carefully reproduces also the look and feel of an old computer. Indeed, its accuracy offers an intriguing side-effect, debunking (and explaining) the classic movie representation of computers packed with blinking lights. In the case of the MR, the lights on the QCM were implemented by cold cathode gas-filled triodes (type Z50T). Their times of ionization/de-ionization were, respectively, 50 and 200 μs, much longer than the clock cycle of the MR that, depending on the type of microinstruction, was 4 or 8 μs. As a result, the lights on the QCM more than blinking, were emitting an incomprehensible and flickering gleam: they were fully on or off only when the machine was stopped and the bit values remained constant.

5   Conclusions and Future Work

Besides any other consideration, the history of computing can be a valuable teaching tool, allowing us to introduce in a soft way basic concepts of computer science to the general public and to students.

The article outlined some of the major results of the HMR project and offered an overview of some of the most significant historic machines preserved at the Pisa Museum of Computing Tools, showing that the reconstructions and the original memorabilia can contribute to the teaching of computer science. The success so far encountered by these initiatives, both in terms of public participation and in the media, seems to confirm the value of this approach.

For the future, we are working to set up a permanent exhibition at the Museum devoted to personal computing, starting from the very first mechanical (yet digital) machines like the XIX century arithmometers, up to the first fully portable computer of the end of the XX century. In the planned setting, the turning point between personal calculators and personal computers will be the Olivetti Programma 101, universally considered a jewel of Italian technology and design. The Museum has in its collections a few P101's, and we hope to be able to restore at least one in working conditions. And, of course, there will be a fully featured simulator.

Acknowledgements. The desk research was carried out in collaboration with the Archives of the University of Pisa and the Library of ISTI-CNR of Pisa. With regard to the archive, a special thanks goes to Daniel Ronco.

The 6-bit adder has been reconstructed in collaboration with the Computer Museum of Novara and the workshops of the National Institute of Nuclear Physics. We remember with great pleasure the days spent working with Andrea Moggi (INFN) and Alberto Rubinelli (the Museum of Novara).

Finally, special thanks go to Elio Fabri, one of the protagonists of the MR, who, with his memories and the documents he preserved, provided us with an invaluable contribution to the understanding of the technologies of the first Italian computer.

References

1. Hackerando la Macchina Ridotta, http://hmr.di.unipi.it
2. Museum of Computing Tools, http://www.fondazionegalileogalilei.it
3. Levy, S.: Hackers: Heroes of the Computer Revolution. Doubleday (1984)
4. Internet Users' Glossary, http://www.rfc-base.org/txt/rfc-1392.txt
5. Cignoni, G.A., Gadducci, F.: Rediscovering the Very First Italian Digital Computer. In: Proceedings of 3rd IEEE History of Electro-technology Conference (HistElCon). IEEE Computer Society (2012)
6. Webb, L.: Tracing the birth of Italian computer science, http://googlepolicy europe.blogspot.it/2013/03/tracing-birth-of-italian-computer.html
7. Cignoni, G.A., Gadducci, F.: Experimental Archaeology of Computer Science. Atti della Società Toscana di Scienze Naturali, Serie B 119 (2012)
8. Sale, T.: The Colossus Rebuild Project, http://www.codesandciphers.org.uk
9. Burton, C.P.: Replicating the Manchester Baby: Motives, Methods, and Messages from the Past. IEEE Annals of the History of Computing 27(3) (2005)
10. Auerbach, I.L.: European Electronic Data Processing – A Report on the Industry and the State of the Art. Proceedings of the IRE 49 (1961)
11. Blachman, N.M.: The State of Digital Computer Technology in Europe. Communications of the ACM 6(6) (1961)
12. Parolini, G.: Olivetti ELEA 9003: Between Scientific Research and Computer Business. In: Impagliazzo, J. (ed.) Proceedings of the 3rd IFIP Conference on the History of Computing and Education (HCE3 2008). IFIP, vol. 269, pp. 37–53. Springer, Boston (2010)
13. Goldstein, G.D. (ed.): ELEA 9003 - C. Olivetti & C. - Milan, Italy. Digital Computer Newsletter, Office of Naval Research 12(3) (1960)
14. Goldstein, G.D. (ed.): ELEA 6001 - C. Olivetti & C SpA. - Laboratorio di Ricerche Elettroniche Milan, Italy. Digital Computer Newsletter, Office of Naval Research 13(3) (1961)
15. Guerraggio, A., Mattaliano, M., Nastasi, P. (eds.): La lunga marcia di Mauro Picone. Università Bocconi (2010)
16. Leclerc, B.: From Gamma 2 to Gamma E.T.: The Birth of Electronic Computing at Bull. Annals of the History of Computing 12(1) (1990)
17. Cignoni, G.A., Ceccarelli, D., Imbrenda, C.: Il restauro del software di sistema della Macchina Ridotta del 1956. In: Atti del Congresso Nazionale AICA. AICA (2009)
18. Cignoni, G.A., Paci, S.: UML Modelling and Code Generation For Agent-based, Discrete Events Simulation. In: Bruzzone A.G., Buck W., Cayirici E., Longo F. (eds.), Proceedings of the International Workshop on Applied Modeling and Simulation (WAMS 2012). DIME Università di Genova (2012)

Computing: Is There a Future in the Past?

Chris Monk

Learning Coordinator, The National Museum of Computing

Abstract. This short summary describes the outcomes from the decision of The National Museum of Computing (TNMoC) to open its doors to visits by students from across the UK. Our experience has inevitably caused us to question the reasons for their visit, the students' understanding of what they see and the relevance their 'day out' has on their understanding of computing.

Keywords: National Museum of Computing, young people, learning guides.

The Rationale for Opening Our Doors to Young People

The Trustees of TNMoC have expressed a clear aim for the museum within its mission statement:

> *"To collect and restore computer systems particularly those developed in Britain and to enable people to explore that collection for inspiration, learning and enjoyment."*

Inspiration, learning and enjoyment are at the heart of what we aim to offer through our learning visit programme.

The Experience over the Past Year

The museum has organised a programme for supported visits that is open to schools, colleges and universities. Visits are supported by 'learning guides' and are a combination of a museum tour plus more interactive activities.

Over 3,000 young people visited the museum over the past year. Their ages ranged from as young as seven year olds through to mature students well into their twenties. Typically most are studying GCSE (aged 15/16) and post 16 courses (aged 17/18). Arriving from all parts of the UK, the students typically stay for 4 to 5 hours. They can be a group of 6 or 60 with most between 15 and 25 in number.

Fig. 1. Student visit to the National Museum of Computing

A. Tatnall, T. Blyth, and R. Johnson (Eds.): HC 2013, IFIP AICT 416, pp. 132–134, 2013.
© IFIP International Federation for Information Processing 2013

Why Do They Come?

The visiting group's teachers express a wish for their students to better understand the history of computing, to support;

- the school curriculum generally, (typically pre 16s)
- the specification of a qualification, (usually GCSE or A/AS Level)
- the teacher's desire to extend and broaden their student's understanding and outlook, (e.g. to encourage a take up of Computing at GCSE)

What Do Young People Think about What They See?

It is important to understand how young people perceive the past and how they make sense of technologies way beyond their life experience. We attempt to encourage them to 'be there' and understand why computing developed in one direction compared to another. The visits are becoming less a collection of 'facts' associated with big machines and more a story that we can illustrate through our collection.

Young people have little experience of any 'past' through which to rationalise what they see. We try to help them get a better sense of time, social context, problem solving and the pace of development.

Their world is essentially 'now'. The computing of today is very bright, attractive and at the heart of their day to day experience. We find it important to link the past to the now, to help capture their attention and interest.

We want young people to better understand why we are where we are and the reasons for that journey. It is vital that they perceive a 'story' not a collection of facts and we want them to understand that they are living in the latest chapter of that story, certainly not at its end.

The past is offering students a chance to 'be there' and think about why decisions were made that have such great impact on what we do today. Where possible we ask students to use the 'story so far' to think about what might come next. 'Future gazing' is an increasingly important outcome for the museum. We would like to do more to listen to young people's predications, desires and fears for the future of computing.

What Next for Our Visits?

TNMoC realises that presenting the past is not enough. We have a responsibility to interpret and explain why we are where we are. Through our visit programme for students we are developing an experience, which will;

- Improve their knowledge and understanding of the past and its story,
- Encourage their perception of building on the shoulders of those from the past,
- Develop their respect and understanding for conservation and restoration,
- Offer opportunities that will, over time, ensure a new generation of enthusiasts, experts and volunteers that can continue looking after the history of computing,

Continuing, developing and improving our learning visit programme is an important contribution by TNMoC to securing the future for 'the past' through the next generation of young people and beyond.

References

1. TNMOC Learning, http://www.tnmoc.org/learn
2. OCR Awarding body,
   http://www.ocr.org.uk/qualifications/gcse-computing-j275-from-2012/
3. DFE Consultation on Computing KS1-4, http://media.education.gov.uk/assets/files/pdf/c/computing%2004-02-13_001.pdf
4. Computing at School, http://www.computingatschool.org.uk/

Bringing Relevance to Computing Courses through History

John Impagliazzo[1] and Mohammed Samaka[2]

[1] Emeritus, Department of Computer Science, Hofstra University, Hempstead, New York USA
John.Impagliazzo@Hofstra.edu
[2] Department of Computer Science and Engineering, Qatar University, Doha, Qatar
Samaka.m@qu.edu.qa

Abstract. This paper shows ways in which computing history can make the delivery of teaching computing courses relevant. The authors' approach involves using computing history as a recurring theme throughout courses by adapting relevant historical stories or material to enhance course delivery and to capture student interest. The use of computing history often makes a positive and constructive improvement in courses by making them more interesting, stimulating, and thereby, informing students with non-technical elements in their computing specialties. This approach to computing studies should prove to be a helpful addition to student studies and provide them with a stronger understanding of the computing field in their careers.

Keywords: Computing history, history in computing courses, computing history and relevance.

1 Introduction

Literature shows that computing history could be an effective pedagogical tool to teach computing courses. History contributes to students' lifelong learning experiences and it encourages them to appreciate the field. History also enables students to gain a better sense of the nature of inquiry, the processes of innovation, and the human dimension [1]. History enables students to explore beyond machines and expand their view on ways in which computing affects society [2]. Historical diversions from basic course material could be simple stories used to enhance student learning. Teachers could use computing history as a vehicle for extra credit or topic enrichment, or for students who enjoy the softer side of the computing field.

Embedding history in computing courses often depends on the initiative of the instructor. In general, computing teachers never studied such history in undergraduate or graduate courses unless they enrolled in a course through their own interest or initiative.

The use of history in courses depends mainly on the creativity and efforts of the individual teacher. Teachers often need to bootstrap themselves and make some effort to incorporate historical topics in their courses. However, the rewards derived from such engagement are satisfying and they outweigh the cost of the efforts involved.

A. Tatnall, T. Blyth, and R. Johnson (Eds.): HC 2013, IFIP AICT 416, pp. 135–143, 2013.

Our experience shows that further exploration on the use of history in computing and related courses is a worthwhile and engaging endeavour.

2   Relevance and Computing History

We believe that history enhances the teaching of computing. Instructors should use history as a vehicle to enrich specialized course studies and to derive other benefits for learning. One reason is the many adages of describing the necessity of understanding and heeding the past because we may be doomed to repeat it in the future. Indeed, the statement by George Santayana that states, *"Those who cannot remember the past are condemned to repeat it"* [3] already exists within the fabric of the computing field. Stories abound on repeating the mistakes of prior happenings; many are well known. Can we explain the cause for the downfall and ultimate demise of Control Data Corporation (CDC)? What caused Digital Equipment Corporation (DEC) to fail? In the mid-2000s, IBM surrendered its personal computer business to Lenovo. Why did IBM do this when "Big Blue" was synonymous with computing machines?

Answers to such questions are quite complex and we do not attempt to answer them here. Nevertheless, they do form a good starting point for student interaction in a classroom setting and stimulate new ideas and concepts. For some students, they may even provide a basis for more exploratory study and research. Computing history also provides fodder for curiosity and intrigue. For example, as far back as 2001 Microsoft started developing its Surface computer, which became a reality as a coffee table in 2004 and formally unveiled in 2007 [4]. Yet, other companies exploited that technology in the manufacturing of tablets and smart phones in the latter part of that decade. Exploring reasons why a company developed a technology while competitors exploit it could be an effective way to engage students in a topic and promote sound (and even heated) class discussion.

Teachers should dispel the notion that the focus of history applies only to past events. We can make history futuristic. Developing new technologies on the successes of others is useful for students to know in a modern age. It is even more useful to avert the mistakes of others, assuming we know those mistakes. Having an inclination or understanding of computing history is one way to avoid such mistakes. Students should view history as an asset. Making computing history relevant to a field of study can enable students to treat it as an asset in conjunction with the technical topics they learn.

Professionals (practitioners and teachers) in the computing field have often ignored the history of their field. They often favour cutting-edge approaches and disregard the adage stated earlier, namely, that those who ignore history are doomed to repeat it. While some organizations have contributed to history preservation, the contributions are isolated and incomplete. Specialized textbooks on technical subjects often do not contain sections on the history of the subject, and when they are included, unfortunately the content often contains myths and inaccuracies. However, in recent times, resurgence is developing where greater awareness of computing history is making strides. Websites such as the IT History Society [5] and conferences such as those held by the Society for the History of Technology (SHOT) [6] address the importance of the topic.

As mentioned before, teachers of specialized computing courses are not likely to have the formal preparation in computing history. However, sufficient resources are currently available and are sufficient to include threads or themes of history in the computing courses they teach. They only need a desire to enrich their class sessions to be successful. Our experience leads us to believe that their students will not regret the enrichment.

3   The Importance of Storytelling

Presenting any history as a series of chronological facts is counterproductive. Storytelling (not gossip or folklore or random rambling) can enrich a subject while connecting students with human elements. We have found that historical storytelling can make computing courses more interesting. Moreover, the computing information and knowledge embedded within these stories are often relevant to some aspect of their own lives. Hence, students tend to remember stories and the computer content within them.

As teachers, we need to adopt more innovative and interesting approaches toward student learning if we expect to achieve student success. Berkeley professor and famed computing theorist Christos Papadimitriou stated [7]:

This narrative mode [storytelling] of thought is fundamental for at least two reasons: First, narrative richness is an essential precondition for the self (the converse is, of course, trivial: there can be no narration without narrator). We think of ourselves almost exclusively in terms of our mental autobiography. Second, stories are in a certain intrinsic sense interesting, in that they are attractive, high-priority memory fodder. Everything else being equal, we are much more likely to remember a story than a logical argument.

There is much truth in this statement. Students, especially those not specializing in computing, are more likely to remember a story about computing than a particular fact about it.

Storytelling can be quite effective. However, teachers should not expect that using this technique is always easy. Stories should evolve naturally. They must be relevant and relate to the topic under discussion. Sources for such stories could emerge from current happenings or events such as a newspaper article, or they might build on some historical background such as a book on computing history. Whatever the source, teachers should make an effort to research historical topics so the stories they tell are meaningful to the topic. We have found that storytelling associates students with different perspectives on computing and it connects them with realistic and relevant things such as people, places, and events. We definitely encourage a dynamic involvement by teachers with an active participation by students to make historical storytelling a memorable component to all computing courses.

4   History in Computing Courses

We now provide a brief illustration on ways in which computing history can complement and enrich some of the computing courses found in a computing curriculum.

4.1   History and Computer Architecture

Computer architecture courses are one area where the history of the subject has received attention. Many textbooks in this area often contain sections, appendices, or sidebar vignettes that contain images of the machines that support the architecture under discussion. Students often find such attention devoted to history interesting and revealing. Introducing students to computers without discussing their "invention" leaves a void in their education and a lost opportunity to question the inspiration of a few among many. We often start such a course with the question, "Who invented the computer?" and we tend to admonish those students who say, "Bill Gates" or "Steve Jobs" in response. A homework activity surfaces and names such as Babbage, Turing, Atanasoff, Zuse, and Mauchly emerge. A few students "get hooked" into the intrigue and before long, they develop an interest in computing history.

The question of the invention of the computer is complex and is not within the scope of this narrative. Nevertheless, it does provide a good starting point to engage students in seeking answers to the question. It also diffuses discussions from an emphasis on "firsts" and changes the focus on strategies used to process data. The discussion easily shifts to ways people or teams designed those machines to achieve the computation of data, not only from the early days, but also from modern approaches to these strategies.

It is natural that computers become part of computing history since computing machines are tangible artefacts and have easy recognition by most people, even to non-specialists in computing. Additionally, as teachers, we wonder sometimes whether our students have ever seen the internals of a computer and its electrical and electronic elements such as resistors, capacitors, flash memory chips, busses, or motherboards. More importantly, do these computing specialists know the manner in which these elements work? Notwithstanding, an overview of the history of the subject would naturally expose such elements at least through images if not through visits to computing museums such as the Computer History Museum in California [8], the Science Museum in London [9], or the Deutsches Museum in Munich [10].

4.2   History and Computer Networks

Another area of computing where history has received some attention is computer networks. One related area is communication networks. The internet as we know it has propelled much of this attention. Making this topic relevant in a modern communications course adds meaning and interesting knowledge. For example, do students know what the word "internet" means? Actually, we could trace the root of the internet to 1957 when the Former Soviet Union successfully launched Sputnik [11]. Students might ask: what does Sputnik have to do with the internet?

Students should reflect on world history and recall the "cold war" threat that existed for decades since 1945, the end of the World War II. In response to Sputnik's launch, the United States formed the Advanced Research Projects Agency [12] in 1958 within its Department of Defense (DoD). The purpose of ARPA was to establish a military advantage in science and technology, since a satellite launch from a seemingly adverse country posed a national security threat.

By 1969, ARPA created the first internet with only four nodes as appears in Figure 1. They called the network ARPAnet. The nodes were located at the:

1. University of California at Los Angeles (UCLA)
2. Stanford Research Institute (SRI)
3. University of California at Santa Barbara (UCSB)
4. University of Utah

Each of the four nodes had a specific function such as special processing or graphics. Together, they operated as a whole and were able to process data, even though they were many hundreds of miles away from each other.

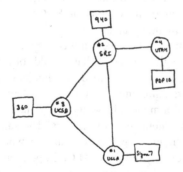

Fig. 1. Classical sketch of the four-node ARPAnet from 1969
Source: http://www.computerhistory.org/internet_history/full_size_images/1969_4-node_map.gif

It is our experience that students find stories such as this one very fascinating. They actually provide fodder for further exploration on topics such as the following.

- How many nodes are on the internet today? How does one count such nodes? Who does the counting?
- How does the internet compare with the world wide web? Are they two entities of the same thing? If not, how do they differ? Can one exist without the other?

These and other related questions lead to class or interpersonal discussions that open up new knowledge based on knowledge students already have. We have found that this approach adds relevancy and enrichment to a topic or subject and makes network or communications classes more inviting.

We could explore other historical episodes that relate computing history to technical topics in a networks or communications plan of study. The outcome would be similar or the same. Our experience shows that using the approach of history or story telling *captures* the imagination of students and makes the teaching of the technical aspects of a course more enjoyable and interesting to students and teachers. Students will definitely explore questions such as those above; teachers could use the results of student findings and exploration as a part of their marks or grades for a technical course (e.g., 5% to 10%) or as extra credit, which students always enjoy receiving for work beyond the expectations of a syllabus.

4.3   History in Other Specialized Courses

Teachers can use computing history in other subject areas where teachers can use stories as a vehicle to generate some excitement and interest. However, the "show and tell" strategy can become limited. With integrated networks and "system on a chip" (SOC) technologies in today's world, it is difficult to demonstrate physical entities compared to demonstrations of valves or vacuum tubes, transistors, floppy disks, and the like that we could do with computers from the past. Yet, even though an entire computer system is in the shape of a small geometric entity or cube, it is possible to establish interesting stories on the evolution of a machine such as the ENIAC that occupied a large room to modern versions of SOCs. We could do the same for specialized areas such as computer graphics or robotics.

The strategy of show and tell becomes limited as we move away from tangible computing entities to intangible ones. What would one show physically about software other than a package or a download of a language product or an operating system? Yet their history remains intangibly rich. We have encouraged students to trace the roots or ancestry of a modern language today such as C#. When students dig into this, they begin to find interesting connections. The same is true with operating systems. Teachers can pose interesting questions such as what is the status of COBOL and FORTRAN languages or why did the IBM OS2 operating system die.

Of course, many charts and timelines exist on tracing the roots of computing languages and operating systems. We have marvelled at the way students enjoy the fascination of seeing ways in which different languages emerged. Additionally, we see that students do appreciate exploring the relevancy of past languages to the languages in use today. With operating systems, student response to learning historical connections is similar. Here again, an optional assignment on a relevant topic would definitely enrich a class related to software.

Occasionally, we have observed that a student begins to develop a keen interest in the study of the origins of programming languages and operating systems. In such cases, we have directed them to communities of special interest such as SIGPLAN of ACM or to some specialized literature of books. Of particular note are the proceedings of two conferences, namely, the "History of Programming Languages" (HOPL) in 1978 [13] and in 1993 [14].

In our experiences, the use of "show and tell" seems to fall short with theory topics. Here, the focus is often on individuals and their circumstances. With topics related to discrete mathematics, algorithms, data structures, or computer theory, we often take the opportunity to explore the life or achievements of the individuals involved. An obvious individual in computer theory is Alan Turing, whose contributions to code breaking, machine learning, and the virtual Turing machine are well known. We have found that students begin to gravitate and to appreciate individuals for their contributions.

The field of computing has a long list of historical contributors such as Leonhard Euler, John von Neumann, and Maurice Wilkes in addition to more contemporary individuals such as Bill Gates, Steve Jobs, Mark Zuckerberg, Larry Page, or Sergey Brin. Whether centuries ago (e.g., Euler), decades ago (e.g., von Neumann), or contemporary pioneers (e.g., Gates), students relate and become interested in the way their subject of study evolved over time and how individuals shaped and reshaped the computing field. They also see the relevancy of the way lives of computing pioneers affect their own paths to their careers. As teachers, we find this student experience fulfilling.

4.4   History and Introductory Courses

Is history useful in introductory computing courses?

We are in the affirmative on this question. In addition to introducing the field of study, these courses often serve as vehicles to support students' interest in a subject area and develop some understanding of the subject's concepts and fundamentals. Introductory courses are often of an overview nature or of a specialized nature such as an introduction to programming. Overview courses tend to include students from diverse specialties; in specialized introductory courses, the majority of students include those with their intended specialty.

Although useful in either setting, we have found that the use history works best in the overview course. The broad scope of the overview course shows students that the field of computing is more than a narrow orientation. In fact, it is more about an exploration of computing where teachers can easily tailor history into their syllabus. The overview course presents many opportunities for students to explore extensions of topics on their own. We have found that history is a perfect way to relate new concepts with people, places, and events. Students appreciate historical excursions and they can relate their finding to relevant topics in their contemporary settings. As before, students also appreciate receiving extra credit for reporting on their findings. Furthermore, if we integrate history in introductory courses, students would expect its appearance in subsequent courses, which would encourage other faculty members to embrace the historical perspective.

4.5   History beyond Technical Courses

History can also be of relevant interest in courses beyond those of a technical nature. One such course is computing ethics or other similar name. Discussion of contemporary issues such as intellectual property rights can form a basis for further explorations such as when did the concept of intellectual property first begin. Computing ethics has emerged as a required topic of study and it is often part of a computing curriculum as an individual course or as an integrated theme.

It would be good to have students explore real case studies associated with computing and identify ethical situations or dilemmas. Unfortunately, repositories of historical case studies are very limited or isolated and they are generally not accessible to the public. Perhaps this is primarily the result of teachers and business entrepreneurs being overly protective of the sensitivity of those projects that were successful or in particular, those that were unsuccessful. Nevertheless, it is important for students to experience real situations such as the lawsuit of Apple v. IBM and ascertain whether any ethical transgressions were at issue in addition to legal ones. Experiences such as these are very relevant to students' understanding of the computing filed as they start their journeys toward their professional careers.

5   Conclusion

In summary, it is our experience that the inclusion of history with specialized computing topics and courses adds a sociological dimension to the subject. This strategy has had the effect of engaging students in these subjects; they also appreciate the relevance of discussions that include people, places, and events. Furthermore, it has the attribute of enriching a topic or course and providing students with an avenue for extra credit as allowed by the instructor.

Although not discussed explicitly in the narrative above, teachers and students should avail themselves of the many online resources available to them such as virtual museums, "walk-through" galleries, and oral histories that provide deeper descriptions and understandings of specialized historical events. A resource such as the *IEEE Annals of the History of Computing* [15] contains an oasis of formal articles, memoirs, anecdotes, and obituaries; it also provides a foundation for many stories about computing distributed across many areas of the field.

Once again, we have found that using history to teach computing courses is a useful endeavour. The rewards derived from the *teaching* experience certainly offset the preparation and the effort. The rewards derived from the *learning* experience should leave a lasting impression long after students complete a course. Such aspects of engagement add relevance to the subjects students learn as they prepare themselves for professional careers.

References

1. Impagliazzo, J., Campbell-Kelly, M., Davies, G., Lee, J.A.N., Williams, M.: History in the Computing Curriculum. IFIP TC 3 / TC 9 Joint Task Group. IEEE Annals of the History of Computing 21(1), 1–15 (1999)
2. Impagliazzo, J.: History: A Vehicle for Teaching Introductory Computing Courses. In: Proceedings of the IFIP 2005 World Computer Conference in Education (WCCE), Cape Town, South Africa, July 4-7 (2005)
3. Santayana, G.: Reason in Common Sense. The Life of Reason, vol. 1 (1905)
4. Microsoft, Surface Table, http://money.cnn.com/2012/06/19/technology/microsoft-surface-table-pixelsense/index.htm

5. IT History Society, http://www.ithistory.org/
6. Society for the History of Technology (SHOT), Annual Conference 2013 (2013), http://www.historyoftechnology.org/annual_meeting.html
7. Papadimitriou, C.: MythematiCS: In Praise of Storytelling in the Teaching of Computer Science and Math. ACM SIGCSE Bulletin 35(4), 7–9 (2003) (Invited Editorial)
8. Computer History Museum, http://www.computerhistory.org/
9. Science Museum, London, http://www.sciencemuseum.org.uk/
10. Deutsches Museum–Munich, http://www.deutsches-museum.de/
11. National Aviation and Space Administration (NASA). Sputnik: The Fiftieth Anniversary, http://history.nasa.gov/sputnik/
12. DARPA History, http://www.darpa.mil/About/History/ARPA-DARPA__ The_Name_Chronicles.aspx
13. Wexelblat, R.L.: The History of Programming Languages, 758 p. Academic Press (1981)
14. Bergin, T.J., Gibson, R.G.: The History of Programming Languages - II, 864 p. Addison-Wesley Pub. Co. (1996)
15. IEEE Annals of the History of Computing, http://www.computer.org/annals

Using Events from the Past to Inform the Future

Martha E. Crosby

Department of Information and Computer Sciences, University of Hawaii, Honolulu, Hawaii, USA
crosby@hawaii.edu

Abstract. Knowledge of the history of computing is an important and relevant topic, particularly for computer science students. Inventions are usually created to solve a particular problem, yet the product evolves and is used for entirely different purposes. Knowing the origin and context gives students additional ways to recall that knowledge. The various implementations make old ideas current. One can infer the past from the future, and from the fact that predictions by most people associated with computer technology have not been particularly accurate. The examples in this paper illustrate how many of the artifacts that existed in early computer and communication systems informed the future.

Keywords: Computer History Education.

1   Introduction

Knowledge of the history of computing is an important and relevant topic, particularly for computer science students. However, students need to know why they are learning something in order to relate it to information they possess. Lee argues: *"little of our literature or open records contains information on the motivation, the innovation and the decision making that led to commercial products, to new methodologies, and significant research results"* (Lee, 1998, p. 11). Students need to understand the relevance of each discovery and its position in a continuum. Often the stories associated with the evolution of the specific technology are as important (or at least as interesting) as the contribution itself. Inventions are often created to solve a particular problem, yet the product evolves and is used for entirely different purposes. The various implementations are what make old ideas current. If the purpose is not to invent but to adapt an idea, the background of the idea's inception may also play a role in the new implementation. Once the idea is clearly understood, it is possible to extrapolate it into a new context. What makes ideas current is not the novelty of the idea in itself but the way in which it is presented. If students are able to see discoveries in their time and context they are more likely to rediscover these concepts as they are implemented in current contexts (Giangrandi & Mirolo, 2006). There are many ways in which students may benefit from the history of computing. Giangrandi & Mirolo, (2006, p. 79) explain that computer history helps students understand the development of scientific knowledge, to bridge the gap between science and

A. Tatnall, T. Blyth, and R. Johnson (Eds.): HC 2013, IFIP AICT 416, pp. 144–148, 2013.

humanities and to enrich cultural background. Other areas where students may benefit from learning the history of computing are presented by (Nakano, Styles, & Draper, 2013, p. 27). They explain that: *"employees who have studied the history of computing can relate to older workers, thus reducing the generation gap in information technology."* Students who are well versed in the history of computing know the outcomes of what was tried before and they bring different points of view to problem solving. Sometimes, the purpose of an idea changes with the available technologies. Anderson (2012, p. 33) gives an example of repurposing of digitization to adapt it to current times with the following quote: *"During the late 20th century and early 21st century, letter writing has given way to email, SMS messages, and tweets, diaries have been superseded by blogs (private and public), and where paper once prevailed digital forms are making inroads and the trend is set to continue."*

2   Events from the Past

Although one can infer the past from the future, it is important that students know that predictions by most people associated with computer technology were not particularly accurate. At one time people thought that fifty storage cells would be enough for any imaginable application. In 1959, there were very few electronic digital computers. However, the sentiment at the time was that the number of computers in the United States would easily meet the demand. People said: "Why would anyone ever want to own a calculator?" Of course the mechanical calculators at that time took an entire desk so it was difficult to imagine having one that could fit in your pocket. If it was hard to envision owning your own calculator, the concept of owning your own computer seemed impossible. In early computers, both time and space were limited but even then most people associated with computer technology realized that optimizing one was usually at the expense of the other. This paper discusses adaptions that were made in hardware, software and data communication and how they informed the future.

In the 1800s Joseph Jacquard created a machine to weave complex patterns using punched cards to automate the process. This concept was adapted to computing by Herman Hollerith, while working for the U.S. Census Bureau. In 1890, he developed the Hollerith Tabulating Machine that used punched cards to take the census. Six years later, Hollerith founded the Tabulating Machine Company later named International Business Machines (IBM). Implementations of time-sharing computers using mechanical relays existed at that time and that technology could have been adapted. However, for almost 30 years, IBM's dominance in the computer field led to the predominate use of punched card technology. Modern computers use control units and separate memory functions, a concept that was heavily influenced by a mechanical calculator called the Z1, invented by Konrad Zuse in 1936. That same year Alan Turing created an abstract model that defined mechanical procedures. Turing's concept of an infinite tape that could be read, written on and erased inspired Random Access Memory (RAM) functions. At the University of Iowa in 1939, John Atanasoff and his student Clifford Berry built the first electrically powered

Atanasoff-Berry Computer (ABC). It was the first computer to use the binary system, to have memory restored when it was booted and to use vacuum tubes instead of mechanical switches to store data. Although each calculation took about 15 seconds, its design was a model for future computers. At Harvard, from the late 1930s to early 1950s, Howard Aiken designed the Mark series of computers that were primarily used for computations by the U.S. Navy. Grace Hopper, a programmer for Harvard Mark I, removed a moth that caused the computer to malfunction. This event initiated the use of the term "bug" to mean the cause of a program error. At the University of Pennsylvania in 1944, John Mauchley and J. Presper Eckert developed a high-speed electronic digital computer called the Electronic Numerical Integrator and Computer (ENIAC). It was primarily used to calculate weapons settings by the U.S. Government and was operational until 1955. The Universal Automatic Computer (UNIVAC), completed in 1951, was the first commercially successful computer in the United States. It was noticed by the public when it only needed 5% of the vote as input to predict that Dwight Eisenhower would win the presidential race.

In the mid-1970s, a special purpose computer built for a chemical company failed to meet specifications and the manufacturers advertised their product in Popular Electronics, a magazine read by many computer enthusiasts. The computer was very primitive but the price finally made it possible for individuals to own a computer. At that time, very few people would have predicted the personal computer movement that followed. Computer languages such as FORTRAN, ALGOL COBOL had been developed in the 1950s, primarily for scientific and business applications. At Dartmouth College in 1964, John G. Kemeny and Thomas E. Kurtz developed a simplified computer language called the Beginners All Purpose Symbolic Instruction Code (BASIC). This was a programming language that could be easily learned giving more people an opportunity to program computers. The BASIC programming language was small and it became the primary language for personal computers. At the same time the personal computer hardware was developing, the addition of application software made the personal computers useful to more people. Since algorithms build on each other, implementations were constantly being adapted to either run faster or use less space. Sorting and searching methods have been continually improved for specific types of problems. Libraries of software are built and improved. Open source mathematical libraries such as SHARE were at first the norm, then for profit application packages gave more people reason to use computers.

In 1961, during the cold war, Baran suggested changing the shape of the national communication network to become a redundant distributed network with no vulnerable central point. Looking into the past and available technologies, he proposed the marriage of computer and communication technologies (Ryan, 2010). Examples that are highly motivating for University of Hawaii (UH) students in this context are listening to audio recordings of locally based computer pioneers telling their stories. For example, W. Wesley Peterson describes his 1961 implementation of cyclic redundancy codes (CRC) in an audio recording. During his narrative he describes how he struggled with the idea. He had figured out how to encode and do parity checks efficiently, then, working with colleagues, everything came together for efficient error detection. He mentions that the CRC codes were used for floppy disk technologies and Ethernet networks. The students are impressed how the CRC codes still remain in use in new storage and transmission technologies. Peterson saw CRC codes, as useful tools for error correction but didn't envision the explosion and wide use and impact that telecommunications would have in the world.

In1971, Norman Abramson, transmitted wireless data packets from a user to a computer network. Those packets, transmitted, between terminals in the engineering building and the computer center at the University of Hawaii, marked the first use of what is now known as an ALOHA channel. ALOHA channels were used in a limited way in 1G first generation mobile phones for signaling and control purposes. The use of ALOHA was expanded in the 1990s by the introduction of SMS texting capabilities in 2G mobile networks, and then even more by the use of General Packet Radio Service (GPRS) in 3G networks in the first decade of this century. It seems clear that the expanding use of smart phones and IP based web traffic in developing 4G networks will lead to an even greater use of ALOHA channels and ALOHA traffic in the next decade. UH students are particularly inspired by the history of the development of ALOHA channels on their own campus, particularly when they see the worldwide application of ALOHA in wireless networks, and satellite data networks.

In 1971, UH researchers and graduate students used primitive tools and with great difficulty provided modern techniques in educational multimedia environments. Researchers at the UH had a grant to bring an experimental computer, developed at UC Berkley, to be the tip for the ARPA network. The computer was called the BCC 500 because it had an architecture that could support 500 interactive users. This was at a time when commercial time sharing computers such as the HP only supported 32 simultaneous users. The communication infrastructure provided by the ALOHA network enabled UH to have many initiatives that are still relevant. Because computers were still very expensive in the early seventies, there was a moratorium on all of the K-12 schools in the state of Hawaii not to buy computers. However, some high school mathematics teachers wanted to teach their students to program. The teachers were able to convince their principals to rent teletypes so they could dial in remotely to the BCC500's BASIC compiler at UH. This enabled high school students from the neighbor islands and other areas of Oahu to learn to write computer programs. The Web Browser Mosaic became available in 1993. That year a graduate student at UH was able to write a thesis comparing the performance of Mosaic to all the other existing search engines and browsers by visiting every node on the Internet. As she traced the historical development of the Internet, she realized that the explosive growth rate of the internet nodes would make her task impossible within the year.

Knowing the origin and context of the computer artifact gives the student more ways to store and recall that knowledge. Many new ideas in computing are often adaptations of previous discoveries. In order to avoid duplication of efforts and re-inventing the wheel, learning about history should encompass more than just the factual information. If witnesses of the circumstances from which breakthroughs were developed don't talk about it, people will not have an opportunity to learn from the past. By paying more attention to the past, we can continue to inform the future.

References

1. Abramson, N.: The Aloha System. In: Abramson, N., Kuo, F. (eds.) Journal of Computer Communication Networks. Prentice Hall, New York (1973)
2. Anderson, D.: The Future of the Past. Communications of the ACM 55(5), 33–34 (2012)
3. Giangrandi, P., Mirolo, C.: "Numerie Macchine": A Virtual Museum to Learn the History of Computing. In: Proceedings of the 11th Annual SIGCSE Conference on Innovation and Technology in Computer Science Education, pp. 78–82. ACM, Bologna (2006)
4. Lee, J.A.N.: History in the Computer Science Curriculum: Part II. SIGCSE Bulletin 30(2), 11–13 (1998)
5. Nakano, H., Styles, M.G., Draper, G.M.: A Call for Champions: Why Some "History of Computing" Courses are More Successful than Others. ACM Inroads 4(1), 26–28 (2013)
6. Ryan, J.A.: History of the Internet and the Digital Future. Reaktion Books LTD, London (2010)
7. Technology in Action Technology in Focus: The History of the PC, pp. 37–47. Pearson Education, Inc. Publishing as Prentice Hall (2011)

The Impact of the Microprocessor

Anthony C. Davies

Emeritus Professor, King's College London, Visiting Professor, Kingston University,
Kingston-upon-Thames, Surrey, UK
tonydavies@ieee.org

Abstract. A description and explanation based mainly on the author's personal experiences of the changes in the curriculum for electrical engineering undergraduates and in the required expertise of practising electronics engineers which occurred from the mid-1960s. The changes began with the introduction of digital system design methods, and increased with the subsequent introduction of microprocessors as widely-used programmable components, for which software design expertise was an essential part of their utilisation.

Keywords: Microprocessor, electrical engineering students, curriculum.

1   The Higher-Education Background in UK

In the 1960s and early 1970s teachers in UK universities had considerable freedom to interpret the syllabuses of courses which they taught. Around 1965, I was teaching a final year undergraduate course for electrical engineers which contained no material on digital electronics. However the syllabus contained the phrase "and/or gates", no doubt intended to occupy only a few minutes of one lecture. I decided to interpret that as an excuse to include a substantial amount of material on digital logic including Boolean algebra, combination logic design, synchronous logic design, which developed into around half of the course content. By the mid-1970s, I was involved in teaching essentially the same material to the first year undergraduates, where it had been transferred against the opposition of the older academic traditionalists. Much the same happened at about the same time in many other UK universities.

Boolean algebra had been included earlier but typically taught by mathematicians who may have known about the original application to logic of a different kind but usually had no idea of the application to switching circuits and electronics. Such teaching did not have a favourable impact on most engineering undergraduates.

In parallel with this it had become common for engineering undergraduates to learn programming in languages such as FORTRAN, used to solve engineering problems, submitting their work by punched-cards or paper tape and receiving the results hours (or sometimes, days, later). By about 1970, they were typically also using electromechanical teletypes for multi-user access to a central computer providing fast return of results. Later, a few had access to and use of a mini-computer such as the PDP-8 for measurement, instrumentation or control applications and this could be in a real-time context.

Errors in programming resulted in wrong answers or crashed programs leading simply to modifications and re-submissions. No concepts such as software

A. Tatnall, T. Blyth, and R. Johnson (Eds.): HC 2013, IFIP AICT 416, pp. 149–160, 2013.
© IFIP International Federation for Information Processing 2013

engineering or software design were involved. It was considered a sufficient education to have a FORTRAN language handbook and see a few examples [1].

Electronic engineering undergraduates were unlikely to be taught about computer architectures or assembly language programming except in a very superficial way.

It was against this background that the microprocessor as an electronic component appeared in the form of the 4-bit Intel 4004, announced in 1971 and the 8-bit Intel 8008 the following year. General availability had arisen by 1973, and the impact was really being felt in industry by 1975, with the availability of 8-bit microprocessors such as the Intel 8080 and Motorola 6800.

2   The Initial Context and Impact of the First Microprocessors

The microprocessor created a shock amongst local electronic component distributors. They found out they had to sell a new kind of component which needed not just the support of a single page datasheet but, rather, huge manuals fall of unfamiliar material plus additional supporting supplies such as a deck of punched cards comprising a cross assembler to run on a mini-computer or mainframe computer, truly a "New World" for which their sales force was totally unprepared and untrained.

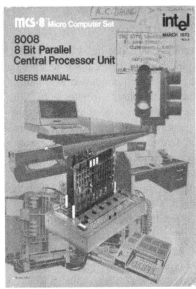

Fig. 1. 126 page User manual for Intel 8008 [2]

A further complexity for both the distributors and potential users of these components in new engineering designs was that each major semiconductor device manufacturer wanted to produce its own unique microprocessor range (see Appendix and Table I). Each microprocessor had a different architecture, a different assembly language and different package pin-outs and needed different 'support-chips' to make a working system. Deciding which microprocessor was the best to choose was a major hurdle for practising engineers as was deciding what was the fundamental expertise needed to use these devices and what was salesman's hype.

At the time there were many companies making integrated circuits, but most were not computer manufacturers. Microprocessors involved making a quite new class of product and so moving into uncharted territory for them. There was no move towards standardisation, each manufacturer hoping to become a market leader. Some 'second-sourcing' agreements were made (for example between Fairchild and Mostek for the F8 and later Zilog and Mostek for the Z80), since this was seen as a sales-advantage with some classes of customer.

3   The Education and Training Responses

All this created a market for short courses of a few days duration run by entrepreneurial engineers who could hire some small rooms in a hotel to present introductory courses focusing on a particular microprocessor type and including hands-on work with inexpensive kits. Typically such courses included simple machine-code and assembly language programming tasks which could be immediately executed on the kits and the participants carried out such assignments as controlling a seven-segment numeric display, responding to the pressing of a push-button, generating simple sequences and waveforms and perhaps even starting and stopping a simple miniature electrical motor.

My assessment of such courses at the time was that they were rather too expensive for many electronics engineers in industry and too detailed in content for the senior managers who could afford the fees but perhaps would have felt that assembly language programming of the kits was beneath their dignity. I therefore had an idea to start running very low cost but useful courses for practising electronics engineers, and accordingly, with the support of my university and IEEE and the aid of two engineers from a nearby industrial research laboratory[1] who had been working intensively with microprocessors, our first short course of weekly evening lectures was run for a fee of only £10 in October 1975 (Figure 2a).

By any standards that was extremely cheap and affordable, our aim was not to make money but to do something useful without the risk of actually losing money. This aim was comfortably achieved and led me to promoting and teaching a sequence of frequent short courses on various aspects of microprocessors over the following years (such as the one illustrated by Figure 2b). Other universities and polytechnics in the UK also began running such courses.

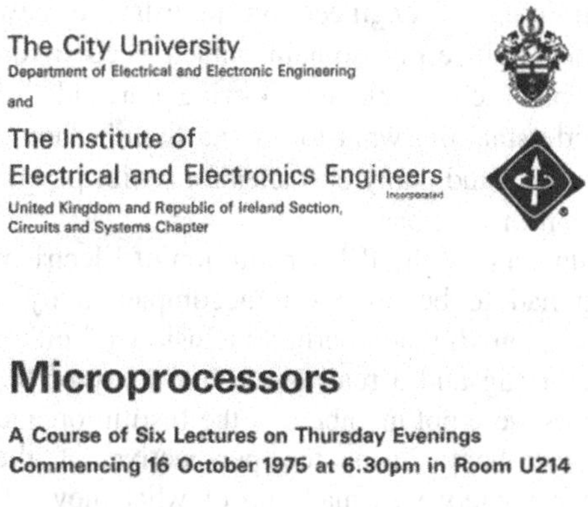

The City University
Department of Electrical and Electronic Engineering

and

The Institute of
Electrical and Electronics Engineers
United Kingdom and Republic of Ireland Section,
Circuits and Systems Chapter

Microprocessors

A Course of Six Lectures on Thursday Evenings
Commencing 16 October 1975 at 6.30pm in Room U214

THE CITY UNIVERSITY

The Institute of
Electrical and Electronics Engineers
United Kingdom and Republic of Ireland Section
Circuits and Systems Chapter

Three Day Introductory Course on
MICROPROCESSORS
at
The Portland Heights Hotel,
Portland, Dorset.

22–24 September 1981

Fig. 2a. First microprocessor short course at The City University

Fig. 2b. Short course in a hotel near a military research establishment

---

[1]   David Wright and Daphne Shipperlee, Standard Telecommunications Laboratories, Harlow, Essex.

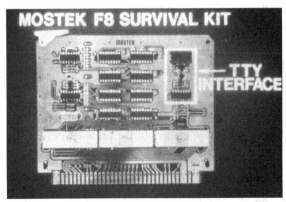

Fig. 3a. Typical single-board 'evaluation kit'

Fig. 3b. Single-chip microcomputer: a new kind of component for the electronic-system designer

4   New Outlooks and the Educational Curriculum

It was clear by this time that a new electronic design paradigm had arisen. There was the prospect of using programmable electronics rather than hardwired logic (which came to be called random logic) in many kinds of electronic products. An obvious consequence was a need for major retraining of engineers in industry, a new responsibility for Learned Societies in the engineering domain, and a need to do something about modernisation of the typical electronic engineering curricula of universities and polytechnics. However understanding what to do and how it should be done represented a challenge, with indecision and many obstacles for senior people in academia and industry and the Professional Institutions.

At the management level (staff and volunteers) of the IEE (Institution of Electrical Engineers) the realisation that something had to be done was accompanied by a general belief that the scope of the Institution did not permit inclusion of either computer architecture or computer programming and a realisation that many of the people knowledgeable about microprocessors were not members of the Institution and maybe not even qualified to become members. From the perspective of the traditionalists in IEE, the British Computer Society was made up of what they felt were mainly hobbyists and amateurs whom they considered to be irreconcilably distinct from the professional engineers of the IEE.

Nevertheless, seeing an urgent need to become involved with microprocessors, they set up a somewhat independent Microprocessor Application Group, with funding and publicity which enabled IEE to have committees, arrange meetings, and generally support this topic, without really either understanding it or admitting it into the scope of IEE. Growth in this subject area enabled them after a few years to incorporate it within the scope of IEE, although arguments continued about whether computer architecture and software engineering belonged in the Institution. For a while there was an uninformed view among some senior members that software engineering meant using computers to solve engineering design problems and they could not or would not recognise that it meant designing software in an engineering manner for any kinds of applications, including embedded software in real time systems incorporating microprocessors.

I recall being at an IEE Council Meeting at which one of the older members suggested that IEE should have nothing to do with Computer Architecture because that would lead to jealousy from the Institution of Civil Engineers.

At about this time, The City University in London started a bachelors degree course called 'Computer Engineering' [3]. Figure 4 shows the cover of a brochure for this course. The intention was that this would be for the 'modern' type of future electronic engineer, in recognition of the importance of computers in all domains, including the use of microprocessors in electronic projects. Getting academic approval and professional institution accreditation proved difficult, and instead of bringing in hoped-for collaboration between the electrical engineering and computer science departments it led to incomprehension and something more akin to warfare.

Nevertheless it provided a route by which much more digital electronics and microprocessor work was incorporated into the undergraduate engineering program.

The typical student experience included similar laboratory experiments to those used in the commercial short courses, e.g. designing and executing simple small assembly language programs on various microprocessor kits, to carry out simple real-time tasks. For the first time electronic engineering undergraduates were introduced to the mechanisms of subroutines and interrupts rather than just using high-level languages to solve problems by sending programs to a computer centre and waiting for the results. It became feasible to 'slide' this laboratory work gradually into that for those on the traditional electronic and electrical engineering degree courses without the opposition of the traditionalists.

The first microprocessor-evaluation kits often had only about one-millionth of the amount of random access memory (RAM) to store programs and data that is today provided in a typical basic laptop computer for home-uses running the Windows operating system.

Initially we made much use of a simple 'kit' for the F8, shown in Figure 3(a), which had a small operating system with a few subroutines for input and output, a teletype interface, a loader for machine code programmes and (almost) 1024 8-bit words of user programmable memory. Programs written in assembly language were translated to machine code by a cross-assembler (written in FORTRAN!) running on a main-frame computer (ICL 1905), with output on a paper-tape which was loaded into the 'kit' using a teletype. Soon after, with the availability of microcomputer systems with more capable operating systems and having storage on 7 inch floppy discs, it became possible to assemble and test the programming tasks in a self-contained portable unit, no longer requiring access to a main-frame computer. Fluency with hexadecimal arithmetic was one of the skills students had to acquire.

It should not be assumed that we 'educationalists' involved in these changes were wise and far-sighted prophets, we were just somewhat less hidebound by tradition than some senior academics and professional engineers. We were aware of Moore's

THE CITY UNIVERSITY

BSc in Computer Engineering

Fig. 4. Computer Engineering Course brochure (shows metallization pattern of Am2909 Microprogram Sequencer)

Law [4], and observed the exponential rise in the complexity of digital integrated circuit chips, but (at least in my case) concluded that this could not go on for long, because the Law indicated that soon there would be a million transistors per chip, from which I concluded (and told others) that designing a microprocessor with so many transistors would be beyond human capability. Of course, that proved completely incorrect, and now single-chip processors with transistor counts of one billion are commonplace (and the fabrication cost per transistor is apparently less than the cost of growing one grain of rice). The first microprocessor chips comprised a few thousand transistors

I also recall a public meeting at which an experienced engineer insisted that there would never be 16-bit microprocessors using silicon technology, because it could be proved from fundamental physics and the laws of thermodynamics that too much heat would be generated. At the time the first rudimentary 16-bit microprocessors were already being developed, and now silicon 32-bit and even 64-bit processors are perfectly feasible and in use.

5   The UK Government Response to Microprocessors

While all this was going on there were members of the UK government who recognised that the introduction of the microprocessor represented a fundamental change for the engineering industry and their products. They perceived that if the UK did not take the correct steps to participate successfully in this change the future prosperity of the UK might be severely damaged.

In addition to commercial applications related to national prosperity this was also the time of the Cold War and so the relationship to military systems and defence could not be forgotten.

It was within this context that in 1979, funding of £15 million was provided to the National Computer Centre for a microprocessor application project (MAP), which invited bids for government financial support for training courses and schemes aimed at updating British industry in the use of microprocessors in manufacturing and in end-products. This source of funding attracted the attention of the universities and polytechnics. In the universities it was often seen as a way of creating additional income by running short courses for industry for high fees and so generating comfortable surpluses. In the polytechnics their funding schemes often meant that any surpluses created by their activities, including short courses, reverted to the local authorities that controlled them and brought no benefit to the polytechnics. This meant the polytechnics often ran short courses charging fees which just covered the direct costs and so spoiled a lucrative market for the universities and also for the small entrepreneurs previously mentioned who were running courses in hotels and making a comfortable income for themselves.

One of the outcomes was that many expensively produced university microprocessor courses attracted few customers and did not create the hoped-for financial surpluses. It could be said that the market was flooded with far more courses than was needed. Nevertheless some did continue successfully and I had personal experience of teaching such short courses in Washington DC and in Berlin as well as in or alongside various industrial companies and government establishments around the UK.

Soon afterwards notice was being taken of what was called the Fifth Generation Computer Project underway in Japan, the purpose of which included research and development to solve some of the difficult problems for which computers had so far been unsuccessful (for example speech recognition, speech understanding, speech synthesis, image processing and recognition and various forms of so-called artificial intelligence). The microprocessor was denoted the 'fourth generation' in computer hardware, and so the Japanese programme was intended to be the next major step.

Shortly after this, the UK Government launched the Alvey Programme (1983-1987), a very well-funded scheme with the aim of moving forward UK research in the computer and information engineering areas with the specific idea of enhancing the position of the UK in associated scientific development and economic prosperity. It was to a large extent based on the assumption that competing with the Japanese Fifth Generation Computer project was necessary. The programme provided a convenient and welcome boost to the funding of related research in UK universities, of particular help to Computer Science, although in retrospect, not much seems to be recalled about the positive outcomes.

There was a sensible realisation that teenage children needed to get some experience of microprocessors, and the many simple and fairly expensive microcomputers becoming available was leading to amateur and hobby groups being formed. One significant consequence was the BBC Micro, based on a design from the Acorn Company (the Acorn Atom) which was chosen from several competing alternatives, and this became widely used to teach programming in schools, clubs and in many university electrical engineering departments. It used a non-standard but somewhat superior form of the BASIC language, with the inclusion of capabilities to support graphics programming and real-time interfacing. The cost was low enough for widespread adoption, and the BBC Micro was powerful and versatile enough to provide an educational foundation for beginners and to be used in simple real-time control engineering applications and experimental work.

Whereas in the early days of semiconductor technology and the move towards integrated circuits, very many of the major electrical engineering companies became involved in fabrication, making their own products, as the complexity of digital integrated circuits increased and the feature sizes of the transistors decreased dramatically (as predicted by Moore [4]), the cost of an up-to-date semiconductor plant became unaffordable for more and more companies. This is now well-known.

In the hope that the UK could remain active and competitive in this field, the INMOS company was formed with government financial support, against a background that most of the British companies which had semiconductor manufacturing capabilities were closing them down or not keeping up with the general advances and instead limiting themselves to specialized niche markets.

Ultimately, INMOS had its government support withdrawn and its activities effectively terminated. However, it was responsible for one very significant product, the INMOS transputer, a microprocessor with a very different architecture specifically intended to support a multi-processor design paradigm. This approach was supported enthusiastically by many UK Computer Science Departments as a basis for both their teaching and research, and brought them more into contact with industry and contract-supported research. However, the final demise of INMOS and the transputer limited the long-term impact of this, and it seems to have done little in most universities to bridge the gap between Electrical Engineering and Computer Science Departments.

6   Some More Technical Details about Microprocessors

Initially, a minimum working system needed several integrated circuits but soon single-chip microcomputers (microcontrollers) appeared, with everything needed in a single 28 or 40 pin dual-in-line package, either mask-programmable for quantity-production (as in the Intel 8048) or with user-programmable memory which could be erased with ultra-violet light and re-programmed for design and experiment and for small-number production runs (as in the Intel 8748).

A significant constraint was the number of pins available when using the industry standard dual in-line packages. The Intel 8008 was in a 18 pin package (Figure 5a) and subsequently packages with 40 pins were generally used for the early microprocessors (Figure 5b). Such large packages were already at the limit of conventional manufacturing and assembly processes for electronic circuit boards. Texas Instruments developed the 9900, a 16-bit processor in a 64-pin dual in-line package, based on their 990 minicomputer. The package was difficult to handle and represented an upper limit for the dual in-line format. Later, totally new kinds of package had to be developed with far more pins (such as the Pin Grid Array) and some with special cooling arrangements. The Intel 80386 was in a 132 pin PGA. Figure 5c shows the Intel 80486 in a 168-pin package with the corresponding socket shown in Figure 5d. Many other types of package were developed to cater for increased miniaturisation and more pin numbers.

The first microprocessors used PMOS technology but this was soon replaced by the faster NMOS and later by CMOS which allowed much lower power consumption. Bipolar technology offered greater speed but could only achieve much lower circuit complexity per integrated circuit and it was used mainly for military applications until CMOS technology "caught up".

Fig. 5a. Intel 8008 in 18-pin dual-in-line package

Fig. 5b. 40-pin ceramic dual-in-line package

Fig. 5c. Intel 80486 in 168-pin PGA (underside)

Fig. 5d. Socket for PGA

7   Languages to Program Microprocessor-Based Systems

Despite the limited performance of the early microprocessors, they enabled the development of home computers and simple desktop computers which began to be used for general office applications such as document preparation and financial calculations. The word processor and the spreadsheet became universally familiar in all office environments.

These small computers provided the means of supporting the programming of microprocessor-based systems. Initially that involved assembly language programming but as the computers became more powerful the use of high-level languages with microprocessors began. This was also a necessary development to enable these small computers to be used by various kinds of beginners (hobbyists, teenagers in schools, and those with no electronics or computer background who were finding interests and applications in such things). Nevertheless, it was still possible to hear 'experts' claiming that high-level languages were inappropriate for use with microprocessors!

In the University teaching environment, there was typically a split between those who preferred the BASIC language and those who preferred languages in the Pascal and Modula-2 style. Most often it was the engineering departments using assembly language and BASIC, while computer science departments understood the conceptual advantages of Pascal and were sometimes rather uninterested in or ignorant about hardware and real-time applications of interest in engineering. The typically limited comprehension of software engineering principles and good software design was an often unrecognised handicap in the engineering departments. Indeed it was often a handicap among practising engineers in industry.

8   Desk-Top Computing

The microprocessor made possible the development of the home computer and the office desk-top microcomputer. Initially with very limited capabilities, they soon improved to make their use normal for document preparation and financial management, as well as providing a basis for the support of teaching of all subjects and the tools needed to design many kinds of microprocessor-based electronic systems. The plentiful diversity of initial products[2] in the market simplified with the release and dominance of the IBM PC and Apple, becoming standards with which other designs failed to compete. The open nature of the IBM PC design stimulated the production of IBM-compatible computers from many sources, often with better performance or lower prices, and this stimulated a huge range of hardware additions and software.

The IBM PC design ensured dominance of the Intel microprocessor range and laid the foundations for the success of Microsoft, while Apple provided an alternative built around Motorola products and supporting somewhat a different conceptual basis, with more emphasis on graphics and the human interface in a closed system which discouraged a market in competing but compatible products. The Apple design may have laid the foundation for their ipad and iphone, and similar products from other manufacturers.

9   Conclusions

The 'birth' of the microprocessor heralded a fundamental change in the educational framework, the practice of engineering design and the products of the manufacturing industries. It is now inconceivable that widely-used products from automobiles to telephones to military weapons systems (including aircraft) would be designed without incorporating microprocessors and microcontrollers.

This has fundamentally altered the education for and practice of the engineering profession.

One could say that it was a 'difficult' birth, but one whose consequences changed lives throughout the world, and laid the foundation for the internet and mobile phones and much that is now taken for granted as essential aspects of modern life.

---

[2]   A table in Personal Computer World magazine in 1980 [5] lists 83 microcomputer systems on sale in UK, of which only a few are generally remembered today (for example, Acorn Atom, Cromemco, HP85, North Star Horizon, Commodore PET, Sinclair ZX80, Tandy TRS 80).

Appendix

Table 1 gives an indication of the somewhat bewildering assortment of microprocessor designs which arose in the early years, with no claim that it is complete. It illustrates the situation that confronted electronics engineers, most of whom had little or no computer experience but who had to choose and learn to understand and use such novel components in products which they had to design. Only with hindsight can it be seen that just a few semiconductor manufacturers (e.g. Intel, AMD, Motorola and Texas Instruments) would survive in this market as the complexity and cost of making state-of-the-art integrated circuits increased. From some ultimately-unsuccessful designs (e.g. the MOS Technology 6502), the ARM computer design developed, and became the central processor used in almost all mobile phones. It is the architecture which supports Blackberry® and the Android operating systems and is used in Kindle e-books.

Table 1. Diversity in early microprocessor designs

Manufacturer	Name	Others (if applicable)	Comments
Intel	4004	8008→8080→8085 →8086	Developed into the 80286, 80386, 80486 range leading to current designs
Motorola	6800	6000→68000 and 6809	Developed to 68020 and current designs. 6809 came too late for success
Fairchild	F8		May have been based on LP8000. F8 was second-sourced by Mostek.
Zilog	Z80	Z8, Z8000	Z80 second sourced by Mostek, development via Intel 8080. Z8 is a single-chip microcomputer.
General Instruments (GI)	LP8000	CP1600	CP1600 was an early 16-bit microprocessor.
Rockwell	PPS-4	Later, R6500 was produced	R6500 was developed from MOS Technology's 6502.
Signetics	2650		Popular for a while with hobbyists.
Texas Instruments (TI)	TMS1000	9900 16-bit microprocessor produced later, but failed to find a significant market.	TMS1000 4-bit microcomputer used in many low-cost embedded-computer applications. Later TI prominence was with signal processing products such as TMS 320 series.
MOS Technology	6501	→ 6502	Used in BBC Micro.
National Semiconductor	SC/MP	Later, 16032 → 32016 → 30032. NSC800 (a CMOS version of Z80)	Pronounced "scamp". Independently and later, 32000 series was a very early 32-bit processor.
RCA	1802 (COSMAC) and 6511		COSMAC was an early CMOS design, offering very low power consumption.
Intersil	IM6100		12-bit CMOS design, with architecture similar to PDP-8 minicomputer.
Ferranti	F100-L		16-bit microprocessor, military sponsor based on FM1600 B minicomputer. Promoted as first European microprocessor, but not commercially successful.
Intel	8048	→8048→8051	Single-chip microcomputer
Mostek	MK3870		Single-chip microcomputer, based on F8.

A more detailed comparison of the wide range of microprocessors and microcomputers was made by Depledge [6].

References

[1] McCracken, D.D.: Guide to Fortran Programming. Wiley (1961)
[2] Intel Corporation, MCS-8 Micro Computer Set, Users Manual, Revision 3 (1973)
[3] The City University, Bachelors Degree Course in Computer Engineering, Syllabuses, London (May 1974)
[4] Moore, G.E.: Cramming more components onto integrated circuits. Electronics 38 (April 19, 1965)
[5] In Store. Personal Computer World, vol. 3(10), pp. 115–118. Sportscene Publishers, London (1980)
[6] Depledge, P.G.: A review of available microprocessors. In: Hartley, M., Buckley, A. (eds.) The Challenge of Microprocessors, pp. 44–53. Manchester University Press (1979)

Part VI

Putting the History of Computing into Different Contexts

The Voice in the Machine: Oral History and Making the Computer Relevant

Thomas Lean

British Library
Thomas.Lean@bl.uk

Abstract. From the beginning computer history has often been more about technical developments than it has been about the social history of the computer and its effects. This paper describes how a greater attention to the social context of developments, representations of technology, the importance of users, software, and other topics, has presented a number of other ways to make computer history relevant rather than concentrating on the machine itself. This paper considers computer history through the medium of oral history, using interviews collected by National Life Stories at the British Library as part of An Oral History of British Science.

Keywords: computer history, social history, oral history, life stories, interviews.

1   Introduction

Given the great complexity of the typical computer it is perhaps of little surprise that the machine itself, in all its technical glory, has cast a long shadow over the history of computing. From its early days computer history has often been more about technical developments far more than it has been about the social history of the computer and its effects. In more recent years, the body of literature concerning the history of the computer from other perspectives has grown, taking in, for example the role and culture of computer users[1], the computer as a business or information machine[2], the role of the military in the development of computing[3], and so on, moving the field on from what has sometimes seemed to be a hagiography of dead white machines. This greater attention to the social context of developments, representations of technology, the importance of users, software, and other topics, has presented a number of other ways to make computer history relevant rather than concentrating on the machine itself.

In this essay I consider computer history through the medium of oral history, using interviews collected by National Life Stories at the British Library as part of An Oral

---

[1] See, for example, Christina Lindsay, "From the Shadows: Users as Designers, Producers, Marketers, Distributors, and Technical Support." In How Users Matter: The Co-Construction of Users and Technologies, edited by Nelly Oudshoorn and Trevor J. Pinch. MIT Press, 2003.

[2] See, for example, Martin Campbell-Kelly and William Aspray, Computer: A History of the Information Machine, Second edition ed. Westview, 2004.

[3] See, for example, Paul N. Edwards, The Closed World: Computers and the Politics of Discourse in Cold War America, MIT Press, 1996.

A. Tatnall, T. Blyth, and R. Johnson (Eds.): HC 2013, IFIP AICT 416, pp. 163–172, 2013.

History of British Science[4]. Launched in 2009, this ongoing project has collected nearly one hundred life story interviews with British scientists and engineers, drawn from a great variety of fields. As history of technology has long preached, technologies have different meanings to different groups, and the computer is no exception to this. Amongst the interviews in the collection are recordings of computer designers, theoretical computer scientists, programmers, and many scientists and engineers who made use of computers in various different fields, presenting many different perspectives on the machine.

Interviews with figures from the history of computing are nothing new. To give a few examples, in the 1970s the NPL computer scientist and psychologist Christopher Evans carried out a series of interviews with computer pioneers about their work. Several organisations, notably The Computer History Museum, maintain extensive collections of oral history, and short interviews also frequently feature in IEEE Annals of the History of Computing often focused on particular issues that interviewees were involved with. On An Oral History of British Science, the development of computing and computers is not the focus of our interviews, which are essentially biographical in nature. This gives our interviews a slightly different perspective to ones more narrowly focused on particular topics, more concerned with an individual's day to day activities, and broadens the questions to include a wide variety of contextual details. Like any source, oral history can have its inaccuracies and biases, it needs to be subject to the same scrutiny as we would any other document and used in concert with other sources for serious academic use. These reservations aside, it is an excellent way of conveying the feel of a place or time, uncovering human interactions around technology that are undocumented elsewhere, and putting a voice to technical developments. In short it presents a number of ways to help make the history of computer relevant to wider audiences.

My aims in this paper are threefold. I touch on computer development as recalled from the point of view of designers, to explore how telling the stories of computers helps us to appreciate them as works of human endeavour rather than as monolithic artefacts. Secondly, I draw on interviews with computer users to suggest how oral history can add a sense of how people interacted with computers in the past, and demonstrate their relevance by uncovering ways in which the computer has shaped the world around us through its impact in science and engineering. Thirdly, and throughout, I aim to demonstrate some of oral history's uses in conveying the story of computing, not just as a historical source to be analysed and interrogated, but as a way of telling computer history in a way that forefronts the people involved and adds context to the machines themselves.

2   Machine Builders

We generally encounter old computers as complete artefacts, things that have been given shape by human activity. However, the inescapable presence of these complete

---

[4] An Oral History of British Science, http://www.bl.uk/aboutus/stratpolprog/ oralhist/oralhist.html Most of the interviews referred to in this article are available through British Library Sounds, sounds.bl.uk/ [accessed 6 August 2013]

artefacts sometimes obscures our view of the processes that created them. The approach of the life story interview encourages not just descriptions of old technology but narratives about development and use. Oral history offers a way of deconstructing finished computer objects by asking designers to tell us the story of how they were built. For example, our interviews with hardware designers reveal the step by step process of building early computers; starting with an outline plan, designing units in detail, having them constructed, adding them to the whole prototype. The computer, our interviewees explain at length, is the result of a gradual process of a machine taking shape, as Geoff Tootill, one of the developers of the 1948 Manchester Baby computer recalled of its construction:

> *The very last thing we could contemplate doing was to design the whole thing and have it all built and wire it all up and then find out why it didn't work. It was essential that the whole thing would work together at every stage as you added one unit after the other. [...] It was necessary that the apparatus should do something which we could see was correct, or if it wasn't correct we could mend it until it was correct at every stage, every chassis that we connected up.*
>
> *[...]*
>
> *Well, we went on with this process of adding the units and making the whole lot do something together at every stage until we got to the stage when we'd made a computer.*[5]

Along the way, in the extended versions of these bit-by-bit stories we learn many other contextual details about their construction: technical challenges that had to be overcome; details of interactions with colleagues; the role of lesser known people, such as technicians; amusing anecdotes; the principles that the machines were built on; their important design details; and the human activity involved in development. They give us the material to consider complete vintage computers as the culmination of processes and various human activities rather than as monoliths. For example, computer designer Raymond Bird recalled how the logical design of the ICT1301 was checked by rather unconventional means:

> *So this machine had masses of gates and shifting registers and all that sort of thing in it, and in order to check over the logical design John Wensley very sensibly said, 'We're going to mechanise, humanise, this, we're going to draw out the whole of the logic design on the conference room floor,' [...] And then human beings acted as pulses. A pulse of information, a voltage which lasts for say a millisecond. So a computer consists of pulses tearing all around the place at a megacycle. So people were stood representing pulses at the correct place in the circuit and then in order to check that a particular operation is correct, say an addition, the number being added would be a stream of pulses, one after the other. [...] There'd be a row of these human beings and they would march onto the machine [...] and told to move to the next point round the machine [...], with each time seeing that the effect of them being at that point at that time*

---

[5] National Life Stories interview with Geoff Tootill. C1379/02

didn't clash with another one, or they'd got somewhere to go and it wasn't shut off to them.[6]

Not only does this insight reveal something of the human story behind the ICT1301, but it also helps to explain some the technicalities inherent in the machine. We learn how information travels about within it as electrical pulses, in an engaging non-technical manner. Whilst the interviews are often rich sources of technical detail about historic developments, our approach has been to try and encourage interviewees to discuss their work in ways that make it intelligible to the general public as well as experts wherever possible. Given that the complexity of computing is something of a barrier in interesting people in its history, this approach presents some promise as a way of explaining technicalities in an engaging manner. While not always as polished as historians' considered explanations, there is a unique value in having technology explained by people who helped create it, particularly when it integrates with an engaging historical story or anecdote.

Of course discussions of technicalities are not the only insight we get from computer designers, oral history allows us to ask for reflections about the work they were involved with, revealing thoughtful insights into how the future of computing looked from the past and adding a further human dimension to stories of machines. The much hackneyed anecdote about IBM's Thomas Watson declaring that the world only needed five computers, is so attractive not only because its amusing when important people get things wrong, but also because it causes us to reflect for a moment on the comparison between then and now. Discussing the motivations and expectations of computer designers for their machines has something of the same appeal because the comparison can be so engaging. Geoff Tootill, for instance recalled his own modest expectations for computing back in 1948 when he was helping to develop the first stored program computer in Manchester.

We thought the culmination of our work would be a large scale computer with not only facilities for subtraction, but also addition, multiplication and division, and a much bigger storage capacity and also a capacity for storing big programs... So we thought that such a large computer would be required for several different tasks, like weather forecasting for example, because we knew that a competent meteorologist could compute what tomorrow's weather was going to be based on today's available data, but unfortunately it would take him a week or a fortnight at the least. So the idea was that a big computer could do this computation in time to give a useful answer about tomorrow's weather. And there were no doubt other tasks like atomic energy calculations. So that we thought there would be scope for another, one or perhaps two big computers in the UK and three or four in Europe and probably half a dozen in the US because they always have big ideas in the US.[7]

Reflections such as these cause us to pause and think about the nature of computing in the past, and how it compares from our reference point of computing in the present day.

---

[6] National Life Stories interview with Raymond Bird. C1379/04
[7] National Life Stories interview with Geoff Tootill. C1379/02

3   Users

As Christina Lindsay points out in a useful essay on the co-construction of the TRS80 personal computer, designers' conceptions of what the user will do with their computer, can differ sharply from what users actually end up doing.[8] The computer is the universal machine, open to a wide range of interpretations and applications; they are not ends in their own right. They are tools to be used for other purposes, a means to an ends, as Professor Sir Maurice Wilkes reminds us in his interview:

> *When I started building the EDSAC I had no doubt about who were going to be our users, they were people like myself. I mean I used to be doing things that would take perhaps a week. Solving a set of ten by ten equations took about a week with a desk calculator machine. Well that could be done rapidly with a digital computer.*[9]

Computer use can be a particularly difficult subject to convey. Whilst the development of computer hardware has at least left obvious, readily interpretable, artefacts behind, the history of computer use and software is rather more ethereal. Punched cards, magnetic tape, and program print outs are perhaps not the most engaging of artefacts, and how much they can adequately represent the history of software and use is debatable. Furthermore the arcane dead programming languages and the complex principles they work on are not easy to convey to wider audiences. Oral history's ability to convey human feelings and activities once more gives us a powerful way to understand historical computer use on a number of levels. For example Stephanie Shirley, an early computer programmer and later pioneer of home working in the software industry, impresses much on the reader the fascination of programming early computers:

> *Well it has some of the beauty of mathematics, it has a lot of logic in it. It has a sort of puzzle element to it. In fact the sort of early, what do they call it, aptitude tests that they used for programming were things like, as they had used for Bletchley Park coding, things like, people who played with crossword puzzles, people who play chess. It's those sorts of, slightly quirky puzzle-solving capabilities. And, programs would take, well, obviously there were different sizes and so on, but, sometimes you would be working on, on a program for months and months and months, so the satisfaction when you did actually complete it and check it, and, most of that time was spent in checking, where you sort of, are nearly there, just got one more bug to get out, made for a very fulfilling life really, that you realised that you had actually created something.*[10]

Computing, as this neatly demonstrates, is about people's interactions with the computer. Recollections of using old computers have the ability to bring dead machines back to some sort of life by capturing the day to day activity that happened around them. Our interviews convey use - the methodical process of checking code, the frustrations of poor reliability, the parsimonious care taken to write programs to fit

---

[8] Christina Lindsay, "From the Shadows: Users as Designers, Producers, Marketers, Distributors and Technical Support."

[9] National Life Stories interview with Professor Sir Maurice Wilkes. C1379/21

[10] National Life Stories interview with Dame Stephanie Shirley. C1379/28

into small computer memories not as simple facts, but as individually recalled human experiences. The following impression of 1950s computer programming from Ferranti programmer Mary Lee Berners-Lee wonderfully demonstrates how the history of computer use can be enlivened by personal reflection and details.

> It's very difficult getting a computer program right, even when one used to do what they called a dry run, imagine work right through your program, going through it instruction by instruction to see what actually happens to the numbers and you pick up a lot of errors like that, and then you go along and try it on the computer and it doesn't work and you're very surprised and you think it's the machines fault and sometimes it was because the machine was not reliable, anything but. But it's more likely in fact to be your fault [...] The program was typed up on punched teleprinter tape, five hole tape, and if you had to make an alteration we'd cut out tiny little bits of sellotape, coloured sellotape, and stuck them over the hole and had little hole punches with which you could punch a new hole if you wanted one and turn pieces of sellotape to cover up the holes you didn't want. And they tended to come off so you thought you'd got rid of a fault and there it came again, and you found your little bit of sellotape had come off, so you were wise to stick sellotape on the both sides.[11]

Use, as this example shows us may not be about complex programming concepts, but about easier to relate to human activities, which may make a good starting point for more detailed discussion and explanation of the more complex principles involved.

Even when machines have been restored to use, we generally encounter old computers today in rather sanitised settings. There are of course exceptions, but the museum gallery is rarely like the machine room or computer development lab of decades ago. Vintage photos and films give us some feel for these machines in their original surroundings, but oral history provides other insights and reflections. From our interviews, computer history gains a sense of place, amidst diverse settings ranging from the decrepit barn where Andrew Donald Booth built some of his earliest computers in the 1950s, to the palatial splendour of Ferranti's Portland Place computer centre, and many other places besides. Not only do we gain descriptions of environments but insights into the personal interactions and social history that was happening in them, for example rocket scientist Bob Parkinson's recollections of using the Rocket Propulsion Establishment's computer in the 1960s and 70s.

> The other way that knowledge transferred round the establishment at that time, not just scientific knowledge but more the knowledge of what the hell was happening, was the computer. In those days it was an Elliott 803, filled a large room with air conditioning, and you ran your programmes by taking a piece of punch tape down there and getting them fed into the machine and getting a piece of punch tape come out which you then went to a teletype machine and printed out. So I used to think of it as down by the river... doing the washing. So there was – there was a queue which we stood and chatted to one another and so anything that was happening got round and that went between division, because it was the computer for the whole thing and you weren't sat at your own little VDU, you were actually meeting other people who were

---

also running computer programs for different purposes. So yes, that certainly at the time acted as a way of, an informal way, of finding out what was going on[12].

4   Wider Effects

In such ways oral history has the ability to help put vintage computers back into their original contexts of use and help us to understand the human interactions that went on in these spaces. However, use goes beyond these immediate contexts to have wider effects. We are often told that one of the key effects of computers has been to speed up calculations, however speeding up the solving of sums is often only a means to an ends. What difference that speeding up of calculations makes is often far more dramatic and far more relevant to understanding computing in a broader sense. As Jon Agar has explored, early computing had an important role to play in several other branches of science, but this was not always just a straight forward matter of speeding up science[13]. Our interviews have explored the differences computing made in several branches of science and engineering, including civil engineering, aeronautics, materials science, geophysics and others, to cover a range of different perspectives on the influence computing made in different fields.

What emerge from these accounts are not always straightforward Whiggish stories of the computer improving things. Rather, we gain more complex accounts with issues to think over, that help to nuance our understanding of the differences computing has made and of the interaction of computing with work in other fields. For example, engineers often talk about having a feel for their work, an instinctive understanding of how mechanisms function or how stresses are distributed in structures. Engineering is not a theoretical activity, but one about the application of knowledge in practical ways, testing that knowledge with experiments and calculations along the way, and building up a sort of tacit understanding of whatever structure is being built and a confidence it will work.

Before computers, doing such work was not necessarily easy or quick, but it provided the all-important 'feel' factor. Structural engineer Michael Parsons, who made key contributions to the design of the Severn Bridge, recalled that back in the 1950s to analyse the effects of a side wind on a suspension bridge involved solving considerable numbers of simultaneous equations with a slide rule.

> *To do five simultaneous equations it used to take me about two hours. Of course now we do it in milliseconds. But I think the position now is that when I was doing this it took me two hours to get an answer and I jolly well had a feel for what the structure was doing. I understood it and I felt the structure was almost a part of me.*

As Parsons continued, for later designers having the computer do the sums may have speeded things up dramatically, but for engineers used to painstakingly building up tacit understanding of their structures, it risked taking something away.

> *Whereas later on people would use a computer programme for analysing suspension bridges and they'd put all these loads on and they'd press the*

---

[12] National Life Stories interview with Bob Parkinson. C1379/68

[13] Jon Agar, 'What difference did computers make to science?', Social Studies of Science (2006).

*button and they'd get all the answers out, pages and pages of answers. But
I always had the feeling that they didn't really know what they were looking
at. Whereas I knew that, if I changed something, I knew what sort of effect
it would have.[14]*

As other interviewees have related, taking designers a step away from
fundamentals and black boxing the calculations in a program, sometimes risked
mistakes, that went unnoticed. Bridge designer Peter Head, for example recalled that
as computer use moved on from engineers devising their own programmes to solve
their problems to using models to predict the performance of bridges potential risk
emerged:

*People started to use them as black boxes. And I can still remember to
this day a particular example, where a young engineer had analysed a
bridge and gone all through the detailed design of a bridge and had come
up with solutions, which weren't quite right. They didn't look quite right.
And so I questioned it and went back and found that there was a
fundamental error in the original coding of some of the members of the
bridge, which had never ever been questioned. [...] And it always worried
me that people tended to use computer models as black boxes and I worried
that engineers would lose the ability to think at a fundamental level about
structural behaviour.[15]*

As these examples show, oral history is an excellent way of conveying some of the
issues raised by the use of computers in wider science and technology. It also gives us
an idea of how computing fitted into scientific and technical organisations and how
the people within them saw the coming of computers. For example as Ralph Hooper,
who led the early design of the Harrier jump jet, recalled the first computer at the
Hawker Siddeley site he worked at:

*We got our first computer in 1958, it was a Ferranti Pegasus computer
by chance. And it was nearly the size of this room, not quite as long
perhaps. And it was done by batch processing I think they called it, and
they got a stack of work together and then fed it through the computer, only
the mathematicians were allowed to use the computer and at that time the
head of maths – there was a small maths section, I forget how many there
were in there, but he was dead scared of this damn computer and he got
into a great tizzy every time he had to go in and use it. His number two was
a much calmer chap and he made best use of it.[16]*

As this example suggests, computers as recalled by interviewees from outside
computing do not always seem to be a dramatic and important part of scientific
workplaces. Indeed, the computer sometimes comes across as an evolutionary step
rather than a revolutionary development, just a better tool to do things they were
already doing anyway, for instance the replacement of slide rules, by scientific
calculators, by personal computers, for individual engineers' on the job calculations.
In many of our interviewees with those from different fields, the computer seems
rather everyday, not unimportant, but part of the fabric of the workplace and part of

---

[14] National Life Stories interview with Michael Parsons. C1379/77

[15] National Life Stories interview with Michael Parsons. C1379/79

[16] National Life Stories interview with Ralph Hooper. C1379/27

the stories of other technologies. It is precisely this part in the stories of other technologies that help these accounts to demonstrate the wider relevance of computing, by tracing its influences through to items in the world around us.

Jet engine designer Ralph Denning, for instance, recalled how collected data about previous designs allowed Rolls-Royce Bristol to work out the fundamentals for designing a jet engine and create software that could quickly produce outline designs for new jet engines. Detailed designers could work these up to full designs, but they also provided a way of quickly developing an optimum design, coping with a large volumes of work, and producing a range of weighed and costed designs for customers. Another civil engineer, Ron Bridle, recalled the flexibility offered by iteration using the computer:

And iteration, the one thing the computer can do that other systems can't do is iterate and iterate and iterate and iterate. And that's a powerful, powerful method then. So you can use methods you couldn't possibly use longhand.

As Bridle continued, this iteration was useful in the development of standard, optimal, engineering components and in planning road layouts:

You could move the [road] alignment, like this, keep iterating, moving the alignment until   you could get minimisation of travel costs, and going up and down, minimisation of excavation costs.[17].

In such ways, oral history with computer users from other fields opens up new ways of appreciating the relevance of computing by showing attitudes towards it more widely, and by giving us examples of its use that link the computer to other points of reference. This linking of the computer's abilities to other things in the wider world can suggest other ways of demonstrating complex principles. For example, iteration goes from being a function of the computer to being about how one decides where to build a road. In such ways we move away from an understanding of the computer as a large complex machine, to one that emphasises its influence in familiar everyday things and in shaping the world around us.

5   Conclusions

As the recent attention to the Alan Turing centenary has amply demonstrated, personal stories can be useful way of interesting a wider public in the history of computing. In this paper I have explored ways in which personal stories gathered from oral histories can help to make the history of the computer more engaging than just focusing on technology. In particular I have suggested how the retelling of stories about early computing development can help us to de-construct computer artefacts, helping us to appreciate the human stories that lie hidden behind them. I have given examples of how oral history can open up a world of past human interactions with the computer. I have suggested how technicalities can be engaged with by anecdotes or personal reflections, and how attention to computer use can illustrate the social history of computing, and demonstrate the relevance of computing more widely than as just 'computer history'.

---

[17] National Life Stories interview with Ron Bridle. C1379/75

Through all of this I have presented ways for people to appreciate the computer as something other than a complex item of technology. Descriptions of the computer as it was when it was in use, the emotions and expectations of designers, and the difference it made to users, all have the potential to act as 'hooks' with which to catch the attention of audiences for whom understanding complicated machines is passé. Oral history reminds us that the history of computing is not just about computers, but about the interaction of computers and people. Hearing stories of computer history, from the people who helped to make that history happen in their own words, is a uniquely personal way of telling the history of computing. It provides us with a powerful way of interpreting computer history for wider audiences and a way of bringing dead computer machinery to life.

Telling the Long and Beautiful (Hi)Story of Automation!

Marie d'Udekem-Gevers

University of Namur, Faculté d'informatique, Namur, Belgique
marie.gevers@unamur.be

Abstract. The purpose of this paper is to suggest and justify a framework for
the history of computing that interests a wide public. The aim is to set the
history of computing in the much broader context of automation, while also
addressing the evolution of ideas. It suggests first a new detailed classification
of programs (in the broad sense). Then it tries in particular to sketch out a
"phylogenesis" of automation from the 12th to 19th centuries in Europe. It
discusses various automatic devices: particularly, clocks and their annexes, but
also organs, games, looms and early computers. Finally, it addresses the stored-
program computer and high-level languages.

Keywords: Automation, Blaise Pascal, Charles Babbage, clocks and their
annexes, conditional branching, languages, programming, regulation, relevance
to the general public, sequence, stored-program computer.

1   Introduction

According to French historian Fernand Braudel [5],
> "History occurs at different levels [...]. On the surface, the history of
> events works itself out in the short term: it is a sort of microhistory.
> Halfway down, a history of conjunctures follows a broader, slower rhythm.
> [...] And over and above this 'recitatif' of conjuncture, structural history,
> or the history of the longue durée, inquires into whole centuries at a time. It
> functions along the border between the moving and the immobile, and
> because of the long-standing stability of its values, it appears unchanging
> compared with all the histories which flow and work themselves out more
> swiftly, and which in the final analysis gravitate around it. [...] In any case,
> it is in relation to these expanses of slow-moving history that the whole of
> history is to be rethought, as if on the basis of an infrastructure. All the
> stages, all the thousands of stages, all the thousand explosions of historical
> time can be understood on the basis of these depths".

To make the history of computing attractive, I would like, following Braudel, to
suggest that we examine, in a general manner, the long-term, multidimensional
history. In particular, I propose to focus on the history of *automation* from Antiquity
to the 'stored program computer', while also addressing the related *mental evolution*
and highlighting the *dematerialization* that occurs on the technical level at the same
time as the *increased autonomy* of the machine.

A. Tatnall, T. Blyth, and R. Johnson (Eds.): HC 2013, IFIP AICT 416, pp. 173–195, 2013.

For the past 10 years, I have had the experience each year of giving lectures (lasting 30 minutes to 30 hours) to students at the University of Namur (Belgium) or on a more sporadic basis during speeches given to a wider public. In my experience, this approach generates a great deal of interest on the part of students. It could, I believe, also be used in a museum setting. In this article, I therefore propose to explain and justify the main thread of my approach.

Long histories, tracing the full evolution of a specific object from its origins, are rare in the field of science and technology. Those relating to automation are particularly infrequent, since they involve a wide range of applications and call on specialists in very diverse disciplines. We can cite two such studies, both published after 1960: the paper by Jean Sablière [49] which at one time was a primary reference in the field, and the more recent article by Brian Randell [44]. The latter is a major contribution to this subject and is essential reading. Randell analyses the origins of computer programming, focusing on the concept of sequence control. To do this, he reviews early automatic devices (pointing out the "pegged cylinder" as a programming medium), Vaucanson's and Jacquard's contributions (underlining that punched media are "clearly separate"), Babbage's contributions, the contributions of some of his direct successors and, finally, the stored-program concept (taking into account, moreover, the ability of the machine to calculate the addresses of the variables, but not envisaging high-level languages).

The current paper revisits Randell's analysis and generalizes it, while supplementing it with additional information. It proposes a broader conception of the notion of a program[1] and provides a detailed typology of this concept. Furthermore, it integrates that concept into the much broader one of automation. The frame of reference that I propose is both generalized and inclusive: it is aimed not only at providing a rigorous definition of any automaton, but also coherently describing the evolution of automation, leading to the development of stored-program computers equipped with software enabling programming in high-level languages. Two comments need to be made at this point. First, it should be stressed that this framework was designed in the spirit of texts written by specialists in computer organization and design, in particular J. P. Meinadier [39] as well as D. A. Patterson and J. L. Hennessy [41]. Second, it should be noted that application of this frame of reference to the history of automation should, in the end, be a tool to help non-computer scientists understand what a computer that enables programming in high-level languages is.

Furthermore, in his introduction, Randell [44] states the following about his own choice of historic milestones:

> *"It is important to realize that many of these particular developments have been selected more because I personally find them interesting than because of any contemporary importance (...)"*

Like Randell, I have selected[2] stages in history that are interesting in order to illustrate the analytical perspective that I have adopted. However, our perspectives do not completely overlap, and the milestones I have chosen differ slightly from

---

[1] The definition proposed here is also broader than that of A. G. Bromley [9] who in analyzing Babbage's machines, reserves the word program for a "user-level application".

[2] Steps not addressed here may, in particular, be found in an article by Randell [43].

Randell's. In contrast with Randell, for example, I have examined in greater depth the history of mechanical clocks and their annexes, highlighting the passage from the wheel (not discussed by Randell) to the cylinder as well as the transition, which from my point of view is fundamental, from stationary pegs to moving ones (which Randell mentions only in passing).

Now that this brief, annotated review of the literature on the long-term history of automation has been completed, we should address the history of different fields that over the centuries were affected by automation. It should be noted that, in general, these fields do not intersect, are unfamiliar with each other and use different vocabularies. Furthermore, these specialized literatures often omit to give pertinent details for those who are interested in automation, since they generally have other preoccupations. For example, a specialist in the history of carillons is interested in the complexity of the melodies played via automation, but not in the programming of those melodies. Overall, the literature pertaining to automata reveal, when compared side by side, many points of confusion, gaps and inconsistencies. It is therefore particularly important to start by providing some definitions. Examples and illustrations will come later. First, let us recall that the word "automaton" comes from the Greek "*automatos*" and thus means etymologically "that which moves by itself." According to Devaux [15], "automation" denotes a mechanism by which the more or less complex sequence of operations takes place spontaneously each time it is triggered. I suggest that an automaton[3] be defined as a machine incorporating automation. Following Sablière [49], Jacomy [29] and Gille [21], let us consider that two principles allow automation to function: regulation (which implies simultaneity in relation to the process being regulated) and programming (which implies precedence in relation to the process being programmed). Let us also note that the two principles are not incompatible. Regulation is synonymous with *feedback* in a broad sense. As defined by Wikipedia, "*feedback describes the situation when output from a phenomenon in the past will influence an occurrence or occurrences of the same phenomenon (or the continuation / development of the original phenomenon) in the present or future*". As to programming (in a broad sense[4]), it can be defined as determining in advance the sequence of operations (or actions or motions) that have to be performed by a machine and then recording this sequence on a medium that serves as a memory.[5] It is useful to emphasize that all programming therefore implies, by definition even, the existence of a memory.[6] A program (in a broad sense) is an ordered set of operations (or actions or motions) performed by an automatic system. I would like to explicitly mention an elucidating distinction between the program as it is conceived by humans and the program as it is 'understood' (i.e. read) by the machine.

Starting from the understanding of Meinadier [39] that there are three major categories of programs which have succeeded each other over time, and adopting his

---

[3] This concept is not taken into account by J. Lafitte [31].

[4] As concerns the semantics of the word "program", my attitude is therefore opposed to that of A. Brennecke [7] which considerably limits the meaning of this word.

[5] Definition adapted from J. Marguin [38].

[6] A so-called "*stored program*" used by the stored-program computer is thus only a special case.

vocabulary, I would also like to propose a new (more detailed) classification of programs (as they are understood by the machine). According to Meinadier's typology [39] (see Table 1), a program is said to be internal (to the machine) if it is fixed. Furthermore, a program is termed "external"[7] by Meinadier if, like Jacquard's loom, it is not unchangeable but rather is (manually) interchangeable. Personally, I will explain this concept later but, as B. Randell [45] suggested to me, I propose to consider the category of external programs as containing two sub-categories, which are above all relevant for comparing calculating machines[8]: the sub-category of exchangeable programs (taken into account by Meinadier) but also the more primitive sub-category of programs that are manually modifiable in situ[9]. In any case, such programs are accessible to the user. Finally, a program is defined as a "stored program" in the last possible case. Meinadier does not note that this last type of program is fully 'manageable' automatically, (as we will describe at length below) i.e. by the machine itself. However, as we are going to see, this point is fundamental.

Table 1. Suggested classification (and evolution) of programs (as understood by the machine)

Programs (as understood by the machine)	
Classes	Feature
1. 'Internal'	Fixed
2. 'External' 2.1. In situ	Modifiable *manually*
2.2. Logically separate from the programmed device	Replaceable *manually*
3. 'Stored program'	Fully manageable *automatically*

We still have to state a basic detail that is rarely addressed in the literature: a machine can have several levels of programming (possibly of the same class). This configuration is quite frequent and applies to most of the automata that will be discussed in the text.

2   Automata Prior to Stored Program Computers

We should begin by stressing the importance of the Mechanicians' School of Alexandria [18] (3rd century BCE - 1st century CE) as pioneers in the history of

---

[7] D. A. Grier [23] stresses that the expression "*external programming*" was employed for the first time in 1951. This was in a "*paper by IBM researchers which attacked the concept [of stored-program computer]. This paper described the IBM card programmed calculator, which was an accounting machine connected to an electronic arithmetic unit*" [23].

[8] This distinction is not however very useful for analyzing the history of pegged cylinders used in musical automata: these cylinders either have mobile pegs (e.g. in carillons) or exchangeable ones (e.g., in organs), essentially as a function of their size.

[9] I would, however, like to stress that there are intermediate cases.

automation. These early mechanicians, using, on the one hand, pegged[10] wheels and, on the other hand, levers, ropes, cylinders,[11] pulleys, etc., were able to build automata, notably in the fields, closely related at the time, of religion and theatre. It is certain that they used the principle of programming. However, in contrast with what certain authors have stated, it seems that they did not use any regulation [25] [26].

We can now move on to the successors of the Alexandrians as concerns automata: the Byzantines[12] and the Arabs. The latter collected the manuscripts of Alexandria and translated them into Arabic. They also refined some of the techniques: we can see that they used the principle of regulation in addition to programming in order to build automata.[13] Furthermore, it has been proven that the oldest description of a "pegged cylinder" used to automate the playing of a musical instrument is the work of the Musa brothers, in 9th century Bagdad [32] [34]. The "flute player" automaton that they described was very sophisticated and based on water power. To produce the desired music automatically, a wooden programming cylinder had to be made, with pegs of the proper dimensions and in the right places, and this cylinder had to be rotated at the proper speed. The Musa brothers provide a great volume of technical details: for example, they state that several melodies can be memorized on a single cylinder. They also explain that if one wanted to have several melodies for the mechanism, it was better to build a wide cylinder (rather than one with a large diameter) [32]. However, it seems that they did not raise the possibility of modifying a cylinder or replacing it, once the automated musical instrument had been made. The program can therefore be described as internal, according to the classification proposed above.

The knowledge of the Arab world was transmitted to the West, in particular by means of translation into Latin, starting in the 12th century, in Muslim-occupied Spain. Let's now turn to Europe.

2.1 Programmed Automata not Used for Calculation in Europe

According to Dohrn-van Rossum [16], from the 12th century, technical innovations were made in Europe to wake the monks: the direct coupling of one or several bells

---

[10] According to their actual shape, the pegs (or teeth or cams) offer, as a general rule, the possibility of producing different movements (from all or nothing [binary effect], all the way to very progressive movement ["continuous" effect]). At the time of the ancient Greeks, it seems that each peg was an equilateral triangle [17].

[11] As underlined by B. Randell [44], Heron of Alexandria did not use 'pegged cylinders' as such but rather their forerunners implying ropes. *"The rope contained eyelets which fitted over pegs protruding from the cylinder, and was fixed to the cylinder with wax. Thus as it was slowly pulled off the cylinder, the cylinder rotated first one way, then another, at various speeds [44]"*. I would like to add that this technique is primitive to the extent that it does not involve any long-term memorization of the sequence of the desired movements: when the rope is unwound, it must be rewound properly around the cylinder and refastened before the process is started again.

[12] See, for example, the water-clock from Gaza (Palestine) circa 530 (see G. Dohrn-van Rossum [16]).

[13] Via conical valves (cf. Hill [25] [26]).

and a water-clock as well as the automation of the repeated striking of one bell (ringing) or of several bells (tune). This automation is based on an internal program.

One of the very rare accounts of this type of programming can be found in the rather rough representation on the reverse of the last folio of a manuscript dating from the reign of James II of Catalonia (1291-1327)[14]: it shows a mechanism consisting of a water-clock (on the bottom), and a set of bells (on top) that the clock would ring at a given interval. According to Farré-Olivé [20]: "*This could be used as an alarm, or as a diversion for a party of assembled guests, or at some gathering of people.*" On the drawing, a set of bells can be seen (only five are shown), above which is a pegged wheel. This pegged wheel can definitely be considered a program: we can imagine that the pegged wheel would rotate and strike the bells, creating a sequence of sounds represented on a musical score, drawn in the top left part of the original document. This program can be characterized as internal. It should be noted that it is more rudimentary than the mechanism proposed by the Musa brothers: a wheel can be seen as a cylinder with a single track... It should also be stressed that the drawing does not give any indication "*of how the pins actuate the hammers placed by the bells below*" [20]. As Farré-Olivé [20] mentions: "*we are presented with a structure conveying the main ideas, without practical details.*"

The next stage in the history of automation is a major event of the Middle Ages, even though it seemed to have passed virtually unnoticed at the time: the invention of mechanical clocks. This probably occurred in the 13th century simultaneously at several European monasteries. It apparently predates the representation of the Catalan clepsydra, but as Farré-Olivé [20] explains:

"*The old water-clocks and the new weight clocks could well have existed side-by-side for a period of time... because the water-clock time measurer would be far less costly to construct than any type of early weight clock.*"

For purely technical reasons, the invention of mechanical clocks led to the passage from unequal hours[15] (as measured by water-clocks) to equal hours[16]. In addition, as Dohrn-van Rossum [16] notes:

"*Mechanical clocks offered the possibility of animating large, heavy automata and of keeping them running more reliably than could be done until then with hydraulic movements.*"

It therefore became possible to build mechanisms known as "monumental astronomical clocks", which were used for entertainment purposes. This involved hoisting the clock and its annexes into a tower (initially a church tower) in order to make them more visible and more audible. According to the classification proposed by Lehr [32], the annexes of mechanical clocks implemented from the 14th century onwards in Europe can be divided into three groups: astronomical and time measurement instruments (astrolabes, dials with representation of astral movements, calendars, etc.), musical instruments (automated mechanical organs, carillons, etc.)

---

[14] The drawing may be a later addition. According to the analysis by Farré-Olivé (p. 374), it was undoubtedly made between 1291 and 1430.

[15] By convention, the period of daylight was always 12 hours in winter and in summer: it was therefore the duration of an hour that varied by the seasons and by the latitudes.

[16] Equal hours imply that the duration of one hour is set as 1/24th of one day.

and devices for the theatre (automata representing, for example, angelic musicians or the Magi, etc.).

The hypothesis explaining the invention of mechanical clocks, as formulated by J.D. Robertson and reiterated by Dohrn-van Rossum [16], is as follows: technology progressed from a bell-ringing mechanism to a clock escapement mechanism controlled by a foliot (see Figure 1). We should identify the basic components of these two mechanisms: a (vertical) crown wheel (which can be considered as an internal program), a verge with two blades (engaging alternatively the wheel teeth) and a weight. The difference lies in the results obtained. In the case of the bell-ringing mechanism, it is the repeated beating of a clapper on a bell. In contrast, the clock escapement mechanism, linked to the weight, will drive a back-and-forth movement of the foliot and its weights: the effect is to divide the flow of time into a succession of units. From this point on, time measurement no longer had to be based on a continuous flow of liquid, as was the case with the clepsydra, but rather on a counting of units [6]. We should also note that the weighted foliot is a regulator of escapement: it sets the duration[17] of the periods of crown wheel movement, separated by periods of rest [40]. A mechanical clock can therefore be described, in the vocabulary adopted here, as a programmed and regulated automaton.

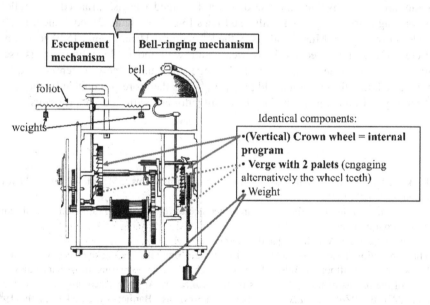

Fig. 1. Diagram of a mechanical clock with both escapement and bell-ringing mechanisms

Hourly bell-ringing involves a much more complex mechanism than the movement of the mechanical clock and, according to Dohrn-van Rossum [16], it was invented only in the early 14th century, probably in the city-states of Italy. Bell-ringing relies

[17] This length of time may be modified by the displacement of two weights.

on the production of a toothed wheel, or "count wheel": the breadth of the bump determines the number of times the bell rings. This is manifestly a case of automation based once again on a centralized, internal program. And this time the invention, though it may appear relatively commonplace to us, was considered very significant at the time. It was only by being combined with hourly bells that mechanical clocks would become widespread, first in the cities and later in the countryside. This led to a secularization of time (public clocks) [16].

A manuscript[18] dating from the mid-14th century shows an improvement in a variant[19] of the programming technique for carillons or organs: the melody to be played was still short and simple, but now it could be modified thanks to the possibility of moving the programming pegs[20]. Of course, there is no proof that the described innovation was ever actually implemented. And while this new feature may seem of little importance from a musical point of view, it is fundamental from the perspective of the present article. Could this not be seen as the first mention of an external program (modifiable in situ) in the history of European, and most likely world, technology?

The next step in perfecting automated carillons led, in the late 15th century, to a greater number of bells and to increased length and complexity of the melodies. For programming, this involved the use of several toothed wheels, arranged in parallel, thus forming a sort of cylinder with fixed pegs [34] (see Figure 2), equivalent to the cylinder drawn by the Musa brothers in the 9th century. Then, around 1530 according to Lehr [33][21], automated carillons were built with moveable cylinder pegs (see Figure 3): this made it possible to change the tunes, now potentially quite sophisticated, that the carillon could play [34].[22] It is therefore certain that by the early 16th century in Europe, mechanicians had built automata with external programs.

---

[18] Kraków, Universytet Jagielloński, Biblioteka Jagiellońska, ms. 551, fol. 47 rev. – 49 rev. (cited by A. Lehr [32]).

[19] The pegs are not located around the circumference of the wheel, but rather on several radii of the programming wheel.

[20] On this subject, see A. Lehr [32] and A. Lehr et al. [34].

[21] This innovation is sometimes attributed to a certain Barthélémy Coecke or de Koecke, also known as the "Buffoon of Aalst." However, such an attribution seems to be pure fancy, in light of the results of in-depth studies on this subject by A. Lehr. According to Lehr ([33] and [34]), the "Zot van Aalst" only became known as "Barthélémy Coecke" in the 19th century, and his role in the improvement, in the 15th century, did not involve the programming cylinder, but rather the technique enabling manual playing of the carillon. Furthermore, the text written by a monk from Saint Michael's Abbey in Old Flemish, mentioning "eenen sot van aelst" and giving rise to far-fetched interpretations, has been commented by L. Rombouts [46].

[22] "A regular grid of holes on the cylinder made it possible to move the cleats and thus modify the piece of music, particularly as a function of the religious calendar. However, these changes were rarely made more than four times each year [...]" (Buchner and Rouillé [11]). See also: http://whc.unesco.org/en/list/943/video

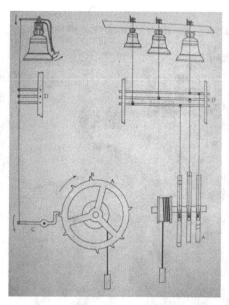

Fig. 2. Diagram of the oldest programming cylinder (with several wheels) for a carillon (late 15th century)

This brings us to the automata developed after the Middle Ages, independently of clocks. We should note first of all that it was difficult to "notate" a programming cylinder for a musical automaton, i.e. to place the pegs in the proper locations to obtain the desired melody. In the 17th century, the idea was developed of using paper tapes to simplify the notation of the cylinders for mechanical organs. First, the punching was performed flat on sheets of paper, and then these punched sheets were glued on the cylinder [14].

We now move on to the 18th century, known as the golden age of automata. Two categories must be distinguished: entertaining or educational automata, and looms, or more precisely, automated machines for the weaving of designs. To illustrate the first category, let's consider the *"Writer"* [57] made in 1770 by the clockmaker and mechanician Pierre Jaquet-Droz. This automaton is capable of writing *any text with a maximum of 40 letters.* This is a very interesting example, since its programming contains two levels. It is, in fact, equipped with an internal program:

> *"A stack of rotating cams, causing three levers linked to the writer's hand to move. One lever controls right-left movements, another back-and-forth movements, and the third vertical movements. There are three cams for the formation of each letter"* (Devaux [15]).

It also contains an external program: a wheel with 40 interchangeable pegs. This wheel *"raises all of the cams, sliding on its [vertical] axis, in order to successively bring the cams for the different letters to the levers"* [15]. Other famous entertaining automata were built in the 18th century, notably by Jacques Vaucanson. The latter moved from making entertaining or educational automata to producing automated looms.

Fig. 3. Staf Nees (1901-1965), Director of the Royal Carillon School "Jef Denyn" (Mechelen, Belgium), programming a cylinder with moveable pegs for a carillon

This leads us quite naturally to address this type of non-entertaining, utilitarian automata. Looms that reproduce designs were the focus of a remarkable innovation. In 1725, Basile Bouchon abandoned raised media for the memorizing of a program and used a medium with punch holes[23], i.e. a punched *paper strip*, that can easily be replaced. Along with Daumas [14], we can formulate the hypothesis that Bouchon was inspired by the process used to mark pegged cylinders since the 17th century. We could say that he simply eliminated one step in the manufacturing process for an external program. As Rouillé [47] notes:

> *"The concepts of zero and vacuum are not natural ones. The use of zero was not generalized in the West until the Middle Ages, and it was only in the 17th century, with Toricelli's experiments on atmospheric pressure that we really became aware of what the total absence of elements meant – a vacuum. Therefore, it is not surprising that we had to wait until the early 18th century for people to envisage control of the repetitive actions of a machine not with pegs on a rotating shaft (...) but rather, as in the case of Bouchon's loom, with punch holes on a paper strip, a medium that took up less space and whose length was no longer limited."*

---

[23] *"(...) the arrangement of the punch holes was established as a function of the design that one wanted to reproduce on the cloth"* (P. Rouillé [47]).

After Bouchon, Jean-Philippe Falcon and then Jacques Vaucanson developed automated machines for the weaving of designs, using external programs on a punched medium. Then in the early 19th century, Joseph-Marie Jacquard further perfected the automated loom and made its use in an industrial setting. As we will see, these looms would also have an influence on calculating machines.

2.2 Calculating Machines

Calculating machines are automata that are quite different from those envisaged up till now in this contribution: in effect, they have the specificity of manipulating symbols. As such, it is relevant to make the distinction between the two varieties of memorized information: first, the data (which can be apprehended at different levels) and, second, the operations (more or less complex and whose sequencing constitutes a program) to be performed on those data.

How do we define a basic calculating machine? Marguin [38] provides the following definition: such a machine *"includes an automatic mechanism to carry tens"*. Let's adopt this definition, while still noting that it is focused on the automation of the rules used for mental calculation, involving position numbering (regardless of the base used). We propose here that each basic[24] mechanism for adding numbers should be considered a form of programming (in the broad sense), since it incorporates calculation rules and is based on a given algorithm to process the various digits that make up the numbers to be added, this algorithm being more or less complex depending on the machine in question. The mechanism for carrying tens is particularly crucial in a mechanical machine that uses toothed gears to represent the digits. As Babbage [3] explains:

> *"The process of addition requires for its completion that an apparatus should be attached to the wheels on which the sum is placed for the purpose of carrying any tens that may occur to the next highest digit. This mechanism may be constructed upon three different principles. It may be:*
> - *Successive in its operation*
> - *It may postpone its operations*
> - *It may anticipate operations".*

One of the first and most famous calculating machines was invented in 1642 by Blaise Pascal. As Marguin [37] states:

> *"It is surprising that automation of the carry operation was invented so late, at a time when machines in general and clock mechanisms in particular had reached a remarkable degree of perfection."*

---

[24] This is not the case for the other basic mechanisms (as listed by Bromley [9]) of non-rudimentary calculating machines: the basic apparatus for storing and transferring numbers.

But we have to understand the mindset of the time:

"Daring to invent a machine with the ability to automatically perform an operation that until then was strictly intellectual was akin to denying the divine nature of man." [38]

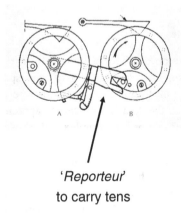

'Reporteur'
to carry tens

Fig. 4. Diagram of the carry mechanism, the basis for the Pascaline

The "Pascaline" [19] is a simple adding machine. We consider here that it is based on an internal program that automates the carrying of digits, thanks to a series of carry mechanisms, each located between two toothed wheels. The central part in Figure 4 is the carry mechanism. It *"is gradually lifted by the B wheel for the units. When it passes 10, it is suddenly released and falls (under its own weight), pushing the A wheel for the tens forward one position."* In the Pascaline, tens are carried successively. Furthermore, it should be noted that in this machine, the storing and computing functions are not separate.

The next important steps in the history of calculating machines occurred in the 19th century and were the work of Charles Babbage. His "Difference Engine"[25], aimed at generating accurate and precise numerical tables, was *"designed to calculate using repeated addition as in the method of finite difference."*[26] There was not yet a separation of the memory and calculation functions. However, it did have two levels of programming: in addition to the internal program (analogous to the Pascaline program, but refined) for carrying the tens[27], it also included a higher level internal

---

[25] Babbage worked on his *"Difference Engine No. 1, from 1822 until 1833"* (Bromley [9]). In 1846, he *"worked on another machine which he called Difference Engine No. 2"* (Bromley [9]).

[26] R. Horton [28] explains: *"When calculating a polynomial using the method of finite differences and after the initial starting values have been calculated by hand, it is possible by using the method of differences to generate the rest of the required table using repeated addition."*

[27] *"In Difference Engine No. 1, that carry propagation was a sequential process"* (Bromley [9]).

program (in the form of a "cam stack" [51]), which dictated the execution of one given sequence of additions, which always remains the same.

In 1834 [42], Babbage began to work on plans for another machine that he called the "Analytical Engine" (see Figure 5). As L. F. Menabrea stresses in his famed "memoir" of 1842, later translated into English and annotated by Ada Lovelace [36]:

"Mr Babbage has devoted some years to the realization of a gigantic idea. He proposed to himself nothing less than the construction of a machine capable of executing not merely arithmetical calculations, but even all those of analysis, if their laws are known."

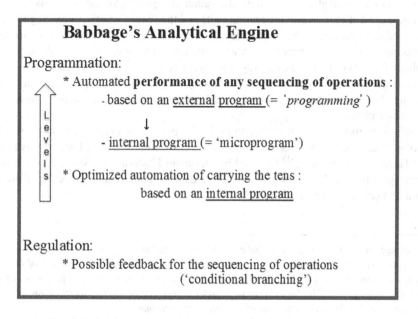

Fig. 5. Definition of the automation of Babbage's Analytical Engine

The aim of this engine was thus to perform automatically any sequencing of operations (set out in writing in a kind of table, examples of which are provided in this same text by Menabrea). According to the classification proposed in the present contribution, the "Analytical Engine" had three levels of programming. Its automation was based on an external program[28] (in the form of a sequence of punched cards[29] inspired by those that Jacquard used in his automated looms), which itself was implemented by an internal program (a sort of micro-program, as it is now

---

[28] *"The highest level is a description of the user-level programs that exist for the machine. What Babbage thought could be done – exploiting the basic micro-programmed operations in order to carry out user-oriented tasks such as solving sets of simultaneous equations, or working out terms in recurrence relations"* (Bromley [9]).

[29] *"All the movements of the cards are relative to the present position, and there is no absolute addressing"* (Bromley [9]).

understood, in the form of a set of pegged cylinders[30]), which in turn controlled notably the sequencing of carry operations, performed by another internal program. We should note that Babbage equipped his Analytical Engine with sophisticated "anticipating"[31] carry mechanisms, located on three "carriage axes" ("with their peculiar apparatus"[32]).

Moreover, the Analytical Engine had to be capable of making a decision on the basis of a result that it had obtained. In other words, it had to enable what is currently called "conditional branching"[33], which is another way of saying it had to be "regulated" (as defined above)[34]. We must also note another significant detail. Another innovation was needed in the Analytical Engine: the splitting of the functions into two organs, the "Mill" (or central processing unit) and the "Store" (with storage registers or cylinders)[35]. However, as A. G. Bromley [8] notes, *"Babbage's store has no structure accessible to the programmer"*. Furthermore, this first "memory" was designed by Babbage for data only: the user's program **always** remains on punched cards.

Babbage's ingenious inventions were largely forgotten, and they are generally (see [50] and [10]) considered as having had practically no impact on the subsequent history of technology.

Let's now move on to the next steps in the history of calculating machines, by looking at those machines that use electrical circuits. In this article, I will not examine the "Tabulating Machines,"[36] patented by Hermann Hollerith in 1884 and which also involve punched cards (but only to memorize data)[37]. These machines only performed a simple mechanization of counting[38].

---

[30] Babbage calls such a pegged cylinder a *"barrel"* with *"studs"*. As noted by Bromley [8], *"The barrel may be thought of as a microprogram store and a single vertical row of studs as a word of that store. [...] In general, the barrel orders its own advance via several of the control levers. [...] The barrel can [...] order a transfer to another vertical up to seven positions either forward or backward relative to present one."*

[31] According to the terms used by Babbage himself [4].

[32] According to the terms used by Babbage himself [3].

[33] *"The idea of conditional control, which had been a convenient feature in Difference Engine No. 1, starts to look like an essential part of the design of the Analytical Engine because of division"* (A. G. Bromley [9]).

[34] We should note that as far back as 1914 Torres y Quevedo [52] used the term 'regulation' to describe the action that today is called 'conditional branching'.

[35] This separation was a consequence of the increase in the size of the machinery, which is itself related to Babbage's determined and successful research in order to minimize the time needed for carry operations (see D. Swade [50] and A. G. Bromley [10]).

[36] On the subject of these machines and their inventor: see, for example, R. Ligonnière [35].

[37] These cards are not the medium for a program, but they do contain qualitative data.

[38] The carry operation was limited here to its simplest expression and was done using base 100. Hollerith himself [27] made the following description: *"A number of mechanical counters are arranged in a suitable frame [...] The face of each counter is [...] provided with a dial divided into 100 parts and two hands, one counting units the other hundreds. [...] A suitable carrying device is arranged so that at each complete revolution of the unit hand the hundred hand registers one ..."*

We will therefore move on to the large numerical calculating machines of the 1940s. They contained at least two levels of programs. Above the internal program (responsible for carry operations and using electro-mechanical or electronic switches) was another program that dictated the sequencing of arithmetic operations. This latter program was either internal (and definitely fixed) (e.g. G. Stibitz's BTL *Model 1*) or external. As explained by W. Aspray [1], on the basis of an unpublished text written by J. H. H. Goldstine and J. von Neumann [22], there were then two possible ways of making an [external[39]] program:

> "*Either all of the connections are made prior to the computation, as in the ENIAC, where one first sets **switches** and **plug cables**, which effectively hard wires the instructions into the machine prior to the computation, or connections are established at the moment in the computation, when they are needed, as in the Harvard Mark I and the Bell Labs relay calculator, in which instructions are fed in as needed from an external **paper tape**. The advantage of the first approach is that, once entered, all of the instructions can be **executed at electronic speed**; the second approach permits indefinitely **long strings of instructions**, does **not require as much time in problem setup**, and can be implemented with less hardware*"[40].

The first approach is, according to the vocabulary used in the present contribution, that of a manually modifiable program in situ, whereas the second is that of a program logically separate from the programmed device and which therefore can be changed manually.

3 Stored-Program Computers

At the end of World War II, the idea for a new design[41] emerged: the computer "*that incorporated the best features of each approach, based on storing instructions as numbers in the computer's internal electronic memory* [1]."[42] This idea was present in the draft written by von Neumann on June 30, 1945 [56] and it is unanimously considered fundamental. It implies that written numerical codes (also later called "machine language"[43]) are now needed to communicate with the calculating machine[44]. The practical consequence of this is that it enables the machine to modify its own programs.

---

[39] This term is not used by W. Aspray [1].

[40] The bold characters have been added by me.

[41] I am deliberately not entering here into the debate concerning the precise paternity and dating of this idea. See W. Aspray [2].

[42] The first computers still used punched strips (or cards), but the program was in the central memory during its execution.

[43] Such a language is defined by D. E. Knuth [30] as follows: "*a language which directly governs a computer's actions, as it is interpreted by a computer's circuitry*".

[44] M. Campbell-Kelly [12] underlines that « *A small-scale experimental computer known as the miniature or baby machine first operated successfully on June 21 1948, and was the first EVAC-type electronic stored-program computer to be completed. [...] Binary programs were put, bit by bit, into the store using manual keys and a 'typewrite' of 32 pushbuttons, each button corresponding to one bit of the store line.* »

However, in the opinion of many commentators, this idea is insufficient to fully define the concept currently identified by the term "stored program computer". To do this, according to B. Randell [45], two other crucial characteristics also have to be taken into account: *"the ability of a program-controlled device to identify some information as a program and to switch to executing that program*[45]*"* and *"the fact that it is possible to calculate addresses, and so make dynamic decisions as to which data to use, or which instruction to obey"*. These two characteristics were absent from the above-mentioned text by von Neumann [56], but the seeds were already present in a slightly earlier text by Turing [54]. As B. E. Carpenter and R. W. Doran [13] explain:

> *"The difference in attitude between von Neumann and Turing is evident in how their central processors deal with instructions. Early calculators had programs on punched tapes through which they stepped, executing each instruction as it turned up. Von Neumann retained this attitude in his 1945 report, for he thought of the processor as receiving a stream of orders from consecutive memory locations. He never explicitly mentions an instruction address register – this was unnecessary, for the next instruction comes from the current position in the memory tape. Turing did have an instruction address register explicitly containing the instruction number IN, i.e. the position of the next instruction. [...] Turing's, concept of memory was much closer than von Neumann's to a random access addressable*[46] *device".*

B. Randell [44] pursues this on the subject of these two drafts from 1945:

> *"In both cases, however, what now seem very awkward techniques of program self-modification were needed to make the machine calculate the addresses of variables – since neither the idea of index registers (B-lines as they were to be called at Manchester, where invented [and operational by April 1949]* [47]*) nor of indirection had yet arisen. However, once all these aspects of the stored-program concept had been provided, [...] machine-level programming essentially as we know it now had arrived."*

Furthermore, one of the applications of the possibility of modifying the program as described above, was not exploited before the 1950s. It is *"the ability of one program to process another, treating it as data"* [13]. However this "aspect" of modification is extremely important from a practical point of view: thanks to this, a programmed

---

[45] B. Randell [44] notes that "the connotation of the computer being able to [...] execute its own programs" is *"surpassing the notion that Babbage had arrived at over a century earlier"*.

[46] A sufficiently large random addressable access store can therefore be considered a practical concretization of the Turing machine's infinite tape (see Turing [53]).

[47] See M. Campbell-Kelly [12].

automaton can help people not only calculate, but also write its own programs.[48] Then, it is possible to invent and use higher-level languages (first, assembly languages and then, operational algorithmic or programming languages) and eventually to know nothing of the specific equipment characteristics of the computer being used when writing a program[49].

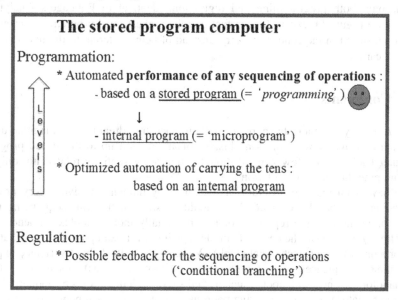

Fig. 6. Definition of the automation of a stored-program computer

The concept of "software" emerged and was clearly differentiated from that of "hardware". As a consequence of storing the program in central memory, this fundamental advance for the *programmer* is combined with increased ease for the *builder*: "*Treating instructions in the same way as data greatly simplifies both the memory hardware and the software of computer systems*" [41]. Obviously, this is also beneficial for the computer *user,* who can go from one program to another instantaneously [41]. "*The commercial implication is that computers can inherit*

---

[48] "*In the early day of automatic computing, programming was considered as some kind of art... With the advent of faster computers, however, the need for writing a program very soon became a nightmare and left no room for artistic feelings. The situation required immediate action in order to reduce the terrible burden. The relief came through the computers themselves: if computers were able to carry such a heavy load of computing, which before had taken years on a desk calculator, they certainly could also assist in writing programs. Indeed they could; it turned out that it was possible to write programs in a notation somewhere 'between' machine code and standard mathematical notation, which was then translated into correct machine code by the computer itself with the aid of a special translation program*" (H. Rutishauser [48]).

[49] The strict definition of a program for a computer scientist is therefore "*an expression of a computational method [i.e. algorithm] in a computer language*" (D. E. Knuth [30]).

ready-made software provided they are compatible with an existing instruction set" [41]. In the end, we can conclude, along with Patterson and Hennessy [41], that the invention of the stored-program concept *"let the computing genie out of its bottle."*

And to close out this long history of *automation,* I find it enlightening to stress that the stored program computer (see Figure 6) still, from a logical[50] point of view, takes into account both programming and regulation, identical to Babbage's Analytical Engine (see Figure 5), except for the fact that the highest-level program is, during its execution, stored in the central memory, instead of being external to the machine (on punched cards).

4   Comments

Since Antiquity, humans have realized their ancestral dreams[51] of manufacturing automata. An overview of the long history of automation up to the stored program computer leads us to a few general thoughts that are essentially related not only to programming, but also to regulation.

We have seen that the programs as designed by humans involve a very precise sequencing that they have in mind. It should be stressed that this sequencing may consist either in a simple repetition or in a potentially more complex sequence. We have already mentioned the cases of simple repetition, for example, of a sound (alarm bell) or a unit of time (mechanical clock). We have also talked about various complex programmed sequences: for sounds (e.g. carillon melodies), movements (e.g. automata for astronomical clocks, such as bell strikers), letters (texts by Jaquet-Droz's Writer automaton), designs (weaving patterns) and, finally (when people dared at last to put intelligence into a machine), calculations (*Formula* of Babbage's Analytical Machine or, more generally, algorithms).

Furthermore, we have illustrated the fact that, to ensure that the machine executes their planned design, people first made fixed programs, then manually modifiable or replaceable ones and finally those that are 'fully' manageable (i.e. which can not only be replaced but also be written and then executed) by the machine itself (see 2nd column of Table 2). These three milestones (respectively called 'internal', 'external' and 'stored program computer' by Meinadier [39] (see 1st column of Table 2) have been shown to be fundamental, and their importance must be stressed. It should be added that, in parallel with this evolution towards greater flexibility and increased autonomy of the machine, we can observe, over time, an increasing dematerialization of the program support (possibly of the highest level), in other words, of the interface enabling humans to communicate with the machine. The major steps in this history involve the passage from raised supports to punched ones (which would seemingly go hand in hand with a mental evolution), then the passage to electrical circuits and finally the use of machine language (see 3rd column of Table 2). It is evident that the fundamental change, from the point of view of the history of the program's support, is

---

[50] From a physical point of view, we should note that the carry operation is performed in binary mode, which is technically quite easy.

[51] For example, Book V 749 of the Iliad contains the following fragment *"The gates of Olympus which open self-bidden [αυτομαται]... "*

the one that accompanies the passage to the so-called 'stored program': since we move from a support enabling a read-only machine with sequential access (or more generally, access relative to the current position[52]) to a support enabling writing and direct access to dynamically calculated[53] addresses (see 4th and 5th columns of Table 2). In the history of books, we can see an analogous evolution from the point of view of access: from the ancient roll of papyrus (which must be read as it is unrolled), we moved to books with pages (invented in the 1st century of the current era). It is striking to note that Turing [24][54] explicitly compared the central (magnetic) memory of Mark II to a book with pages:

> "It is as if information in the magnetic store were written in a book. In order to find any required piece of information it is necessary to open the book at the required page."

Table 2. Suggested classification (and evolution) of programs (such as they are understood by the machine) and corresponding medium type

Programs (as understood by the machine)		Corresponding Medium type		
Classes	Practical feature	Human/machine communication	Practical feature from machine's point of view	Machine access characteristics
1. 'Internal'	Fixed	Using pegs / electrical circuits	Read-only	Sequential access
2. 'External'				
2.1. In situ	Modifiable *manually*	Using pegs / electrical circuits	Read-only	Sequential access
2.2. Logically separate from programmed device	Replaceable *manually*	Using pegs / holes	Read-only	Sequential access
3. 'Stored program'	Fully manageable *automatically*	Using symbols (a 'machine language')	Writable	Random access (and calculated addresses)

---

[52] A. G. Bromley ([8] and [9]) uses the term 'relative addressing' in this instance.

[53] It is only with addressable memory that the notion of an address for an instruction takes on its full meaning. The predecessors of stored program computers which were controlled by, for example punched tape, "could largely get by without addresses because of the fact that they could control the moving of the tape (q. v. Turing machines)" (B. Randell [45]).

[54] Cited by M. Campbell-Kelly [12].

The concept of regulation has been addressed only briefly in this contribution. However, let's note that, when assimilated with conditional branching, it helps to increase the autonomy of a calculating machine, by enabling it to make decisions when the program is being run.

The brief and recent history of computing has now been placed within the longer history of automation. This has revealed deep-seated trends in the evolution of technology. I believe that this is likely to be of interest to a broad public.

Acknowledgements. I would like to thank Professors Brian Randell and Pascal Verroust (members of IFIP WG 9.7) and Luc de Brabandère (mathematician and philosopher) for reading the original manuscript and for helpful criticism and suggestions. I am also indebted to Professor Rita de Caluwe (*Universiteit Gent*) as well as to Philippe Slégers (member of the Association Campanaire Wallonne) and Serge Joris (administrator of the World Carillon Federation) for providing information about carillons. I would also like to acknowledge Richard Horton (Conservator Engineering & Metals, Babbage Project Engineer, Science Museum, London) and three professors at the University of Namur: Dr. Vincent Englebert, Dr. Ir. Laurent Schumacher and Dr. Wim Vanhoof for their help. Finally, I would like to thank Virtual Words Translations, which translated the original French text into English.

A preliminary, less detailed version of the present article was the subject of two presentations in 2011: one in French at Collège Belgique (slides are available on the website) and the other in English at the international conference "History and Philosphy of Computing" in Ghent (Belgium).

Figure 1: Basic drawing by G. Oestmann (with permission of the author) in G. Dohrn-van Rossum, p. 109, annotated M. d'Udekem-Gevers.

Figure 2: From A. Lehr *et al.* 1991, p. 89 (with the permission of M. Lehr).

Figure 3: From the Royal Carillon School "Jef Denyn" Mechelen (with the permission of K. Cosaert, director of the Royal Carillon School).

Figure 4: Drawing by Serge Picard, from Musée des arts et métiers (Paris), "Blaise Pascal", *Les carnets*, with the permission of Anne Chanteux (Head of the Multimedia Centre and of the network of technical museums and collections); annotation by M. d'Udekem-Gevers.

References

1. Aspray, W.: John von Neumann and the origins of modern computing. The MIT Press, Cambridge (1990)
2. Aspray, W.: The stored program concept. IEEE Spectrum, 51 (September 1990)
3. Babbage, C.: On the Mathematical Powers of the Calculating Engine. Unpublished Manuscript (1837), reprinted in: Randell, B. (ed.): The Origins of Digital Computers: Selected Papers, 3rd edn., pp. 19–54. Springer, Heidelberg (1982)
4. Babbage, C.: Passages From the Life of a Philosopher, ch. VIII. Longman, Green, Longman & Roberts, London (1864),
   http://www.fourmilab.ch/babbage/lpae.html

5. Braudel, F.: On History. University of Chicago Press, Chicago (1982)
6. Braunstein, P.: Préface. In: Dohrn-van Rossum, G. (ed.) L'histoire de l'heure – L'horlogerie et l'organisation moderne du temps, pp. IX–XVII. Editions de la Maison des sciences de l'homme, Paris (1997)
7. Brennecke, A.: A Classification scheme for Program Controlled Calculators. In: Rojas, R., Hashagen, U. (eds.) The First Computers: History and Architecture, pp. 53–68. MIT Press, Cambridge (2000)
8. Bromley, A.G.: Charles Babbage's Analytical Engine, 1838. Annals of the History of Computing 4(3), 196–217 (1982)
9. Bromley, A.G.: The Evolution of Babbage's Calculating Engines. Annals of the History of Computing 9(2), 113–136 (1987)
10. Bromley, A.G.: Difference and Analytical Engines. In: Aspray, W. (ed.) Computing Before Computers, pp. 59–98. Iowa State University Press, Ames (1990)
11. Buchner, A., Rouillé, P.: Les instruments de musique mécanique. Gründ, Paris (1992)
12. Campbell-Kelly, M.: Programming the Mark I: Early Programming Activity of the University of Manchester. Annals of the History of Computing 2(2), 130–168 (1980)
13. Carpenter, B.E., Doran, R.W.: The other Turing machine. Comp. J. 20(3), 269–279 (1977)
14. Daumas, M.: La petite mécanique et les origines de l'automatisme. In: Daumas, M. (dir.) Histoire Générale des Techniques, vol. 3, pp. 172–195. Presses universitaires de France, Paris (1969)
15. Devaux, P.: Automates et automatismes. Que sais-je? Presses universitaires de France, Paris (1942)
16. Dohrn-van Rossum, G.: L'histoire de l'heure – L'horlogerie et l'organisation moderne du temps. Editions de la Maison des sciences de l'homme, Paris (1997)
17. Drachmann, A.G.: The Mechanical Technology of Greek and Roman Antiquity. Munksgaard, Copenhagen (1963)
18. Drye, E.: Alexandrie, la naissance de la mécanique. La Revue 20, 28–34 (1997)
19. Ellenberger, M., Collin, M.M.: La machine à calculer de Blaise Pascal. Nathan, Paris (1993)
20. Farré-Olivé, E.: A Medieval Catalan Clepsydra and Carillon. Antiquarian Horology 4(18), 371–380 (1989)
21. Gille, B.: Les mécaniciens grecs: la naissance de la technologie. Seuil, Paris, Collection Science ouverte (1980)
22. Goldstine, H.H., von Neumann, J.: On the principles of large scale computing machines. Unpublished text, reprinted In: Taub, A.H. (ed.) John von Neumann Collected Works, vol. V, pp. 1–32. Pergamon Press, New York (1961)
23. Grier, D.A.: The ENIAC, the Verb 'to Program' and the Emergence of Digital Computers. IEEE Annals of the History of Computing 18(1), 51–55 (1996)
24. HB1, Programmers' Handbook for Manchester Electronic Computer Mark II (Turing, A.M. ed.) (March 1951); Errata March 13 (1951)
25. Hill, D.R.: Arabic Water-Clocks. Sources & Studies in the History of Arabic-Islamic Science, History of Technology Series 4. University of Aleppo, Aleppo (1981)
26. Hill, D.R.: Technologie. In: Rashed, R. (ed.) Histoire des Sciences Arabes. Le Seuil, Paris (1997)
27. Hollerith, H.: An Electric Tabulating System. Reprinted in: Randell, B. (ed.) The Origins of Digital Computers, Selected Papers, 3rd edn., pp. 133–143. Springer, Heidelberg (1982)
28. Horton, R.: E-mail to the author (January 20, 2012)
29. Jacomy, B.: Une histoire des techniques. Seuil, Paris (1990)

30. Knuth, D.E.: The Art of Computer Programming, 2nd edn. Fundamental Algorithms, vol. 1. Addison-Wesley, Boston (1975)
31. Lafitte, J.: Réflexion sur la science des machines. Cahiers de la nouvelle journée 21, Librairie Bloud & Gay, Paris (1937)
32. Lehr, A.: De geschiedenis van het astronomisch kunstuurwerk. Zijn techniek en muziek. Nijhoff, Den Haag (1981)
33. Lehr, A.: Van Paardebel tot Speelklok (2e herziene druk). Europese Bibliotheek, Zaltbommel (1981)
34. Lehr, A., Truyen, W., Huybens, B.: Beiaardkunst in de Lage Landen. Drukkerij Lannoo, Tielt (1991)
35. Ligonnière, R.: Préhistoire et histoire des ordinateurs. Robert Laffont, Paris (1987)
36. Lovelace, A.A.: Sketch of the Analytical Engine invented by Charles Babbage, by L.F. Menabrea, from the Bibliothèque Universelle de Genève, 1842, No. 82, with notes upon the Memoir by the Translator (October 1843), http://www.fourmilab.ch/babbage/sketch.html#NoteB
37. Marguin, J.: Le reporteur et la naissance du calcul mécanique. La revue 2, 26–32 (1993)
38. Marguin, J.: Histoire des instruments et machines à calculer. Hermann, Paris (1994)
39. Meinadier, J.P.: Structure et fonctionnement des ordinateurs. Larousse, Paris (1971)
40. Mesnage, P.: La construction horlogère. In: Daumas, M. (dir.) Histoire Générale des Techniques, vol. 2, pp. 289–310. Presses universitaires de France, Paris (1965)
41. Patterson, D.A., Hennessy, J.L.: Computer Organization and Design (3rd ed.). Elsevier (2005)
42. Randell, B.: The Origins of Digital Computers: Selected Papers, 3rd edn. Springer, Heidelberg (1982)
43. Randell, B.: From Analytic Engine to Electronic Digital Computer: The Contributions of Ludgate, Torres, and Bush. Annals of the History of Computing 4(4), 327–341 (1982)
44. Randell, B.: The Origins of Computer Programming. IEEE Annals of the History of Computing 16(4), 6–14 (1994)
45. Randell, B.: Comments to the author (June 12, 2012)
46. Rombouts, L.: Zingend brons – 500 jaar beiaardmuziek in de lage landen en de Niewe wereld. Davidsfonds, Leuven (2010)
47. Rouillé, P.: Trous de mémoire. La revue 2, 34–41 (1993)
48. Rutishauser, R.: Handbook for Automatic Computation. In: Bauer, F.L., et al. (eds.) Part a, Description of ALGOL 60, vol. 1, Springer, Heidelberg (1967)
49. Sablière, J.: De l'automate à l'automatisation. Gauthier Villars, Paris (1966)
50. Swade, D.D.: The Difference Engine: Charles Babbage and the Quest to Build the First Computer. Viking, New York (2001)
51. Swade, D.D.: Automatic Computation: Charles Babbage and Computational Method. The Rutherford Journal 3 (2010), http://www.rutherfordjournal.org/article030106.html
52. Torres y Quevedo, L.: Essais sur l'Automatique. Sa définition. Étendue théorique de ses applications, Revue de l'Académie des sciences de Madrid (1914), reprinted In: Randell, B. (ed.) The Origins of Digital Computers, Selected Papers, 3rd edn., pp. 89–107. Springer, Heidelberg (1982)
53. Turing, A.M.: On computable numbers, with an application to the Entscheidungsproblem. Proc. Lond. Math. Soc. 42(2), 230–265 (1936), http://www.cs.virginia.edu/~robins/Turing_Paper_1936.pdf

54. Turing, A.M.: Proposals for Development in the Mathematics Division of an Automatic Computing Engine (ACE), Report E882, Executive Committee, NPL (1945), reprinted with foreword by Davies, D.W. as NPL report. Com. Sci. 57 (April 1972)
55. Unesco, http://whc.unesco.org/en/list/943/video
56. von Neumann, J.: First Draft of a Report on the EDVAC. Contract no. w-670-ord-4926. Techn. Rep., Moore School of Electrical Engineering, University of Pennsylvania, Philadelphia, PA (1945),
http://www.virtualtravelog.net/entries/2003-08-TheFirstDraft.pdf
57. Youtube,
http://www.youtube.com/watch?v=Pd_21_pfSRo&feature=related

Competing Histories of Technology: Recognizing the Vital Role of International Scientific Communities behind the Innovation of the Internet

Christopher Leslie

Polytechnic Institute of New York University, Brooklyn NY, USA
cleslie@poly.edu

Abstract. One way to make the history of computing relevant is to explain how different histories are in competition with each other and how they support quite different technology policy. The prevalent history that the US military created the Internet hides the international spirit of goodwill and cooperation that made a particular implementation of Internet happen. This is not just an academic issue. The success of the Internet encourages us to ask how we can continue to innovate the technologies of the Internet or new technologies of a similar power. The myth that the military created the Internet also supports the idea that it was designed on purpose according to a plan. This could not be further from the truth. In fact, the most interesting thing about the Internet is that, in its history, it had a tendency to violate the plans set forth. The international community invigorated the kind of inquiry that would lead to the Internet, not the United States in isolation. In order to create something like the Internet, then, we need to provide an environment for international exchange and cooperation, not maintain proprietary secrets and work in a disciplined environment of practical research.

Keywords: History of the Internet, packet switching, technology policy, innovation.

1 Introduction

The facts seem simple: The United States military funded a project to build, test, and improve a packet-switched network in the 1970s that provided the groundwork upon which the modern Internet was built. This story has been told many times, but the facts are not the most interesting thing in the discipline of history; to the historian, the implication of these facts is more important. Is this a story of military contracts providing technology to civilians? Is this a story of American ingenuity and technological superiority? Or is it a story of how academic researchers and commercial enterprises made a technology by innovating science developed for the military? One way to make the history of computing relevant is to explain how different histories are in competition with each other and how they support quite different technology policies. Because the Internet has been so successful, it is

A. Tatnall, T. Blyth, and R. Johnson (Eds.): HC 2013, IFIP AICT 416, pp. 196–206, 2013.

important to tell the right history of its development so that future innovation can be supported. Unfortunately, the story of the Internet is frequently told in such a way that hides the vital role of the international scientific community.

Historians of technology frequently rail against "whiggish" histories, or histories that interpret the past by explaining how we arrived at the present, as if there were a clear, linear path from an identifiable origin to the modern day. The history of the Internet is sometimes referred to in such a manner. *Where Wizards Stay Up Late* [1] is a perfect example. This book combines interviews with many people who helped manage projects that built up to the Internet, and the authors provide an indispensable resource for someone who wants to know about the Internet's history. *Nerds: 2.0.1: A Brief History of the Internet* similarly relates a tale for dramatic effect of the slow building of technology until the present day [2]. Both of these texts are useful, but an unintended consequence of their approach is that it seems as if technological devices grow with their own inertia, one development adding itself to the next until the perfected whole is achieved. Shorthanded accounts of the history of the Internet proliferate in newspapers and college history and media studies courses, promoting the idea that the Internet grew linearly and inevitably from a simple idea into a complex version in the present. An historian of technology would protest that these versions of the story make the development seem inevitable and free from connection to the economic, legal, political, social, ideological circumstances, let alone from dependence on existing technology. This might suggest that there is only one best way to make a worldwide computer network or, by extension, any other technological innovation. Although this approach is good for television series and mass-market books, it is not suitable for those interested in technological innovation. Given the success of the Internet, engineers and computer scientists interested in inventing in a similar environment need a more nuanced history.

Teleological approaches have been shunned for twenty years, and historians have begun offered alternatives to this approach. Janet Abbate's *Inventing the Internet* [3] was one of the first, telling as it did the ways in which Internet history was woven together with a larger institutional framework and existing technological achievements. Milton Mueller's *Ruling the Root* [4] adds counterfactual histories, hypothesizing for readers how things could have worked differently, to his discussion of how a new form of internet governance emerged at the end of the 1990s. Martin Campbell-Kelly and Daniel D. Garcia's recent article "The History of the Internet: The Missing Narratives" similarly makes hypothetical forays into what could have brought together widespread computer networks besides TCP/IP and examines the consequences and opportunities of each; it is not as if the Internet grew from the ARPANet "as a tree from a tiny acorn" [5]. As well, Byung-Keun Kim [6] makes an effort to describe the multiple histories of networks that led to the Internet, and Luis Arroyo has documented a 1972 commercial packet-switched network designed independently in Spain [7]. At this conference, we have heard more about local histories of computers that are evidence of large community of professionals engaged in innovating computers and networks. The history of this community, with its multiple efforts to advance computing technology, needs to be elaborated because it helps to explain why the growth of the Internet was not inevitable, but one that relied on a particular ethic of cosmopolitan cooperation. This version of the history of the Internet is more appropriate for engineers and computer scientists who hope to innovate new technology because it helps them to draw connections between the technological, political, and economic framework that enabled certain aspects of Internet innovation while at the same time forestalling other possibilities.

In this paper, I would like to build on these studies by employing a notion of the user from Science and Technology Studies. As pointed out by the contributors to the volume *How Users Matter* [8], it is difficult and even inappropriate to separate a technical, design stage of a technology from its social, consumer diffusion to users. In fact, the idea that a technology is developed without an end user in mind runs counter to both intuitive notions of how design is accomplished and also anecdotal studies of innovation, which both suggest that the concept of the end user is always on the mind of designers. This concept harkens back to Bruno Latour's 1987 critique of the diffusion model [9], wherein Latour points out that if so many people unthinkingly accept a technology (as it is proposed in the diffusion model), it would seem as if objects themselves compelled users to work with them – but what, he asked, is this "inertia that does not depend on the action of people" that propels them? Latour states that the simple belief in diffusion does not account for the "long translations" that were necessary to bring different actors into an alliance that would, for instance, produce vaccinations or the Diesel engine. Latour's diffusion model points to the active role that users take in the development of technology as well as lends credence to the idea that creating juxtapositions of hypothetical users with technological systems is an important aspect of innovation.

I would like to extend this analysis of "translations" with the study of the history of the Internet. Recounting the story of the complex interactions between users behind the innovations that led to the Internet is similar to Latour's effort to counter the mythic, passive society that is constructed in order to support the theory of diffusion to simple users. The story of the Internet's adds to Latour's translation model the necessary substrate of the international scientific community. The TCP/IP Internet did not succeed because it was a good technological innovation that either was inevitably accepted by large groups of users based on its merits nor, as is sometimes asserted by my students, because it was enforced through the military and cultural might of the United States over other alternatives like the proposed OSI model. Basing the Internet's eventual success on the diffusion model hides the work of the many actors that added their insights to create a flexible protocol that would work in unexpected circumstances. It was the efforts of these individuals – and their ideal of communication that would function through networks that were locally administered, as would be the case in international contexts where national governments have control over communication or in business communities where networks are designed to aid the enterprise – that accounts for the Internet's success. The translational activities of these user groups, however, is not often told when one considers the history of the Internet.

Before the conference, a group of us was fortunate enough to visit The National Museum of Computing at Bletchley Park on Sunday. One of the clearest indications that the international community is essential to the history of the Internet is the museum's exhibit on Donald Davies. Donald Davies, at the National Physical Laboratory in the England, made a proposal for a "national message switching network" for commercial applications. A paper written by Davies his colleagues uses the word "packet" for the first time and describes a common-carrier network. The

IFIP conference as well has allowed us to think about why this story matters. At the conference, Gauthier van den Hove's insight that one way to make the history of computing relevant is to utilize it as inspiration for the present. Several presenters have done the same, and it is something that I know is successful based on my own teaching of courses like Hypertext in Context at the Polytechnic Institute of NYU. I think one reason why people do not think it is useful to study the history of technology is because they think technology proceeds on its own logic, the determinist version of history that Tilly Blyth in her paper said that she wants to combat.

Learning how to tell the history of a technological advance like the Internet is essential. As a field of the humanities, history is more complicated than ascertaining the facts. Historians try to understand not only the story of what happened and determine why it happened that way, but also to understand what is at stake with the common histories that are told. As pointed out by computer historian Mike Mahoney [10], histories of computing are rhetorical devices used by developers and funders of technology to make what they are doing seem natural. It is the job of the historian, then, to make sure that the right histories are being told of the right developments. If the U.S.-centric story is the history of the Internet, a certain kind of innovation policy is implied: one must enhance the ability of national projects in partnership with the military. But what about the other history of the Internet, the one that focuses on the international community? If this story is plausible, then it implies a different kind of technology policy, one that enhances international cooperation.

2   The Military Origin Myth

One of the most common myths about the Internet is that it was started as a military communication project to withstand a nuclear attack. Like many myths, this reflects reality to a certain extent, even though the founders of the Internet have gone to great lengths to revise the record to state that this idea is distorted (Larry Roberts, for instance, is quoted by Andreu Veà [11] as saying that ARPANet had "nothing to do with nuclear war or survivability"). One of the technical achievements of Internet technology is the use of packets, which means that a long message is split into short units of a predetermined length. As documented by Les Earnest [12], the first time that packetized data was used in communications was for the SAGE missile defense system. SAGE was a network of computers designed to integrate twenty-two radar stations around the perimeter of the United States and it was designed to detect an aircraft carrying a heavy payload – in other words, to prevent the Soviet Union doing to the United States what the United States had done to Japan in 1945: detonating a nuclear device over its cities. SAGE was not exactly a success; it became operational in 1954 and it could track aircraft and send out intercepting fighter jets. However, with the use of ballistic missile that could carry nuclear weapons, the SAGE system was obsolete almost before it began.

Nevertheless, as documented by Paul N. Edwards [13] and others, SAGE was successful in unexpected ways. It pioneered important technologies, such as computer screens, modems, and computer memory, not to mention transmission of information in packets. This system would not have survived a nuclear attack, however, for two reasons. One was because it had a centralized command center, so disabling the command center would have ended the system's capabilities. The other was that the system used ordinary telephone lines for transmissions; certainly, the copper wires used for the telephone network in the 1950s could not have withstood a nuclear attack.

SAGE is visible not only in the histories of the Internet but also in mass media. Feature films such as *Fail Safe* (1964), *Dr. Strangelove, or How I Learned to Stop Worrying and Love the Bomb* (1964), and *WarGames* (1983) all depict computer systems that resemble SAGE. This visibility, however, hides a robust international community that existed at the time SAGE was developed. As documented by William Aspray [14], computing had already spread to fifteen countries by 1955, and surprisingly, government did not play a large role in countries outside the United States and Britain. Even in the U.S. and Britain, where government played a larger role, an equal number of computers were built by universities as were built by government. This transfer of technology would later be accomplished by commercial means, but as Aspray points out, it was initially accomplished by the mechanisms of "international science": "reports, professional journals and monographs, visits, secondment, and professional conferences" (356). This is not surprising, given the robust international scientific and technical community that had developed over centuries, and yet it is often omitted from the histories of the Internet.

The use of data packets for SAGE was not the only thing that was used in the creation of the Internet; the Internet is an example of packet-switched technology. The first large-scale test of packet switching began in 1969, when the Advanced Research Projects Agency, an agency of the Department of Defense, established a computer network for research purposes. However, there are ten years between the use of packets in SAGE and the packet-switched network known as ARPANet. How did this idea find enough advocates in these ten years so that the idea would seem obvious to the ARPA leaders that the time had come for packet-switching? The innovation of implementing a switched network was thought about in three different places in the late 1950s and early 1960s. Leonard Kleinrock's 1961 doctoral dissertation at MIT provided mathematical models to support the idea of packet switching, proving that it would work. Paul Baran, working on a military communication project for the Air Force, reported in 1964 that a switched network was the most reliable way to set up a survivable emergency communication network. Finally, Donald Davies at the National Physical Laboratory in the United Kingdom made a proposal for a "national message switching network" (225-6) for commercial applications; it was not until the next year that it was brought to Davies's attention that Baran had made a similar proposal [15]. Although some have suggested that packet-switching was developed independently by two or three different researchers, it would be more accurate to state that the research was conducted collaboratively.

The thesis that direct international cooperation was essential for the development of the Internet is supported in this period. Davies and three colleagues used the word "packet" in a paper presented by R. A. Scantlebury at the same ACM symposium in 1967 where Larry Roberts made the first public presentation of the funding priorities for the ARPA network [16]. These three individuals who made well-known testimonials for packet switching discussed the idea with the head of ARPA and convinced him to use packet-switching for his network. In preparation for developing the British network, Scantlebury (along with K. A. Bartlett and P. T. Wilkinson) developed a single-bit handshaking procedure for transmitting data over a serial link reliably, a protocol that was eventually adopted for the ARPANet in a modification to the IMP software in 1972. The adaptation of the "odd/even" packet acknowledgement improved network efficiency by 10 to 20 percent [17]. The international academic transfer of technology as described by [14] clearly extended to the age of the ARPANet; additionally, it is important to note that Davies and his team sought commercial applications for their network and were not interested in military research or survivability in the event of nuclear attack.

Of the three people – Kleinrock, Baran, and Davies – one of them did in fact design a network to withstand a nuclear strike. Baran's network [18] was innovative in the way that it created redundant pathways between important locations in the network. Baran imagined that telephone lines were part of the network, but also there would be microwave transmitters, FM radio transmitters, buried cables, satellite links, and other paths that the messages could take. This robust and redundant network would have survived a nuclear attack; it also would have been inordinately expensive for widespread use. The Air Force declined to pursue his plan for a defense communication network, and so the project was ended. The main legacy of this network (with regard to the Internet, anyway) is that Baran's paper inspired Donald Davies and influenced the decision of ARPA to start the widespread use of a switched network. (Interestingly, Arroyo [7] suggests that this work was not discussed with the researchers working on the Spanish network.)

The ARPAnet was the one project that was built and expanded, while Baran's project was never tested and Davies' did not get far. Although ARPANet was a defense department project, there is one definite way in which it was not a network to survive a nuclear attack: that is because it, like SAGE, used telephone lines for its connections. In this way, it is quite different from the network that was imagined by Paul Baran but never built. Nevertheless, the myth that the Internet was designed by military generals as a communication network to withstand a nuclear attack is quite pervasive, even though the Internet pioneers (including Baran) have tried hard to discredit it. This myth supports other widespread myths about the Internet. If we believe the myth that the Internet was invented to survive a nuclear attack, it is much easier to believe the myth that the Internet was started and perfected by the United States before it was sent out to other countries. This myth is very satisfying to Americans, but it is not very ethical.

The development of the Internet depended on the international community of researchers from the start. One of the three early proponents of switched networks was Donald Davies from Great Britain. The fact that he heard of the idea from the U.S., tested it out in the UK, and then came to a computer conference in the United States and talked to the leader of the ARPANet project demonstrates how these ideas were fully discussed and shared in an international atmosphere. In fact, the word we use to describe this technology – *packet* –makes more sense in the context of British English. Baran had called the technology message-switching, but the British influence is shown in the original ARPAnet documentation, which called the technology "packet-switching." A "packet," in British English, is a small, flat package, and this connection does more than provide evidence of the British influence on Internet technology. The idea of the helpful post office that knows how to deliver packages was described in Klienrock's paper. Furthermore, as pointed out by the Oxford English Dictionary [19], the packets that one receives in the mail are related to the packet boats that carried them; the first packets were standard shipping of letters between two points, such as England and Ireland. Thus, by appreciating the international community behind the early Internet technology, one can see how it was built by translating ideas from successful networks already in operation to electronic networks. This shows how users translate new ideas from concepts in other domains in order to actively support innovation.

3   From ARPANet to Internet

The ARPANet was publically demonstrated at the 1972 International Conference on Computer Communications, and as noted by Abbate and others, it was at this conference that the International Networking Working Group (INWG) was formed, with Vinton Cerf in charge of the group (this group would become IFIP Working Group 6.1 [20]). With the success of a national project for networking, the idea of the group was to "take the lead in creating an international network of networks" (quoted by [1]). The group quickly allied itself with the International Federation for Information Processing (IFIP), giving it "visibility and legitimacy within the international computer science community" [3]. It is, perhaps, not surprising that the international conversation around the innovation of packet switching before ARPA financed its networking project was embodied in the conception of the user as an international scientist after ARPAnet was established.

In the wake of the INWG's second meeting in 1973, Cerf edited and distributed a draft of was then called the "International Transmission Protocol" created with an international group of researchers who had experience in packet switching [20]. By 1973, Davies had an operating packet-switched network in his laboratory, and that same year, the first connections were made for the CYCLADES network in France, which "links several major computing centers" [21]. Although today one might be tempted to see these as distinct projects, it is clear that there was an active exchange of ideas among the researchers involved; furthermore, what one might see as different networks today may not have been so distinct at the time: as noted by [6], "ARPANet was not notably different to several other embryonic internetworking research projects": the UK's EPSS, CYCLADES, and the European Informatics Network (25). It is clear that the ARPANet, at this point in the story, was not the only packet-switched network in the world.

What is more, the ARPANet was not the Internet: The ARPANet would have to adapt its implementation of packet-switching in order to connect heterogeneous networks, and this shows evidence of additional international collaboration. Cerf and Robert Kahn started working on what they called the "Internetworking" project at this time: how could someone send a message between different networks? They presented their ideas to a 1973 meeting of the INWG at the University of Sussex [1]. In one of their first published papers on this topic, they note that the design goal is to establish protocols that eliminate the problems when "dissimilar networks are interconnected." This 1974 paper [22] acknowledges that the "early discussions of international network protocols" were helpful, and mentions Scantlebury and Davies by name. In addition, they thank and cite the work of Louis Pouzin, the French researcher behind CYCLADES. In creating a protocol that could easily work between networks, it was clear that the restrictions and capabilities for each network were different because they had different physical properties. To accommodate this, one of the key ideas in TCP/IP is that each packet needs a wrapper. Packets that originate on different networks might be set up differently, and this wrapper would help the networks carrying the message work with it, even though they could not know what the contents were. Cerf and Kahn acknowledge that they borrowed the solution from the French computer science community. CYCLADES had a slightly different implementation, and this difference resulted in an innovation that was applied directly to the TCP/IP protocol. The name CYCLADES comes from a group of Greek islands, and this name was used for the network because the researchers wanted to inspire islands of computing. In other words, they thought about creating a mixed networking environment much like Cerf and Kahn were trying to make. Thus they borrowed the idea of the datagram created in this heterogeneous environment and imported it into their design.

With the switchover to TCP/IP in 1983, once can say that the Internet had truly arrived: after all, the "i" in IP stands for internetworking. The power of TCP/IP was demonstrated many times in the expansion of the Internet. This is especially shown in the international community, where different kinds of computers and different kinds of national networks would have prevented a less flexible network from working. An excellent example of this was China's first connection to the TCP/IP network. There was no way that China could be directly connected to the U.S. Internet during the Cold War; the United States had strict laws about exporting technology to communist countries at this time. However, the U.S. was friendly to its partners. As part of the networking project known as CSNET, the U.S. made several international connections, including one to West Germany.

CSNET was established from 1979-1982 at the University of Wisconsin by Lawrence Landweber, who noted that there were 120 computer science departments at the time, even though only 25% (15 of 61) ARPANet sites were at universities [23]. The network that emerged from funding by the National Science Foundation had three tiers: a top tier of full ARPANet connections, a second tier that send TCP/IP packets over commercial X.25 lines so that researchers could use services like mail, telnet and FTP, and an e-mail only service. Along with setting up the service, Landweber held a series of meetings that came to be known as Larry's Networkshops, which "formed an important way, along with BITNET, to spread the Internet overseas" [24]. The first meeting in 1982 was held in London, where German researchers described plans for Deutsche Forschungsnetz (DFN), active projects in Norway and Sweden were described, the U.K. described the Coloured Book, and CERN described an early version of HEPnet. At the 1983 networkshop, Landweber announced that CSNET would go international, and the next year, Israel became the first connection outside the U.S. Connections to Korea, Australia, Canada, France, Germany, and Japan followed.

Landweber's effort to support the story of international connections shows how today's ubiquity of TCP/IP was not inevitable. As told by Andrew L. Russell [25], at the time TCP/IP was thought of as a temporary solution to international networking that would later be supplanted by protocols under development by the International

Organization for Standardization known as Open Systems Interconnection (OSI). Remarkably, Vinton Cerf had resigned as chair of INWG after becoming "discouraged by his international adventures in standards making" (40). By 1985, the U.S. Department of Defense recommended a transition away from TCP/IP and in 1988, Russell writes, the U.S. Department of Commerce mandated that all government computers use OSI by 1990. Russell [26] has characterized this conflict as a "protracted international struggle" (56), even though today the discussion is largely forgotten. It is clear, however, that the international community involved in networking research resented a top-down approach to generating standards, an attitude that is nicely summarized in David Clark's 1992 dictum "We reject: kings, presidents, and voting. We believe in: rough consensus and running code" [27]. By 1992, Clark was able to refer to the defeat of OSI as an example of how the grassroots commitment to Internet development had provided the world with a working network, but the ability of the international community to successfully resist top-down demands for standards was far from certain.

An example of how "running code" became the default standard for the Internet is seen in the story of how China was connected to the international Internet. West Germany had a robust computer industry, and through a contract with the World Bank, Siemens Corporation had supplied computers to China and helped connect computer science researchers in both companies. Werner Zorn, who was responsible for organizing German visitors to China, was dismayed that he could not send e-mail to his Chinese colleagues: "A turnaround time of 14 days is even considered fast if one does not want to resort to the extortionately expensive telephone or telex, which are not available everywhere" [28]. He then tried to set up a modem connection between the two countries, but the phone lines in China were not reliable enough to sponsor communication. He ended up using the CSNET software – modified to the Chinese setup of Siemens computers, of course – to send TCP/IP packets through a satellite connection that China had with Italy, and then through the European networks to Zorn's university computer [29]. Finally, his colleagues could exchange email messages with the rest of the world. The development of TCP/IP utilized a conception of a user who was an international scientist managing a local network, and this definition of a user enabled Zorn to connect his Chinese counterparts to the Internet in spite of Cold War prohibitions about the export of technology.

In stories like this, one sees how it was not the inevitable progress of a military objective that led to the widespread adoption of the Internet, but instead the value of translational work of individuals who sought to enhance their access to the value of the versatile networking protocols that were developed with the help of the international community, and how the desire to connect different networks in different countries helped TCP/IP to become the dominant networking standard. If we want to be unfriendly to the United States, we could say that the U.S. researchers stole these ideas from their foreign colleagues and used them for their own work. But the reality is that this sharing has a long tradition in the history of science, and the Internet is no different than any other scientific endeavor. The idea of sharing ideas in an international forum and then making the ideas work in one's home environment is one of the established principles of the scientific community. The myth that the Internet is a U.S. invention, then, hides how it was developed and tested with the conception of an ideal user who was a member of an international group of scholars.

4   Conclusion

Dispelling the myth that the United States created the Internet in isolation is crucial if one wants to recreate the environment that brought about the Internet in the first place. If the military made the Internet, then it would seem that one needs to give more money to the military to continue this kind of innovation. If the United States developed the Internet on its own, then there is no need to foster international cooperation. If the Internet was made according to a plan, then one needs to keep research tied to a clearly specified timeline with clear goals and deadlines. However, the way to invent the Internet (or the next generation of Internet technologies) is quite opposite to what these myths would lead us to believe. The technologies behind the Internet were invigorated by the international community, not by the United States in isolation. In order to create something like the Internet, then, it is necessary to foster an environment for international exchange and cooperation, not maintain proprietary secrets. The historian has an important role to play in making sure this environment is available. If we allow the myths of the Internet to perpetuate, we give support to misguided projects that will not be able to create the innovations of tomorrow.

Clearly, the popular history of the Internet needs to be revised. Sponsoring insular, high-tech research projects is not the way to create the next generation of Internet technologies. The story of the academic, international Internet is one that encourages us to foster heterogeneous connections. It is the role of the historian to remind policy makers, educators, and the users of the Internet that it was not planned from the start. It was hacked together by users of different projects to help them do the kind of work they found most valuable. In order to make the history of computing relevant, it is the task of the historian to show how the cosmopolitan tradition of science is responsible for the Internet we know today, and in order to foster this kind of innovation in the future, this community must be supported.

References

1. Hafner, K., Lyon, M.: Where Wizards Stay Up Late: The Origins of the Internet. Touchstone, New York (1996)
2. Segaller, S.: Nerds 2.0.1: A Brief History of the Internet. TV Books, New York (1999)
3. Abbate, J.: Inventing the Internet. MIT Press, Cambridge (1999)
4. Mueller, M.L.: Ruling the Root: Internet Governance and the Taming of Cyberspace. MIT Press, Cambridge (2002)
5. Campbell-Kelly, M., Garcia-Swartz, D.D.: The History of the Internet: The Missing Narratives. J. of Information Technology 28, 18–33 (2013)
6. Kim, B.K.: Internationalizing the Internet: the Co-evolution of Influence and Technology. Edward Elgar Publishing, Northampton (2005)
7. Arroyo, L.: The First Worldwide Public Packet Switching Network. In: A Century of Broadcasting: Proceedings of the Second Region 8 IEEE Conference on the History of Communications. IEEE, Piscataway (2010)
8. Oudshoorn, N., Pinch, T. (eds.): How Users Matter: The Co-Construction of Users and Technology. MIT Press, Cambridge (2005)
9. Latour, B.: Science in Action: How to Follow Scientists and Engineers through Society. Harvard University Press, Cambridge (1987)

10. Mahoney, M.S.: Histories of Computing. MIT Press, Cambridge (2011) Haigh, T. (ed.)
11. Veà, A.: The Unknown History of the Internet: Engineering the Worldwide WiWiW Project. In: A Century of Broadcasting: Proceedings of the Second Region 8 IEEE Conference on the History of Communications. IEEE, Piscataway (2010)
12. Earnest, L.: Internet Creation Myths, `http://www.stanford.edu/~learnest/net.htm`
13. Edwards, P.N.: The Closed World: Computers and the Politics of Discourse in Cold War America. MIT Press, Cambridge (1997)
14. Aspray, W.: International Diffusion of Computer Technology, 1945–1955. Annals of the History of Computing 8(4), 351–360 (1986)
15. Campbell-Kelly, M.: Data Communications at the National Physical Laboratory. Annals of the History of Computing 9(3/4), 221–247 (1988)
16. Davies, D.W., Bartlett, K.A., Scantlebury, R.A., Wilkinson, P.T.: A Digital Communication Network for Computers Giving Rapid Response at Remote Terminals. In: Proceedings of the First ACM Symposium on Operating System Principles, SOSP 1967, pp. 2.1–2.17. ACM, New York (1967)
17. McQuillan, J.M., Crowther, W.R., Cosell, B.P., Walden, D.C., Heart, F.E.: Improvements in the Design and Performance of the ARPA Network. In: AFIPS Fall Joint Computing Conference, vol. 2, pp. 741–754 (1972)
18. Baran, P.: On Distributed Communications, 1: Introduction to Distributed Communications Networks. RAND Corporation, Santa Monica (1964)
19. Oxford University Press: Packet, n. and adj. OED, `http://www.oed.com/view/Entry/135850` (accessed August 11, 2013)
20. McKenzie, A.: INWG and the Conception of the Internet: An Eyewitness Account. Annals of the History of Computing 33(1), 66–71 (2011)
21. Roberts, L.G.: The Evolution of Packet Switching. Proceedings of the IEEE 66(11), 1307–1313 (1978)
22. Cerf, V.G., Kahn, R.E.: A Protocol for Packet Network Intercommunication. IEEE Transactions of Communication 22(5), 637–648 (1974)
23. Comer, D.: The Computer Science Research Network CSNET: A History and Status Report. Communications of the ACM 26(10), 747–753 (1983)
24. Malamud, C.: Exploring the Internet: A Technical Travelogue. Prentice Hall, Englewood Cliffs (1993)
25. Russell, A.L.: The Internet that Wasn't. Spectrum 50(8), 39–43 (2013)
26. Russell, A.L.: "Rough Consensus and Running Code" and the Internet-OSI Standards War. Annals of the History of Computing 28(3), 48–61 (2006)
27. Clark, D.: A Cloudy Crystal Ball: Visions of the Future. In: Proceedings of the Twenty-Fourth Internet Engineering Task Force, pp. 539–543. Corporation for National Research Initiatives, Reston (1992)
28. Zorn, W.: How China was Connected to the International Computer Networks. The Amateur Computerist Newsletter 15(2), 36–49 (2007)
29. Zorn, W.: China's CSNET Connection 1987 – origin of the China Academic Network CANET. Asia Internet History Project, `https://sites.google.com/site/internethistoryasia/book1/personal-essay-werner-zorn` (accessed April 21, 2013)

History of Computer Science as an Instrument of Enlightenment

Yakov Fet

Institute of Computational Mathematics and Mathematical Geophysics of
Siberian Branch of Russian Academy of Sciences, Novosibirsk, Russia
fet@ssd.sscc.ru

Abstract. This report focuses on the dangerous problems that are currently facing the society – the negative phenomena in development of education and science. The most important way to solve this problem seems to be education and enlightenment. It is assumed that in the history of Computer Science, the intellectual and moral heritage of this history contains a wealth of material that can be used for the dissemination of knowledge, education, and human qualities. It is proposed to significantly expand the publication and dissemination of relevant non-fiction and biographical literature.

Keywords: history of computing, cultural heritage, global problems, Rome Club, Aurelio Peccei, human qualities, education, enlightenment, Norbert Wiener, John von Neumann, Leonid Kantorovich, Aleksey Lyapunov, Donald Knuth, Andrey Ershov, Aleksander Aleksandrov.

1   Introduction

The study of the history of science, familiarity with the life and activities of outstanding individuals – scientists, engineers, inventors, has always been an important part of the cultural and scientific heritage.

In the middle of the 20th century, a new stage began in the development of science, and, as we can say, in the history of human society! That was – the invention of electronic computers, the unprecedented pace of their improvement and dissemination, the creation of global information networks, as well as new means for storage and processing of huge amounts of data.

New information technologies have a strong influence on the society. They can bring people prosperity and physical and spiritual well-being. They pave the way to unprecedented opportunities for development of all areas of human activity.

2   Danger

Unfortunately, the achievements of information technologies, like some other results of scientific and technical progress, have their reverse side.

A. Tatnall, T. Blyth, and R. Johnson (Eds.): HC 2013, IFIP AICT 416, pp. 207–212, 2013.
© IFIP International Federation for Information Processing 2013

The creator of cybernetics Norbert Wiener was well aware than the new means of communications and the mass media can turn to the people their dangerous consequences. Even at the dawn of computers, in 1948, in the first edition of his famous book "Cybernetics" Wiener wrote:

> One of the lessons of the present book is that any organism is held together in this action by the possession of means for the acquisition, use, retention, and transmission of information. In a society too large for the direct contact of its members, these means are the press, both as it concerns books, and as it concerns newspapers, the radio, the telephone system, the telegraph, the posts, the theatre, the movies, the schools, and the church...
>
> That system which, more than all other, should contribute to social homeostasis is thrown directly into the hands of the most concerned in the game of power and money, which we have already seen to be one of the chief anti-homeostatic elements in the community.

Today these dangerous events became threatening. The uncontrolled use of the media in the interests of commercial structures deeply influence the fall of morality, tastes and mental abilities of the population.

For example, the Vice-President of the Russian Academy of Sciences academician Aleksander Aseev in his recent interview[1] noted "the general decline of morality in modern Russia" as well as "rapid contamination of the research and education sector of the country".

This case relates to Russia. But it can be assumed that similar signs could be observed in some other countries.

3   Human Qualities

The considered events can be seen as one of the global challenges facing the society today. It is not the first time when history poses to the reasonable minded scientists some complicated tasks related to the protection of society against various threats. As you know, in the middle of the 20th century several prominent scientists and humanists created an international social group, which received the name of the "Club of Rome". One of the organizers of this Club and its first President was the famous Italian social activist, scientist and industrialist, Aurelio Peccei (1908–1984).

The main objective of the Club of Rome was to attract attention of the world community to the global problems threatening the existence and well-being of mankind. To do this, the members of the Rome Club, together with visiting scientists from different countries and professions, prepared so-called "Reports of the Rome Club". One of the first Reports considered environmental hazards associated with unnecessarily high consumption of natural resources and the pollution of environment.

---

[1] Newspaper *"Science in Siberia"* / May 22, 2013. – P. 3. (In Russian).

In 1977, Aurelio Peccei published his famous book "Human Quality"[2]. The main idea of Peccei was that for successful solving complex and dangerous natural, economic, and many other problems of the community, the community should first of all improve the human qualities of its members. Peccei wrote in his book:

> *In the end the problems come to the human qualities and the way of their improvement...*
>
> *Until our so-called technologic society becomes as well a human society, violence will proceed its triumphal demonstration and we will continue to fight special cases of this general phenomenon without understanding the origins of the violence...*
>
> *The main problem is – how can we get the spark which will kindle the flame of developing the human qualities...*

These conclusions were written by an experienced, wise, and honest man, whose whole life was dedicated to one purpose: to help people in solving their extremely complex, vital issues. These are also valid with respect to all the issues that we are concerned about to-day. Watching the current negative events, we must unconditionally agree with the conclusions of Aurelio Peccei. The only remedy that we can offer in order to *kindle the flame* could be the enlightenment.

The History of Science as well as History of Computer Science are quite important tools. A special part in the dissemination of true human culture and high moral principles is played by the study of biographies of outstanding scientists, engineers, and inventors. There are good reasons for the opinion that in the scientific community the level of morality is much higher than in most other sections of society.

Dissemination of reliable information about our heroes and the instilling of their human qualities in our contemporaries, seems to be an efficient instrument for enlightenment.

4   Some Examples

At different times, the lives of distinguished personalities, their scientific achievements and moral honesty served as the source of education and emulation. Naturally, it concerns also the heroes of Computer Science. We can cite here some examples from well-known memoir literature:

Norbert Wiener

> *Norbert Wiener was deeply concerned about his younger colleagues. He displayed lavish attention to the new teachers of the Faculty of Mathematics. He invited them for breakfast and dinner, and in the first few weeks often went to their rooms.*
>
> *Norman Levinson wrote: he asked me to check the manuscript of his new book. I found a gap in the proof and proved a Lemma to correct this deficiency. Wiener then sat down at the typewriter, typed my Lemma, put my name down and sent to the journal. It is not often that a distinguished Professor acts as a Secretary of his young pupil.*

---

[2]   *Aurelio Peccei. Human Quality / Pergamon Press, 1977.*

His colleagues and students have kept alive the memory of him as a teacher. They also remember the inspiring enthusiasm with which he treated all kinds of rigorous intellectual activity. Amar Bose said: "I could never thank Wiener enough for the education that he gave me. And most of all – he gave me faith in the incredible potential inherent in each of us"[3].

John von Neumann

Von Neumann was always ready to help anyone who came to him for advice. He was sincerely interested in any difficult problem. Von Neumann taught me mathematics more than anyone else. As for the nature of creative thinking of a mathematician, I learned from him more than I could learn without him in my whole life. If he analyzed a problem, the need for its further consideration disappeared.

Only a great mind could make such significant contributions to science as was made by von Neumann. Impeccable logic was the most characteristic feature of his thinking. He seemed a perfect logical machine with carefully fitted gears. Listening to von Neumann one begins to understand how the human brain has to work.[4]

Leonid Kantorovich

Academician Israel Gelfand said:

The talent of Kantorovich is obvious. But the talent as such is not much of a gift: you should be able to use it. Meanwhile, the scientific gift is not all a person needs. The humane is primary, the scientific is secondary.

Why do I consider Leonid Kantorovich to be a genius? It is very simple – he combines in himself two cultures: the first one pertaining to the humanities and the second one pertaining to mathematics... In the 20th century, very few people were capable of such a synthesis...What we see is an integral inner spirituality that equally affects all areas of his work[5].

Igor Poletaev about **Aleksey Lyapunov**

The scientific truth was his sacrificial altar, and the search for the truth was his religion. His attitude to cybernetics resembled the attitude of a priest to his religion. His self-denying and chivalrous serving the truth was supplemented with his fascinated personality and his ability to be precise and understandable at the same time. < ... >. Even disputable opinions sounded attractive and almost convincing, when he was talking. Every conversation with him was an intellectual event and an aesthetic experience[6].

---

3   *David Jerison and Daniel W. Stroock*. Norbert Wiener / Proc. of Symposia in Pure Math., Vol. 60, 1997 / The Legacy of Norbert Wiener: A Centennial Symp. in Honor of the 100th Anniv. of His Birth. – Providence, RI: AMS.

4   *Eugene P. Wigner*. In: Yearbook of the American Philosophical Society, 1957.

5   *I.M. Gelfand*. Leonid Kantorovich and the Synthesis of Two Cultures / In: Leonid Vital'evich Kantorovich: A Man and a Scientist. Vol. 1. / – Novosibirsk: SB RAS Publ. House, 2002 (- in Russian).

6   *Ya. Fet*. Stories about Cybernetics / Novosibirsk: SB RAS Publ. House, 2007. – P 40 (- in Russian).

Donald Knuth about **Andrey Ershov**

The conference on Algorithms in Modern Mathematics and Computer Science held in Urgench, in 1979, was one of the most memorable events of my life. Although Andrey and I were officially listed as co-chairmen of that meeting, the truth is that Andrey took care of 99 % of the details, while I was able to relax and enjoy the proceedings and to learn important things from the many people I met there. Such an experience is a once-in-a-lifetime thing, and I hope it will be possible for many other computer scientists to participate in a similar event if someone else is inspired to follow Andrey's example. During that week I got to know him much better than ever before, and I was especially struck by the brilliant way he filled numerous roles: a conference leader, organizer, philosopher, speaker, translator, and editor[7].

Aleksander Aleksandrov

Professor Aleksandrov wrote[8]:

Primarily in general education and, therefore, especially in the school teaching there should be, I think, historical education. It must give account of the development of nations, their material and spiritual culture, and science in particular. It should contain vivid descriptions of the dramatic events and remarkable personalities that would serve as cultural and educational lessons for young people. Thousands of Shakespeare's dramas and Tolstoy's novels were composed and performed in history. History is marvellous, inspiring, and gives us profound lessons.

5   Our Activities

Of course, biographical information about the heroes of the history of science, history of Computer Science, is continuously published in various books, magazines, and virtual museums. We should note the archives of Charles Babbage Institute, the databases of the Society of Information Technologies, the "IEEE Annals of the History of Computing", and a number of other sources. An important event in this series was the publication in 1999 of the report "History in the Computing Curriculum"[9] prepared by the IFIP Joint Task Group.

Considerable attention to biographical materials is paid in the Proceedings of IFIP Congresses, conferences on the history of Computer Science, which are periodically held in different parts of the world by the WG 9.7 as well as this London conference "Making the History of Computing Relevant".

---

[7] *Donald Knuth.* In: "Programming" / Moscow: Nauka, 1990, No. 1.

[8] *Academician A.D. Aleksandrov. Reminiscences. Publications. Materials* / Moscow: Nauka, 2002. – P. 307 (- in Russian).

[9] *J. Impagliazzo, M. Campbell-Kelly, G. Davis, J.A.N. Lee, M.R. Williams.* History in the Computing Curriculum / Annals of the History of Computing, vol. 21, no 1, January–March 1999. – Pp. 4–16.

However, in most known publications the authors focus their attention on the description of scientific and technical developments and achievements. Very seldom will you find here less formal information about the personal features of the protagonists. Apparently, there is a need for special books, maybe a special international journal, with an emphasis on personal characteristics of the scientists.

6   Conclusion

It is appropriate to say here about investigations on the History of Computing which are conducted in Russia. In particular, for a number of years, our Institute carries out corresponding research. We are publishing a series of scientific-biographical books about Russian and foreign Computer Pioneers. Presenting in these books the life and the work of our heroes, we pay special attention to their personal qualities. Some examples of the book titles are: "Essays on the History of Computer Science in Russia", "Leonid Vital'evich Kantorovich: a Man and a Scientist", Aleksey Andreevich Lyapunov. 100th Anniversary of the Birth"

As of today, we have published 11 books, with the total volume above 5000 pages. Naturally, our books are printed in Russian. However, an English translation of the Summary, Foreword and Contents is included in each volume. We hope that reading of these reference materials is sufficient to get an idea of the corresponding Russian book. In addition, we are printing each year a booklet «Book Series "History of Computing"» (in English), which contains the brief details of all previously published books.

Probably, it would be useful to select definite parts of the mentioned books and publish them in English.

Part VII

Celebrating Nostalgia for Games – And Its Potential as Trojan Horse

The Popular Memory Archive: Collecting and Exhibiting Player Culture from the 1980s

Helen Stuckey, Melanie Swalwell, and Angela Ndalianis

Department of Screen and Media, Flinders University, Australia
Helen.stuckey@flinders.edu.au

Abstract. Memories of playing games with computers have an important role in terms of documenting people's personal relationships with computing history. This paper presents and discusses the Popular Memory Archive (PMA), an online portal of the "Play It Again" game history and preservation project, which addresses 1980s games, produced in Australia and New Zealand. As well as providing a way to disseminate some of the team's research, the PMA taps into what is, effectively, a collective public archive by providing a technique for collecting information, resources and memories from the public about 1980s computer games. The PMA is designed to work with online retro gamer communities and fans, and this paper reflects on the PMA as a method for collecting and displaying the memories of those who lived and played their way through this period.

Keywords: Computing History, Digital Preservation, Videogames, Games History, Online Communities, Fan Cultures, Museum 2.0.

1   Introduction

It can be difficult to engage people with the histories of computing who don't already have a personal investment in the story. Digital games offer a useful vehicle for talking about what might be regarded by some as a dry topic. Games were the way in which many people first came into contact with computers, particularly in the 1970s and 1980s, when games offered laypeople the chance to have playful and personal experiences with the then new micro-computers.

Since their inception digital games have developed a complex and layered history, which has left its mark on the memories of game players. Yet the dramatic speed with which game technologies (software and hardware) have developed and continue to develop renders game technologies defunct at an exponential rate, to the extent that game fans have become a significant resource for mapping game history. This paper discusses the ambitions of the Popular Memory Archive, an online exhibition and database being created as part of the Play it Again Project and how it aims to collect information, resources and memories from the public about 1980s computer games.

1.1   A Played History

Videogames are important cultural artefacts in their own right but they are also intrinsically tied to the history of computing. In reflecting on how audiences might

A. Tatnall, T. Blyth, and R. Johnson (Eds.): HC 2013, IFIP AICT 416, pp. 215–225, 2013.

engage with the history of early computing it may be valuable to look at the importance that play has had in the story of computing and how playing games with technology has historically played such a significant role in both engaging users and showcasing emerging technology. Alan Turing famously wrote a chess program in 1947 before a computer existed that was powerful enough to run it [8]. This aspiration of creating a computer capable of playing chess was to be the goal for many early computer scientists working on Artificial Intelligence. From the beginnings of computing history games have often been used to demonstrate the capacity and accessibility of the incipient technology. In 1951 the Australian software engineer John Bennett wrote a version of the game "Nim" to showcase the Ferranti computer at the 1951 Festival of Britain. For the display Ferranti built a special "Nim" playing machine – Nimrod, with the number relays mounted behind clear perspex to demonstrate their workings and a panel with rows of coloured lights for the gameplay. Festival goers were invited to play against the computer and watch its mathematics' ability in action. The demonstration was meant to show off the scientific prowess of the British computing company to the nation. The guidebook explained *"It may appear that, in trying to make machines play games, we are wasting our time. This is not true as the theory of games is extremely complex and a machine that can play complex games can also be programmed to carry out complex practical problems [8]."* In 1951 Ferranti understood the power of games to make computers relevant or at least exciting to the public. Later Bennett recorded his disappointment with a public who mostly just wanted to play rather than engage with the maths and science behind Nimrod's electronic brain [3]. But no one can deny the impact that these early encounters with playing with the computer had on some people. Despite the fact that over half a century has passed since the public got to play with Nimrod, traces of the fascination it held for them can still be found online. A 2011 query to *The Guardian*'s Notes and Queries page includes a request from an unknown author who remembers playing "Nim", as a schoolboy, at the Festival of Britain and wants to know what the computer was. He received two replies, one which perhaps would have delighted Bennett with its tidy description of the Ferranti's hardware and operations whilst the other respondent speaks to the game, how it played, strategies for playing and confession of how as a 16 year old, he spent long hours at the display trying in vain to beat the machine [22].[1]

1.2   Playful Memories of CSIRAC

Although the user group for these early monolithic computers was small the enduring fascination of playful engagement is a consistent theme of people's remembrance of them. CSIRAC, now on display at the Melbourne Museum, is the only surviving first

---

[1] To celebrate the 50th anniversary of Nimrod hobbyist and early computing historian Peter Goodeve created a charming simulation of Nimrod where you play by manipulating the buttons on photographs of the original 1951 display. Goodeve states that the program is built like the original where the logic is performed by "Gates' and "Flip-Flops". He explains that where he had access to detailed descriptions of the original logic he followed it almost exactly. http://www.goodeveca.net/nimrod/simulation.html

generation computer in the world. Built in Australia in 1949 it was the fourth computer built in the world. CSIRAC's immense scale and massive racks of valves clearly communicate to audiences at the Museum that this is a different beast than that which sits on their desktop: it is a metaphoric 'dinosaur', a wonder from another age.[2] It is not the hardware operations, however, that captures the public imagination. The stories that enliven the CSIRAC display are those of the personal and creative relationships that people had with the system. These include how CSIRAC's first programmer, software engineer Geoff Hill was able to program CSIRAC to play popular tunes such as "Colonel Bogey" which it would perform on public display in the 1950s.[4–6, 9] Featured also are the games that the teams created to play with the machine. Of particular fascination was the ability of operator Kay Thorne to beat the machine when playing Dick Jenssen's "The Way the Ball Bounces".[4] These narratives and the artefacts that accompany them, the music and the games, are able to communicate to contemporary audiences both a sense of the constraints that governed the operations of these machines and their creative potential. The ingenious ways that people found to make games using the simple input systems and displays convey some of the excitement that these individuals had in interacting with these early systems - playing with the machine and playing the machine. These artefacts express what happens when the principles of binary arithmetic and digital logic become more than mathematics and become an invitation to play.

2   Play It Again

The Play it Again Project which is the focus of this paper is not situated at the dawn of the computer age but rather at the moment when the computer found its way into the homes and hearts of ordinary people. It is designed to capture the memories of those people who played their way through the era of the first home computers. Play It Again is a game history and preservation project focused on locally-written digital games in 1980s Australia and New Zealand. It is a collaboration with the Australian Centre for the Moving Image (ACMI), the New Zealand Film Archive (NZFA), and the Berlin Computerspiele Museum. This paper presents and discusses the Popular Memory Archive being generated by the "Play It Again" team. The Popular Memory Archive is both a technique for collecting information, resources and memories from the public about 1980s computer games, and a way to display the results of the team's research into 1980s histories of digital game production and consumption. In this paper we discuss the Popular Memory Archive as a strategy for exhibiting and documenting the history of early digital games. This is based on the premise that there is cultural significance in these early encounters - like our friend whose unforgettable game of 'Nim' as a schoolboy in 1951 had him questing 60 years later to learn more about the computer he first played upon. And that these personal epiphanies and remembrances can contribute to building a better understanding of the history of games and computing.

---

[2] The use of the term "dinosaur" here is not meant as pejorative but the special value that dinosaurs have for museums where their breath-taking scale and ability to evoke wonder offers a sense of spectacle that make them perennial favourites with audiences.

3   History of Production

The Popular Memory Archive seeks to balance a history of production, in the specific national contexts of 1980s Australia and New Zealand, with a history of use and reception. In researching the history of production, we have sought to compile information on as many locally-produced 1980s games titles as possible. The Play It Again project has identified more than 900 locally-written titles (700+ from Australia and 200+ from New Zealand). From this, the team has selected a shortlist of 50 or so titles which will be featured in an online exhibition.

Alongside this online exhibition, there will be an associated online program of 'events', in the form of a curated blog with a program of guests which changes monthly. Our selection of game titles for the shortlist has been conducted with this unfolding public program of guests in mind, to ensure that particular curatorial themes are illustrated. Curatorial themes include: the work of pioneering companies, including Beam Software; the rise of the bedroom coder; local scenes and local themes; legal issues for game archivists; and a focus on the collector. It is envisaged that these curated discussions amongst invited guests will draw out valuable reflections from them and attract contributions from others wishing to join the conversation.

Other criteria informing our selections of games are: important game designers; formal innovation/pushing technical limits; popular or nationally significant platforms; overall representation and balance; and consideration of the quality of the games. Selections have been informed by archival research, interviews and conversations with game designers, as well as systems we already have hard and software for. As much as possible, the project focuses on a breadth and depth of platforms, themes, and contrasting attributes.

4   History of Consumption

In seeking to understand the rise of the micro-computer and the cultural significance of videogames, the Popular Memory Archive moves its focus beyond a technology history to a history of use and interactions. This is in keeping with Patricia Galloway's call for the importance of personal knowledge in comprehending personal computing [10]. It also echoes the observation Oudshoorn and Pinch make: "*Whereas historians and sociologists of technology have chosen technology as their major topic of analysis, those who do cultural and media studies have focused primarily on users and consumers*"[23]. Rather than understanding our object of study – 1980s games – as an archaeological and static object that exists in the past, we instead consider it as a dynamic form that continues to have a presence in game culture, living on through the energies of retro gamer communities and informing both contemporary game design and player cultures.

The Popular Memory Archive is centrally concerned with making links with a wider audience, and connecting historical research into early gaming with those who lived and played their way through this period. The collation of information about selected game titles is intended to drive the program and act as a prompt to elicit participation and materials from audiences.

Videogames are more than inert, digital code. Games theorist James Newman argues that the act of playing a videogame cannot be adequately considered or appreciated without a deep understanding of the ways in which it is enmeshed within and informed by its cultures and communities, all of whom contribute to the collective knowledge of videogame culture [19–21]. Recognising that game culture in the 1980s was highly participatory, hands on, and often characterized by a DIY ethic, the project aspires to create a history of games as they have been used and experienced. We want to hear about what people did with early computers and games: what games they wrote; what these games mean and meant to them, now and then; what records they have; and what difference their involvement with games made. For the duration of the Popular Memory Archive's active life (expected to be around 18 months) users will be able to submit comments, images, video and other files to the site. Participation will be possible through uploading game capture, screenshots, photos, and the like. Participation will be encouraged through low barrier engagement such as "liking", "played", "owned". We are also considering including a link to a more detailed set of questions that visitors could complete to provide richer information for other visitors and future researchers.

5   Fan Knowledge

Before detailing what we expect the Popular Memory Archive to deliver, we need to detour briefly to foreground an earlier (and still ongoing) phase of the research, namely our engagement with fan communities. It was fan communities who, years ago, took the initiative to document and preserve retro games, long before there was any institutional discussion on the cultural value of videogames. Operating outside institutional structures, such groups have been able to advance their work with minimal bureaucracy: they are agile, highly focused on what can be niche-fields of inquiry, and able to draw on the combined knowledge of large communities, who operate along gift economy lines [1, 2, 13, 14, 18]. Whilst many have also been involved with creating specialised techniques to help with game preservation, it is the collective intelligence that fans have of games which is of most interest to us in this context. Fans have knowledge about the playing of games, the played games and the played with game [7, 16, 19–21].

The research team, ACMI and NZFA recognize that much knowledge about the history of digital games is currently held by the gamer community. Elsewhere, we have reported on interviews conducted with two long time expert fan groups, Lemon64 and World of Spectrum, discussing the potential advantages in collaboration for both the Museum and fan groups [26]. In considering our approach to exhibiting information about - and seeking to collect documentation of - games, we have looked to the databases created by retro computer game fan sites such as Hall of Light, World of Spectrum and Lemon64. Some of these sites have existed for nearly two decades and have evolved over time, refining their catalogues and the opportunities they present for engagement as the web has grown to support more complex data and more possibilities for participation. Having engaged in this protracted iterative design process, these sites have produced archives that strive to address the complex nature of videogames and also reflect how an active user community searches and engages with this material. Sites such as these - built around digitally native content by a digital literate community - provide excellent resources, operating as blueprints for memory institutions who are hoping to work with online knowledge communities to develop resources, share information and create a broader community engagement with the history of computing.

6   What We Expect to Get from the Popular Memory Archive and the Significance of This

We expect the Popular Memory Archive to generate oral history-like fragmentary recollections from users, whether stimulated by the monthly hosted discussions, or spontaneous reminiscences. Depending on our audience - which we expect will comprise a mix of retrogamers, collectors, occasional players, and other users who are simply interested in the issues - we believe contributions are likely to have some particular qualities.

Fan discourse issues from a situated knowledge that is based on lived experience. Fans and players typically understand games as a set of experiences. Retrogamer sites - sometimes motivated by nostalgia and by a personal past with the software and hardware - often frame games in an intimate dialogue. For example the comments section at Lemon64 for "The Way of the Exploding Fist" ("WOTEF") includes people's memories of the first time they played "WOTEF". These focus not just on the game, but where and who they played with, the time it took for the tape to load and their first encounters with the infamous "Bruce Lee" scream on the loading tape.

Many retro game sites are platform specific and the romance of particular machines and their idiosyncrasies plays a major role in the hearts and minds of their user communities. Comments on such sites often offer a combination of personal passion and specific knowledge. *"Forget all that Street Fighter rubbish, this is a proper fight! Get the right move at the right time and that tension of knowing one blow could land you on your arse"* reflects [funky-springer] at Lemon64 on "WOTEF" in response to [melante]'s reminiscing *"While IK+ ("International Karate+") can be even more fun thanks to the 3 player action, this was, and still is my favourite fighting games of all time (Street Fighter can't hold a candle to this one) Besides, this was also responsible for making me start studying karate."* These two comments situate "WOTEF" within a comparative discussion of the beat-em-up - of which it was one of the first for the home computer (the first karate simulation) - but they do so in the voices of people who cared, including one who was inspired enough by their experiences with the game to go and study karate [28].

6.1   Context

The Popular Memory Archive will deliver context, which is critical for creating an understanding of games for future users and researchers [17]. It can be difficult to appreciate the innovation and achievements of early video games as rapid technological change renders the most sophisticated features of 1980s games as crude to contemporary audiences. For example, the revolutionary sense of fluid control that "WOTEF" offered players through its intuitive mapping of the fight moves to the joystick is lost to a generation raised on the precision and speed of current peripherals. An understanding of both the social and material conditions of the consumption and reception of these early games is difficult to collect, preserve and display. Documenting player memories is one way to approach this dilemma and to record the experience of these games when their technology was state of the art and their designs were breaking new ground, offering new kinds of experiences.

6.2   Non-traditional Archives

We believe that the Popular Memory Archive will yield a range of digital primary source materials and documentation, such as ephemera, images, and game capture. As part of our research, we have reviewed a number of Facebook communities who are using social media to reconnect and document their shared history. Two groups have particularly interested us: "Sharpies, Sharps and Skins a 1960-1970's Melbourne Subculture" and "I got Drunk at the Crystal Ballroom", a group dedicated to sharing memories of Melbourne's punk and post-punk subculture of the late 1970s and early 1980s. In reconnecting these groups, these Facebook pages serve as ad hoc memory institutions, archiving photos and collecting both individual oral histories and shared conversations. The "Crystal Ballroom" users have uploaded photos and scans of ephemera, and post links to footage they filmed back in the day, as well as linking out to videos of the bands from the era. This visual archive is supported by individual memories and altogether the discussion documents a detailed family tree of Melbourne's 1980s indie band scene. The collective remembering produces a richly-textured history, and a 'tested' one at that as people are quick to correct erroneous and boastful statements. The momentum created through these social media has also resulted in the development of more traditional archives. The "Sharpies" site, for example, has already supported the biography of one of its members and its user group are currently working on a book of images, short stories and biographies documenting Sharpie culture, with a second to follow[3].

7   Significance for the Museum

What is the significance of the Popular Memory Archive for the Museum? For some years, Museums have been inquiring how Web 2.0 can be used effectively to provide

---

[3] *Rage: A Sharpies Journal 1974-1980* by Julie Mac. Forthcoming *SNAP* an illustrated (100 photos) collection of small anecdotes and snippets from and about Sharpies sourced through the online community to be followed by the collection of longer pieces entitled *TAILS.*

access and engagement with collections, and there are an increasing number of examples of institutions working with online communities. Galaxy Zoo, for example, invites hundreds of thousands of amateur astronomers to contribute to mapping the obscure corners of the universe. As detailed on the website, maintained and developed by the Citizen Science Alliance (which include partners NASA and Origins), *"the CSA works with many academic and other partners around the world to produce projects that use the efforts and ability of volunteers to help scientists and researchers deal with the flood of data that confronts them"*. What Galaxy Zoo's 'citizen scientists' contribute to the project is not just data, but, through their forum discussions, they help crowd-source what is significant about the findings [24]. In this way the focuses of fan discourses help to build the cultural value of their subjects, and in turn contribute to shaping their value for the Museum [7, 15, 20, 21].

In thinking about how to engage with game history, the 2010 "Preserving Virtual Worlds" report identifies the important work of lay historians and their efforts in building online collections, as well as developing tools for emulation and preservation. The report proposes that one of the immediate steps that archives and museums can take to assist in the long term preservation of games is the development of systems that are accessible by, and can accept contributions from, the gaming community. Rather than being informed by a static view of game data preservation, the Popular Memory Archive offers an alternative model for documenting the cultural memory around early digital games. Lisa Gitelman reminds us that *"Despite the ubiquity of the phrase raw data... data are always already 'cooked' and never entirely 'raw'"*. Raw data *"are the starting point for what we know, who we are, and how we communicate. This shared sense of starting with data often leads to an unnoticed assumption that data are transparent, that information is self-evident, the fundamental stuff of truth itself."*[12] Gitelman posits understanding data "as a matter of disciplines" - from our perspective, that of games - and in doing so, a richer understanding of data as 'cooked' phenomena emerges. Rather than being understood as bits of information or *"abstract objects useful in the production of knowledge about the past"*[12] , in this project we reimagine the data we collate as a part of a collective phenomenon that extends to players. Through the collection of player memories we aim to activate this period of gaming history.

7.1   Moving beyond the Object Focus

Operating online, the Popular Memory Archive already entails a shift beyond the Museum's historic object focus. But the Popular Memory Archive will do much more than this. For instance, to pick up on an earlier point about fans' passion, passionate voices are engaging in a way that the measured tones of the Museum are not. In examining the effects of "Discussion exhibitions" at the Science Museum, London, Ben Gammon and Xerxes Mazda note that one of the motivations for visitors to read the comment of others is that the emotive language of visitor's comments is more compelling than the display didactics [11]. In contrast to the careful neutrality of Museum language, the passion of the retro gamer and fan captures a sense of the lived experience and its importance to the user. Oral histories, even fragments thereof, provide a nuanced and embodied relationship with the work.

7.2   Reality Check

It is always tempting in the planning stage of a project to delude oneself by envisaging an ideal response. We are very aware that the idea of *"build it and they will come"* has not always served the Museum well as it has moved into the online space. And we are very aware that it has taken over 10 years for Lemon64 to amass its 98 comments on *"WOTEF"*. It is therefore our intent to work with these fan sites to collect and reuse relevant content related to our fifty selected games. This sourced material will be featured in the Popular Memory Archive with its curated "discussion" on Australian and New Zealand game history. This naturally opens up new preservation questions as the online digital preservation environment is a hall of mirrors, but that's for another paper. There are additional challenges foreseen in a further ambition to offer 'play in the browser' versions of some of the games. This creates a series of technical challenges but also complex rights management issues as many of the work are orphanware, their publishing rights obscured by the volatility of the history of the games industry. In addition to these are the philosophical and quality issues for the Museum in providing an emulated experience.[4] These include technical challenges but also rights management and the quality of, and philosophical issues regarding the authenticity of, the emulated experience.

8   Conclusions

The Popular Memory Archive is not just trying to reach new online audiences but to activate existing expert audiences whose memories and skills are needed to understand the games of the 1980s era. Games are, and were, a popular media form, and so we want to hear the voices of the community who played them. Ideally the Popular Memory Archive will reflect how an online exhibition/collection can blend the voices of game designers, players and retro computing hobbyists with those of the museum professional to produce a richer understanding of this era in computer culture. The Popular Memory Archive has the potential to engage the Museum in a more transparent process of meaning making, by placing on display the ambition to allow invested communities to shape narratives, become part of the information exchange, and work to directly build the archives. It will also, in turn, provide rich contextual content that helps new audiences make connections to these objects.

It is hoped that the online catalog/exhibition will offer more than a traditional static and authoritative catalog entry reflecting the more discursive, inclusive and questioning practice of exhibition and events [25]. We feel, however, that the significance of this project is to be found in the very possible scenario where games from this era stop working. Whilst "Play It Again" will be making it possible to play selected games from this era again without needing a sophisticated knowledge of emulators, if and when these games stop working, the Popular Memory Archive will

---

[4]   Further to the quality issues of emulation is a loss of control over what audiences are actually experiencing interacting with web based media whose performance may be affected by the set-up of the client machine.

have netted popular memories, together with ephemera, artefacts and other documentation. Whilst these memories may be fragmentary, told in different voices, together with different artefacts and documentation, they will allow future researchers to piece together a sense of what it might have been like to play these games in 1980s Australia and New Zealand.

8.1   Postscript

Whilst games were not always part of the official history of computers even the earliest computers had games played upon them. These early games help illustrate both how people interacted with these machines and often capture the zeitgeist of the times. At the conference one of the participants shared with the authors his memories of playing "Moonlander" on the DEC GT40, a PDP-11 using the light pen. What he remembered fondly about "Moonlander" was that a successful landing was rewarded with the discovery of a McDonald's restaurant on the moon.[5] This playful humour offered a quirky juxtaposition to the challenges of calculating deceleration on the physics simulator. The DEC-11 "Moonlander" was created by DEC consultant Jack Burness. An earlier text version of the game existed for the PDP-8 created in 1969 by Jim Storer when moon landings were a global obsession.[6] "Moonlander" features strongly in people's memories of the DEC particularly as it was one of the first computer games played with a graphical interface. It launched the popular genre of lunar landers for the arcades of the 1970s and home computers of the 1980s. [27]

Collecting and displaying memories of gameplay help contemporary audiences understand not just how that technology worked but how interacting with these systems could delight and enthral their users. Stories of playing computer games are thus important in the history of computing because they speak to the creative and personal relationships users had with the technology.

Acknowledgement. This research is supported under the Australian Research Council's Linkage Projects funding scheme (project number LP120100218).

References

[1]   Baym, N.: Tune In, Log On: Soaps, Fandom, and Online Community. SAGE (1999)
[2]   Baym, N., Burnett, R.: Amateur experts: International fan labour in Swedish independent music. International Journal of Cultural Studies 12(5), 433–449 (2009)
[3]   Bennett, J.: Autobiographical Snippets. In: Bennett, J.M., et al. (eds.) Computing in Australia - The Development of a Profession, p. 55. Hale and Iremonger (1994)
[4]   CSIRAC: Australia's First Computer,
      http://museumvictoria.com.au/csirac/index.aspx (accessed July 12, 2013)

---

[5]   The late 1960s saw McDonald's restaurants proliferate across America with the introduction of their distinctive signage and architecture. In 1968 the 1000th store opened in the USA. The first UK McDonald's opened in 1974.
[6]   The first moon walk occurred on the 20th June 1969 as part of the Apollo 11 NASA mission.

[5] Demant, D.: Why the Real Thing Is Essential for Telling Our Stories. In: Tatnall, A. (ed.) HC 2010. IFIP AICT, vol. 325, pp. 13–15. Springer, Heidelberg (2010)

[6] Demant, D., Tatnall, A.: Institutional Nostalgia – Museum Victoria's Cabinet of Computing Curiosities. In: Tatnall, A. (ed.) Reflections on the History of Computing. IFIP AICT, vol. 387, pp. 348–361. Springer, Heidelberg (2012)

[7] Donahue, R., Kraus, K.: Do You Want to Save Your Progress?: The Role of Professional and Player Communities in Preserving Virtual Worlds. DHQ: Digital Humanities Quarterly 6 (2012)

[8] Donovan, T.: Replay: The History of Video Games. Yellow Ant (2010)

[9] Doornbusch, P.: Computer Sound Synthesis in 1951: The Music of CSIRAC. Computer Music Journal 28(1), 10–25 (2004)

[10] Galloway, P.: Personal Computers, Microhistory, and Shared Authority: Documenting the Inventor – Early Adopter Dialectic. IEEE Annals of the History of Computing 33(2), 60–74 (2011)

[11] Gammon, B., Mazda, X.: The Power of the Pencil Renegotiating the Museum Visitor Relationship. Exhibitionist, 26–33 (Fall 2009)

[12] Gitelman, L. (ed.): "Raw Data" Is an oxymoron. MIT Press (2013)

[13] Jenkins, H.: Fans, Bloggers, and Gamers: Exploring Participatory Culture. New York University Press (2006)

[14] Jenkins, H.: Interactive Audiences? The "Collective Intelligence" of Media Fans. In: Fans Bloggers and Gamers Exploring Participatory Culture, pp. 134–151 (2002)

[15] Kraus, K.: "A Counter-Friction to the Machine": What Game Scholars, Librarians, and Archivists Can Learn from Machinima Makers about User Activism. Journal of Visual Culture 10(1), 100–112 (2011)

[16] Lowood, H.: Found Technology: Players as Innovators in the Making of Machinima. Digital Young, Innovation and the Unexpected, 165–196 (2007)

[17] Mcdonough, J., et al.: Preserving Virtual Worlds Final Report (2010)

[18] Ndalianis, A.: Chasing the White Rabbit to Find a White Polar Bear: Lost in Television. In: Pearson, R. (ed.) ReadingLost: Perspectives On A Hit Television Show, pp. 193–310. I.B.Tauris (2009)

[19] Newman, J. (Not) Playing Games: Player-Produced Walkthroughs as Archival Documents of Digital Gameplay. The International Journal of Digital Curation 6(2), 109–127 (2011)

[20] Newman, J.: Best Before: Videogames, Supersession and Obsolescence. Routledge (2012)

[21] Newman, J.: Playing with Videogames. Routledge (2008)

[22] Notes & Queries: Speculative Science (2011), http://www.guardian.co.uk/ notesandqueries/query/0,,-1958,00.html (accessed: July 8, 2013)

[23] Oudshoorn, N., Pinch, T.: Introduction: How Users and Non-Users Matter. In: Oudshoorn, N., Pinch, T. (eds.) How Users Matter The CoConstruction of Users and Technology, pp. 1–25. The MIT Press (2003)

[24] Owens, T.: Digital Cultural Heritage and the Crowd. Curator: The Museum Journal 56(1), 121–130 (2013)

[25] Srinivasan, R., et al.: Digital Museums and Diverse Cultural Knowledges: Moving Past the Traditional Catalog. The Information Society 25(4), 265–278 (2009)

[26] Stuckey, H., Swalwell, M.: Retro-Computing Community Sites and the Museum. In: Agius, H., Angelides, M. (ed.) The Handbook of Digital Games. IEEE/Wiley

[27] Technologizer Forty Years of Lunar Lander (2009), http://technologizer.com/ 2009/07/19/lunar-lander/ (accessed July 9, 2013)

[28] The Way of the Exploding Fist - Comments, http://www.lemon64.com/ ?name=way+of+the+exploding+fist (accessed: August 12, 2012)

The Introduction of Computer and Video Games in Museums – Experiences and Possibilities

Tiia Naskali, Jaakko Suominen, and Petri Saarikoski

University of Turku, Digital Culture, Degree Program of Cultural Production and Landscape Studies, Pori, Finland
{tiia.naskali,jaakko.suominen,petri.saarikoski}@utu.fi

Abstract. Computers and other digital devices have been used for gaming since the 1940s. However, the growth in popularity of commercial videogames has only recently been witnessed in museums. This paper creates an overview of how digital gaming devices have been introduced in museum exhibitions over the last fifteen years. The following discussion will give examples of exhibitions from different countries and provide answers to the following questions: Can digital games and gaming devices be used as promotional gimmicks for attracting new audiences to museums? How can mainframe computers be taken into account in digital game related exhibitions? How has the difference between cultural-historical and art museum contexts affected the methods for introducing digital games? Is there still room for general exhibitions of digital games or should one focus more on special theme exhibitions? How are museum professionals, researchers and computer hobbyists able to collaborate in exhibition projects?

Keywords: Digital games, museums, exhibitions.

1 Introduction – Pulling in with Digital Games

The popularity of digital games has increased during the last few decades. The playing of games plays an important role in many people's lives, and the average age of players is, in many countries, almost 40 years-old. In Finland, for example, the average age of the digital game player was 37 years-old in 2011, while a total of 73 % of Finns played digital games. Further, a total of 54% of the Finnish population reported playing digital games at least once a month (48% of females and 60% of males) (Karvinen & Mäyrä 2011).

Players' earlier experiences in gaming affect the way in which they choose the games that they play, as well as how they experience these games. The playing of games has become a part of players' life histories. Games are linked to changes in players' social relationships, as well as the uses of media and technologies, and their consumption of forms of popular culture. Thus, digital games work as mediators between many different and important sectors of contemporary cultures. Little by little, people are becoming more and more aware of these connections.

A. Tatnall, T. Blyth, and R. Johnson (Eds.): HC 2013, IFIP AICT 416, pp. 226–245, 2013.
© IFIP International Federation for Information Processing 2013

When people recollect their game histories and articulate these recollections, they often express feelings that can be interpreted in the context of nostalgia. At least in certain cases, they long for older games or situations related to the playing of games (Suominen 2008). Even though this nostalgic interpretation and explanation might be quite obvious and even self-evident, it nonetheless provides possibilities, not only for introducing retro or game and historical related consumer products to the market, but also possibly to museums. One way to take advantage of these sentiments is to create types of exhibitions that deal with questions of digital games, such as computer and video games, and consider different gamer generations as target audiences, which would like to replay and re-experience classic games, potentially introduce those games to their children, or without earlier experiences, get to know the history of a phenomenon that is important in their current lives.

A possible starting point for the creation of such an exhibition is the notion that game-related (positive) feelings are often collective, social and personal, as well as being individual at the same time (Suominen 2011a. and also Suominen & Ala-Luopa 2012.). Many players and non-players recognize some game cultural icons such as Pac-Man, Super Mario and other game characters or individual game products. Likewise, they also recognize gaming platforms and technologies such as the Commodore 64 and Sinclair Spectrum home computers, coin-fed machines and home consoles. They might place these gaming icons into a section of a particular era and way of life, and then associate them with a certain phase of their own lives. At the same time, the experiences with an iconic digital character or other forms of game cultures are very personal because people situate the experiences with some particular moments and memories of their own lives. The sociologist Fred Davis (1979, 122–123) has thus divided nostalgia into collective and private.

Even though the collective importance of digital games and their history has emerged somewhere from "the below", from everyday experiences and digital game hobbyists' interest, there is a growing tendency towards institutionalizing their importance. One reason for this is the fact that gamer generations are employed in the workforce and in such positions, they are able to institutionalize something that is important for them. Games and their historical value have indeed been noticed on an institutional level. This can be seen in a growing number of game exhibitions and an interest in games. (Barwick, Dearnley & Muir 2011, 378–380; Saarikoski 2010, 132) Because of popularity, nostalgia and the fact that researchers and heritage institutions have gradually started to take notice games as a part of cultural heritage, it is tempting to use them in exhibition attractions and at least drawing cards, as a means for attracting new visitors to the museums. Even though since the late 1990s some specialised game museums have been established (such as in Berlin, 1997), digital games have more commonly been presented in temporary and, in some cases, traveling exhibitions.

The aim of this paper is to provide an idea about the variety of possibilities for exhibiting digital games in museums. We cannot comprehensively cover every museum exhibition in the world that is related to digital games, but we will nonetheless present examples from different countries and different types of museums. In addition to the review of past exhibitions, we introduce some possibilities for future exhibitions and briefly consider the question of collaboration between different actors for creating better game exhibition experiences.

Fig. 1. Examples of two different museum exhibitions of games: one from the Berlin computer game museum in 2012. Photo: Tiia Naskali.

Fig. 2. And one from Salo Art Museum in 2009. Photo: Petri Saarikoski.

2 The Variety of Game Exhibitions

Digital games have been exhibited in various types of museums, such as in cultural historical museums, art museums and galleries, museums of photography and moving image, and museums of media and communication. (See the table 1)

Table 1. Some examples of game exhibitions from the 1990s to the present

Exhibition	Time	Museum	Permanent/ Temporary/ Traveling	Approach
Videotopia	1996–2011	traveling exhibition (worldwide)	traveling	art/ science/ cultural history
Game On	2002–	traveling exhibition (worldwide)	traveling	cultural history/ art
Level X	4.12.2003– 8.2.2004	Tokyo Metropolitan Museum of Photography, Tokyo, Japan	temporary	one company/ art/ cultural history, focused on the history of Nintendo Famicom console
I am 8-bit	18.4.– 19.5.2005	Gallery Nineteen Eighty Eight, Los Angeles, United States	temporary	art
C:/DOS/RUN – Remembering the 80s Computer	25.8.– 9.10.2005	The Film Archive, Wellington, New Zealand	temporary	art
READY – Commodoren kulta-aika [The Golden Age of Commodore]	9.3.– 28.5.2006	Rupriikki Media Museum, Tampere, Finland	temporary	cultural history/ one platform
Mikrokerhoista koteihin. Satakuntalaisen tietokoneharrastami sen juurilla [From Computer Clubs to Homes]	27.9.– 12.11.2006	Satakunta Museum, Pori, Finland	temporary	cultural history

Table 1. (*continued*)

Videogame Nation	14.5.– 20.9.2009 12.2.– 5.9.2011	The Arts Centre Urbis, Manchester, UK Woodhorn Museum, Northumberland Archives, Ashington, UK	temporary, traveling	cultural history
WoW: Emergent Media Phenomenon	14.6.– 4.10.2009	Laguna Art Museum, California, United States	temporary	art/ focused on cultural products based on World of Warcraft - game
Pelaa! Digitaaliset pelit Pongista Trineen / Taide pelissä [Play! Digital Games from Pong to Trine / Art in Games]	20.11.2009– 31.1.2010	Salo Art Museum, Salo, Finland	temporary	cultural history/ art
Game On 2.0	2010–	traveling exhibition (around the world)	traveling	cultural history/ art
Pongista Pleikkaan [From Pong to PlayStation]	from May 2010 to December 2011 24.4.2013– 26.1.2014	Elektra Sähkömuseo [Museum of Electricity], Hämeenlinna, Finland Museum of Technology, Helsinki, Finland	temporary, traveling	cultural history
Computer Games – The evolution of a medium	21.1.2011–	Computerspiele Museum, Berlin, Germany	permanent	art/ cultural history
Pac-Man – vanhempi kuin Porin taidemuseo - project [Pac-Man - Older than Pori Art Museum]	14.5.2011	Pori Art Museum, Pori Finland	temporary	cultural history/ one game, focused on the Pac-Man -game
SUPER I am 8-bit	11.8.– 10.9.2011	Iam8bit Headquarters, Los Angeles, United States	temporary	art

Table 1. (*continued*)

Game story – A history of video Games	10.11.2011–9.1.2012	Grand Palais Southeast Gallery, Paris, France	temporary	art/ cultural history
Finnish Games Then and Now	5.-10.6. 2012	Rupriikki Media Museum, Tampere, Finland	temporary	cultural history
The Art of Video Games	16.3.2012–	traveling exhibition (United States)	temporary, traveling	art
Game Masters	28.6.–28.10.2012	ACMI (Australian Center for the Moving Image), Melbourne, Australia	temporary, traveling	art/ cultural history
	15.12.2012–28.4.2013	Te Papa, Wellington, New Zealand		
Spacewar! Video Games Blast Off	15.12.2012–3.3.2013	Museum of the Moving Image, New York, United States	temporary	cultural history/ one game, focused on the Spacewar! - game
Applied Design	2.3.2013–20.1.2014	The Museum of Modern Art, New York, United States	temporary	art

Digital games can be related to different kinds of contexts because of their above mentioned versatility. Games are audio-visual products that include music and other sounds, moving images and graphic design, different kinds of narrative and game genres, as well as various user interfaces and national specialities. Games are also closely attached to the hardware they are made for, which distinguish them from movies and many other audio-visual products, which can be copied and played more easily with different platforms. These tangible and intangible features provide multiple – and multimodal – ways for examining games and relating them to different kinds of exhibitions and museums. Games are easy to relate to art, movies, design, and technology and game development. Additionally, they are part of youth culture, popular culture and different kinds of subcultures. (Barwick, Dearnley & Muir 2011, 378–384.) Because of their versatility, it's important to contextualize and present them properly, because otherwise, exhibitions can merely feel like an arcade – both in the meaning of a game centre and their shopping mall-like setting.

Game exhibitions from around the world have attracted many players to see and play games in museums (Suominen 2011b). Interactivity, participation, the possibility to handle objects and play games interests many visitors. It has often been noted that audiences want to do something other than just looking at and reading about things (Taivassalo & Levä 2012, 8 ; Taivassalo 2003, 9–11). In this sense, games are not used as the subjects of exhibitions, but they have in some cases, played an instrumental pedagogical role in museums. Games are hard to explain without the personal experience of playing, and this is the reason why game exhibitions usually provide the possibility to play games with an emulator or with another platform. In some cases, there are also possibilities for playing games on their original digital platforms, which makes the experience more real. (Saarikoski 2010.) However, James Newman (2012) has recently contested this argument and noted that the playing experience, quite obviously, always differs from the original – even if there has been any sort of original playing experience, because games have originally been released for many different platforms and they have been played with various user interfaces e.g. VDUs and so forth.

Despite the fact that a majority of the population plays games, these game and technology related exhibitions have attracted young people, particularly male-visitors, who usually don't visit museums very often. This target group is noticed in museums that design game exhibitions, which has been one of the goals for many exhibitions, for example at *Game On* and the *Pelaa!* exhibition. (Saarikoski 2010, 136) Further, exhibitions about the Commodore 64, *READY – Commodoren kulta-aika* (2006) at the Rupriikki Media Museum, attracted first-time visitors to the museum, and in all likelihood, this example is not unique (Naskali 2012, 73, 89). It is for these reasons that games can be used as promotional or pull in products for attracting new audiences, particularly male-visitors.

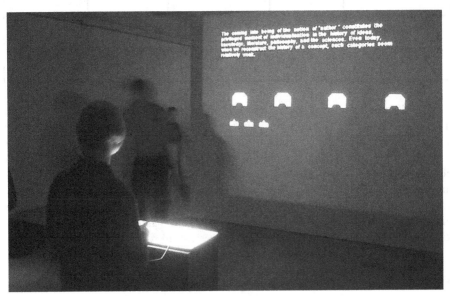

Fig. 3. A photo from the Game On! exhibition in 2003. Photo: Petri Saarikoski.

Nevertheless, digital gaming and digital technologies have their own unique cultural history while at the same time, the cultural heritage of digital technology is constantly emerging (Suominen & Sivula 2013). Games themselves are important and that is why games should not be used only as promotional gimmicks. We claim that it is controversial to only use games as tools for attracting visitors to museums, because, then, the original idea of the exhibition can be neglected and be easily ignored.

3   From Micro to Mainframe and Vice versa – How Older Computer Systems Can Be Taken into Account in Digital Game Related Exhibitions

Exhibitions range from object-oriented to concept-oriented. In object predominated displays, there is no interpretive information involved and the arrangement simply relies on the objects to speak for themselves. A concept-oriented display, on the other hand, relies solely on interpretive information, and there are no objects or, if there are, they are of only minimal importance. Nevertheless, a combination of both is usually the best solution because the exhibition doesn't then include too much text for the audience to read and objects are also properly selected and interpreted. (Dean 1996, 3–5; Heinonen & Lahti 2001.) An exhibition that combines digital games and mainframe computers can operate, for example, with the technological process of computers and its close relationship to game development. In addition, it can focus on specific computers and their purposes, significance and attitudes toward them. Further, these exhibitions are able to touch upon totally different aspects of society and culture.

From a historical point of view, it is always intriguing to examine how games have been developed alongside technology; such as how mainframe machines have turned into smaller personal computers (PCs), game consoles and mobile devices at the same time in which digital games have extended from simple Tennis for Two and Pong types of games in different sorts of directions and forms. This process provides various possibilities for exhibition design. For instance, the exhibition *Spacewar! Video Games Blast Off* at the Museum of the Moving Image in New York (US) was about the Spacewar video game and it included an ia. model of a PDP-1 mainframe computer with a playable simulation of Spacewar! -game (from 1961–62).

Different purposes and attitudes towards computer games reveal social and cultural meanings that computers and gaming have had and still have nowadays. Digital games have been part of computers from the very beginning and they were first made for testing a computer's capacity and training people to use them. Therefore, 50 years ago digital games had, at least on some level, more serious meanings and serves the same purposes that they have now (Saarikoski & Suominen 2009, 18–19; Mäyrä 2008, 52–53).

Fig. 4. Picture from a PDP-1 computer at the Game On! exhibition at the Helsinki City Art Museum 18.9.-14.12.2003. Photo: Petri Saarikoski.

Even though the above mentioned key figures of the history of modern digital games, such as Spacewar!, have already been recognized in museums, there are some more or less blind spots in the history of digital games that museum curators would be able to deal with in new exhibitions. For example, exhibitions could also display early experiences with several games and simulations such as chess, military strategy games, flight simulators or business simulators; and would be able to introduce these in various contexts, not only in relation to the history of gaming, but also in relation to business, transport and military history (on examples of these games in Finnish context, see Saarikoski & Suominen 2009).

Another noteworthy issue is the mainly forgotten double meaning of early computer games. For example, games such as NIM and its variants were used, on one hand, as experiments in the development of computer logics. On the other hand, the games introduced the vast potential of computers and popularized computing technology for public audiences in newspaper and magazine articles and public exhibitions in the 1950s and the 1960s (Paju 2003; Jorgensen 2009. Picture of the Nimrod machine for playing of NIM in the early 1950s, see: http://en.wikipedia.org /wiki/File:Nimrod_in_Computerspielemuseum.jpg). Thus, the introduction of NIM machines in museums would function at the same time as an introduction to the history of computing technologies and games, as well as an introduction to the creation of the history of computing and games.

It is essential to provide the opportunity for the audience to use these objects. The playing of games makes the visit more interesting and experiential, and it further helps them to understand the subject, which might be otherwise hard to comprehend. For instance, it would be of interest to compare different platforms and their capacity with the possibility to play games with them. That could be one way to make the meaning of mainframe computers in the evolution of computing concrete, when the visitors can themselves experience the difference. However, it's almost impossible to play games using the original objects, at least for the long-term, because there are probably only obsolete and fragile games and platforms available. The problem can be solved, however, on a certain level, with emulation. Emulation refers to the capability of a device or software to replicate the behaviour of a different device or software via backwards compatibility, which makes software or hardware able to interpret older versions of data. Another possibility is the migration of data to a new format, which unfortunately doesn't always include the interactive quality of playing game (Guttenbrunner, Becker & Rauber 2010; Barwick, Dearnley & Muir 2011, 382–384).

4   Different Museums, Different Contexts

The museum as an exhibition site makes the subject of the exhibition and displayed objects that are more significant and valuable, essentially because of the institution's primary function to preserve cultural heritage.[1] A digital game exhibition in a museum increases the appreciation and knowledge about games, gaming platforms and their meanings to our culture and society. However, there are obvious differences between museum contexts. An art museum, for example, offers an alternative way to introduce digital games in comparison to the cultural-historical context. Art as a point of view gives the exhibition design various opportunities to approach games and place the objects (and other exhibition material) (Turpeinen 2005, 147–148; Naskali 2012).

Fig. 5. Three different examples of games in art context: one from Ljubljana in 2009. Photo: Jaakko Suominen.

---

[1] ICOMs Museum definition: http://icom.museum/the-vision/museum-definition/

Fig. 6. Example of games in art context from Bratislava in 2009. Photo: Jaakko Suominen.

Fig. 7. Example of games in art context from Finland in 2011. Photo: Petri Saarikoski.

Digital games have inspired many artists and their artwork, and games can be considered as art itself. The relationship between art and digital games can be perceived from at least four different perspectives: 1) games as art, 2) artistic features in games, 3) game related subjects in art and 4) interactivity and other playable features in art. In one way or another, these approaches have been included in several temporary exhibitions such as *The Art of Video Games* (US, 2012-), *C:/DOS/RUN – Remembering the 80s Computer* (New Zealand 2005), *I am 8-bit* (US, exhibitions from 2005-), *Serious Games* (UK 1996-1997), and also in the *Applied Design* exhibition[2] (US, 2013-2014) that approach video games along with other designs from the interaction design point of view (Naskali 2012).

Because of their artistic features, games can inspire patrons to pay more attention to the visual appearance of the exhibition. Digital games, with their audio visual qualities and gameplay remind the visitor, in many ways, of more contemporary and media art because of the soundtracks, music, graphics and lights of the moving image. This can also affect the way in which they are presented in the museum environment. Games can be seen, for example, as artworks but such an approach requires that the exhibition design and object placement needs to support this. It would also be interesting to display the original game and the art piece influenced by the game alongside one another (Naskali 2012).

It is perhaps more straightforward to try alternative presentations in art museums, because of their visual and aesthetic function, and due to the fact that the audience is also used to seeing experimental pieces of art and presentations when they go there. For example, texts don't have to always be on the wall, like in a small *Pac-Man* exhibition in Pori Art Museum (Finland 2011) where the text was printed

Fig. 8. The Pac-Man cube in Pori Art Museum. Photo: Janne Karvinen.

---

[2] This exhibition is produced by The Museum of Modern Art (MoMA), which has started to collect games for their collection. http://www.moma.org/explore/ inside_out/2012/11/29/video-games-14-in-the-collection- for-starters/

in the cube[3]. This idea got its inspiration from an art exhibition design and the art museum that provided the environment without walls. Otherwise, in this case, the exhibition approach was mainly cultural-historical. Games could also elicit questions from the audience, for example about the artistic qualities of digital games, instead of placing information, that they have already interpreted, onto the wall (Turpeinen 2005, 189–191; Naskali 2012, 85).

A game exhibition that introduces the subject from a cultural-historical point of view usually provides a history of platforms, games and gaming with their broader meanings and related phenomena. Exhibitions are usually about one or a few platforms and/or games, or it can provide a larger holistic story about digital games. (Saarikoski 2010, 134–136). It is very common, however, to combine both art and cultural historical approaches in game exhibitions like in the following exhibitions: *Computer Games – The evolution of a medium* in Computerspiele Museum (Germany, 2011-), *Game On* (traveling exhibition from 2002-, also *Game On 2.0* from 2010-), *Game Story – A History of Video Games* (France 2011-2012), and the smaller and first of this kind of exhibition in Finland, *Pelaa! exhibition* (Finland, 2009–2010).

Fig. 9. A Pac-Man in Flesh game performance in Pori Art Museum. Photo: Petri Saarikoski.

---

[3]   The audience was free to take the cube in their hands and to read the text in any order that they wanted. It also made it easier to notice all kinds of audiences because the cube was light and movable and it could be red from the distance that felt comfortable (Naskali 2012).

The museum is able to provide frames for the temporary exhibition approach and display, but this can also be simply background information. That means that in the exhibition displays in art museums or cultural historical museums, the approaches do not have to be, and do not have to automatically be the same. Nevertheless, the museum type can still inspire the exhibition design on a new level and bring something new to the way of introducing games.

5   From Generalism to Specialization

Although there is no established tradition for designing game exhibitions, partly because of their novelty in a museum environment, there are some features that seem to be part of many game exhibitions. According to Petri Saarikoski, who has participated in several game exhibition projects, like the *Pelaa!* exhibition in Finland, these exhibitions usually consist of old and new games, part of which are set aside in vitrines and part of which are still playable. In addition, there are different kinds of by-products, like magazines, controllers and toys. There can also be a screen display on the wall that presents game aesthetics, gameplay, designer interviews, or a space where visitors can listen to game music or see documentations about games. The approach usually provides information about the history of games, game cultures and their meanings (from a wider or more detailed perspective, and the texts are thus placed on the walls). An exhibition usually provides lectures for the audience and game demonstrations. (Saarikoski 2010, 134) Even if there is nothing wrong with this type of display, it can be considered as "already seen", if there are only small variations.

Fig. 10. An example of a national exhibition of games and game industry: Finnish games then and now, Tampere 2012. Photo: Taru Muhonen.

It is challenging to design exhibitions on the history of games for different kinds of audiences and make the subject understandable and interesting. It is problematic, in many situations, to ignore the changes in the digital gaming and cultural and historical contexts, but it is further troublesome if these changes are presented mechanically and chronologically. General exhibitions are able to offer a great overview of games and game cultures and related phenomena, but they can also be too generic. (Saarikoski 2010, 137) Whereas special theme exhibitions, like for example the *Game Masters* exhibition in ACMI (Australian Centre for the Moving Image) and Te Papa (New Zealand's national museum), which is about the most influential game designers, can provide more details and a more inclusive experience to the audience than a general exhibition that provides, in the worst-case scenario, only a little information about this and that.

Special themes in exhibition design can inspire people to find and provide new approaches to the subject, such as interactivity in subcultures, like demoscene[4] and retrogaming[5], different types of combinations of art and games (as we mentioned in the previously section), platform "wars" and user group rivalries, a comprehensive review of particular games or platforms or so forth. The history of games can be explored, for example, from art history, the software and hardware industry, technology, social history, knowledge and the historiography of games' point of view (Mäyrä 2008, 30–32). Although the possibility to play games is significant (in game exhibitions), because the audience can re-memorize and experience these games and have social interaction with other visitors and their experience (Saarikoski 2010, 136–137). Sociability is perhaps a more important point of view than some sort of nostalgic return to some type of authentic and original gaming experience.

It appears that the interest in general exhibitions has already started to decrease and more original and special theme exhibitions have become popular, particularly if we look at the game exhibitions that have been displayed lately. Many people have already seen the general version since game exhibitions have been increasingly displayed worldwide from the beginning of the 21st century. At the same time, people who design these exhibitions, are getting more experience and new ideas about how to display games. This will probably influence future game exhibition design

---

[4] A demo is a short, most often non-interactive program that displays audio-visual content in real-time. Demoscene or the scene is a worldwide community of hobbyist interested in computer demos (Reunanen 2010,1).

[5] Retro gaming is very popular at the present. "Retrogamers" or hobbyists respect old game cultures and collect and play them with the original hardware, if possible, or with new hardware via emulators. Retrogaming, as a phenomenon, tells about how older game cultures have become part of today's game culture. It can be seen, for example, in remix versions of old game music and sounds, using old game aesthetics in different kind of products like toys and clothes, and in different phenomena. The phenomenon can inspire people to find interesting games, platforms, controllers and other material for the exhibition design and approaches to the subject. Together with the fact that gaming has become part of our everyday life, retro gaming cultures provides one possible frame for exhibition design that operates with time (Suominen 2008; Saarikoski 2010).

approaches and the objects that they display. For example, at some point, it appears that the dominance of video games and games cultures of the 1970s, 1980s and the early 1990s is decreasing in exhibitions, while newer games and game cultures begin to interest the public more, in the process where retrogaming and nostalgic focus transfers on new devices, applications and phenomena. In addition, exhibition related happenings and events will probably become diverse and more interactive (Saarikoski 2010, 136–137; Naskali 2012, 87), They can consist of game design workshops, eSport events, artistic performances, game music concerts and workshops, as well as collector's markets etc.

6   Possibilities for Collaboration

It would be ideal if museum professionals, researchers and computer hobbyist and professionals would be able to collaborate in game exhibition projects. In many projects, like *Game On* and all exhibition projects in Finland, this have already been accomplished. This type of collaboration has many benefits. It brings about better exhibitions, increases value and information about collections, helps to maintain museum objects, produces wider historical awareness amongst computer professionals, hobbyists, users and so forth.

A simple museum object, without text, does not communicate with the general audience very well, except with professionals (af. Hällström 2011, 82–83). An object requires interpretation that makes it part of the collection or exhibition theme (Heinonen & Lahti 2001, 152–153). Museum professionals have specialised knowledge about different audiences, museum environments and techniques, and they know how to execute functional and impressive exhibitions. They also have experience with preserving different kinds of objects (even if they are not necessary that familiar with preserving digital content such as games). Researchers can bring along their knowledge on the history of games, different kinds of game cultures and digital cultures to the game exhibition creation process. Together with museum professionals, they are able to make the exhibition narrative, select topics and produce content for different audiences. That turns the exhibition into more than just a general display with a gaming room. That is what makes the exhibition relevant.

Hobbyists and game collectors are, in many ways, important partners in exhibition projects. In Finland for instance, they are the only ones who have, to date, preserved old games, gaming devices and other related objects. The most important group of hobbyists in Finland is Pelikonepeijoonit (The Arctic Computer and Console Museum), which serves game software and keeps games functional (Barwick, Dearnley, & Muir 2011, 375–376). They are enthusiastic, not only about the subject, but also about their memories, feelings and personal aspects, which can also be used in exhibition design, in addition to the collective perspective. That can make the subject more approachable (Newman & Simmons 2009, 1–6). Hobbyists are also able to organize various workshops and game demonstrations.

Fig. 11. A group of organizers of Pelaa! exhibition: Mikko Heinonen from Pelikonepeijoonit (The Arctic Computer and Console Museum), Leena Järvelä from Salo Museum of Industrial and Cultural Heritage SAMU, Juha Köönikkä, Petri Saarikoski and Jaakko Suominen from the University of Turku. Photo: Marjatta Hietanen.

In addition, it would be important to collaborate more with game companies in exhibition projects, partly because of the legal issues present in many countries. Further, many old games are impossible to play nowadays. Emulation of the original hardware requires permission from the hardware manufacturer and transferring the game to different media platforms requires the approval of all rights-holders involved in the game. Another solution is to adapt copyright laws in order to make video game preservation easier (Guttenbrunner, Becker & Rauber 2010, 75; Naskali 2012, 83).

7   Conclusion

In this paper, we have provided an overview of some aspects of exhibiting digital games in museums. We have argued that due to games' general increased importance, they have to be taken into account more carefully in museums as well. Even though there has been a plethora of game exhibition projects, particularly over the last 15 years, the tendency in the future is to put more emphasis on permanent collections, as well as special thematic exhibitions instead of general overviews of digital games cultures.

One has to obviously, always consider several key aspects: what is the museum context for the exhibition (what type of museum: cultural historical museum, art museum, museum of science and technology, museum of communication, games, computers etc.), what is the role of game in its in entirety (main topic, supporting role, or an instrumental role in introducing something else), what is the context of the introduction of games (popular cultural, artistic, everyday life, certain era, military, technological, design, innovation process etc.), how to use freshly multimodal and interactive affordances of games, and naturally, ponder the question, who is the audience?

In this paper, we have also argued that the collaboration between museum professionals, academic researchers and computer professionals and hobbyists is one of the most important key factors for creating the best possible way for making an exhibit of digital games.

Acknowledgements. We would like to thank the Kone Foundation for funding the Kotitietokoneiden aika ja teknologisen harrastuskulttuurin perintö (The Era of Home Computers and the Heritage of Technological Hobbyist Culture) research project.

Exhibitions

1. Applied Design: http://www.moma.org/visit/calendar/exhibitions/1353. Accessed 16 July 2013.
2. The Art of Video Games: http://americanart.si.edu/exhibitions/archive/2012/games/. Accessed 16 July 2013.
3. C:/DOS/RUN – Remembering the 80s Computer:
   http://www.filmarchive.org.nz/google-search?sp-q=C%3A%2FDOS%2FRUN+Remembering+the+80s+Computer. Accessed 16 July 2013.
4. Computer Games – The evolution of a medium:
   http://www.computerspielemuseum.de/. Accessed 16 July 2013.
5. Finnish Games Then and Now: http://www.uta.fi/english/news/item.html?id=74723. Accessed 16 July 2013.
6. Game Masters Exhibition: http://gamemasters.acmi.net.au/#!/home/. Accessed 16 July 2013.
7. Game On, Game On 2.0: http://www.barbican.org.uk/bie/game-on. Accessed 16 July 2013.
8. Game Story – A History of Video Games: http://www.grandpalais.fr/en/event/game-story-history-video-games-grand-palais-southeast-gallery. Accessed 16 July 2013.
9. I am 8-bit, SUPER I am 8-bit: http://iam8bit.com/. Accessed 16 July 2013.
10. Pac-Man - vanhempi kuin Porin taidemuseo [Pac-Man - Older than Pori Art Museum]: http://www.doria.fi/bitstream/handle/10024/86817/gradu2012naskali.pdf?sequence=1. Accessed 16 July 2013.
11. Pelaa! [Play!] – game and art exhibition: http://www.pelitutkimus.fi/vuosikirja2010/ptvk2010-12.pdf. Accessed 16 July 2013.
12. Pongista Pleikkaan [From Pong to PlayStation]: http://www.elektra.fi/pages/pp.html, http://www.tekniikanmuseo.fi/pongistapleikkaan.html. Accessed 16 July 2013.
13. Spacewar! Video Game Blast Off: http://www.movingimage.us/exhibitions/2012/12/15/detail/spacewar-video-games-blast-off/. Accessed 16 July 2013.

14. READY – Commodoren kulta-aika [The Golden Age of Commodore]: http://www.facebook.com/media/set/?set=a.119949721351056.194 87.119920721353956&type=3. Accessed 16 July 2013.
15. Serious Games: http://www.berylgraham.com/serious/. Accessed 16 July 2013.
16. Videogame Nation: http://www.videogamenation.net/Home.html. Accessed 16 July 2013.
17. Videotopia: http://www.videotopia.com/. Accessed 16 July 2013.
18. WoW: Emergent Media Phenomenon: http://lagunaartmuseum.org/wow-emergent-media-phenomenon/. Accessed 16 July 2013.

References

1. Barwick, J., Dearnley, J., Muir, A.: Playing Games with Cultural Heritage: A Comparative Case Study Analysis of the Current Status of Digital Game Preservation. Games and Culture 6(4), 373–390 (2011), http://gac.sagepub.com/content/6/4/373. full.pdf+html (accessed July 16, 2013)
2. Davis, F.: Yearning for Yesterday. A Sociology of Nostalgia. The Free Press, New York (1979)
3. Dean, D.: Museum Exhibition – Theory and Practice. Routledge, London (1996)
4. Guttenbrunner, M., Becker, C., Rauber, A.: Keeping the Game Alive: Evaluating Strategies for the Preservation of Console Video Games. The International Journal of Digital Curation 5(1) (2010)
5. Heinonen, J., Lahti, M.: Museologian perusteet. Suomen museoliitto, Helsinki (2001)
6. Hällströmaf, J.af.: Näyttelyviestintä. Suomen museoliitto, Helsinki (2011)
7. ICOM (International Council of Museums), Museum definition: http://icom.museu/the-vision/museum-definition/
8. Jorgensen, A.H.: Context and Driving Forces in the Development of the Early Computer Game Nimbi. IEEE Annals of the History of Computing 31(3), 44–53 (2009)
9. Karvinen, J., Mäyrä, F.: Pelaajabarometri 2011: Pelaamisen muutos. Informaatiotutkimuksen ja Interaktiivisen median laitos/yksikkö -TRIM: Research Reports 6. Tampereen yliopisto, Tampere (2011), http://urn.fi/urn:isbn:978-951-44-8567-1 (accessed July 16, 2013)
10. The Museum of Modern Art (MoMA), video game collection. Antonelli, P.: Video Games – 14 in the Collection, for Starters. Inside/Out, A MoMA/MoMA PS1 Blog (2012), http://www.moma.org/explore/inside_out/2012/11/29/video-games-14-in-the-collection-for-starters/ (accessed July 16, 2013)
11. Mäyrä, F.: An Introduction to Game Studies. Games as Culture. Sage Publications, London (2008)
12. Naskali, T.: Digitaaliset pelit museossa – kokemuksia ja havaintoja näyttelyjen suunnittelusta ja toteutuksesta. Digitaalisen kulttuurin pro gradu (2012), http://www.doria.fi/bitstream/handle/10024/86817/gradu2012na skali.pdf?sequence=1 (accessed July 16, 2013)
13. Newman, J.: Best before: Videogames, supersession and obsolescence. Routledge, Milton Park (2012)
14. Newman, J., Simmons, I.: Make Videogames History: Game preservation and The National Videogame Archive. DiGRA (2009), http://www.digra.org/dl/db/09287.32127.pdf (accessed July 16, 2013)
15. Paju, P.: Nim-pelin rakentaminen ja käyttö Suomessa. Wider Screen 2003/2-3 Digitaaliset pelit ja elokuva (2003), http://www.widerscreen.fi/2003-2-3/huvia-hyodyn-avuksi-jo-1950-luvulla/ (accessed July 16, 2013)

16. Reunanen, M.: Computer Demos—What Makes Them Tick? Licentiate Thesis. Aalto University, School of Science and Technology, Faculty of Information and Natural Sciences Department of Media Technology (2010), https://aaltodoc.aalto.fi/handle/123456789/3365 (accessed July 16, 2013)
17. Saarikoski, P.: Peleistä taiteeksi: digitaaliset pelit taidemuseossa – Salon taidemuseon Pelaa! -näyttely 2009. In: Suominen, J., Koskimaa, R., Mäyrä, F., Sotamaa, O. (eds.) Pelitutkimuksen vuosikirja (2010), http://www.pelitutkimus.fi/vuosikirja2010/ptvk2010-12.pdf (accessed July 16, 2013)
18. Saarikoski, P., Suominen, J.: Pelinautintoja, ohjelmointiharrastusta ja liiketoimintaa - Tietokoneharrastuksen ja peliteollisuuden suhde Suomessa toisen maailmansodan jälkeen. In: Suominen, J., Koskimaa, R., Mäyrä, F., Sotamaa, O. (eds.) Pelitutkimuksen Vuosikirja (2009), http://www.pelitutkimus.fi/wp-content/uploads/2009/08/ptvk2009-02.pdf (accessed July 16, 2013)
19. Suominen, J.: The Past as the Future. Nostalgia and Retrogaming in Digital Culture. Fibreculture (11) (digital arts and culture conference (perth) issue) (2008), http://eleven.fibreculturejournal.org/fcj-075-the-past-as-the-future-nostalgia-and-retrogaming-in-digital-culture/ (accessed July 16, 2013)
20. Suominen, J.: Pac-Man kaihon kohteena ja kokeilujen välineenä. Wider Screen 1-2/2011 (2011), http://www.widerscreen.fi/2011-1-2/pac-man-kaihon-kohteena-ja-kokeilujen-valineena/ (accessed July 16, 2013)
21. Suominen, J.: Retropelaamista tutkimassa – välitilinpäätös. In: Suominen, J., Koskimaa, R., Mäyrä, F., Sotamaa, O., Turtiainen, R. (eds.) Pelitutkimuksen Vuosikirja (2011), http://www.pelitutkimus.fi/vuosikirja2011/ptvk2011-08.pdf (accessed July 16, 2013)
22. Suominen, J., Ala-Luopa, S.: Playing with Pac-Man: A Life and Metamorphosis of a Game Cultural Icon, 1980-2011. In: Wimmer, J., Mitgutsch, K., Rosenstingl, H. (eds.) Applied Playfullness. Proceedings of the Vienna Games Conference 2011: Future and Reality of Gaming, pp. 165–176. Braumüller Verlag, Vienna (2012)
23. Suominen, J., Sivula, A.: Gaming Legacy? Four Approaches to the Relation between Cultural Heritage and Digital Technology. ACM Journal of Computing and Cultural Heritage: Serious Games for Cultural Heritage 6(3) (July 2013)
24. Taivassalo, E.-L.: Museokävijä – Valtakunnallinen museoiden kävijätutkimus 2003. Helsinki, Suomen museoliitto, Gummerus (2003)
25. Taivassalo, E-L., Levä, K.: Museokävijä 2011. Suomen Museoliiton Julkaisuja 62 (2012)

Part VIII

The Importance and Challenges of Working Installations

Computer Conservation Society (CCS) – Its Story and Experience

Roger Johnson

Birkbeck University of London, Dept. of Computer Science, UK
r.johnson@bcs.org.uk

Abstract. There were three main motivational drivers for founding the Computer Conservation Society as a joint co-operative venture of the Science Museum and the British Computer Society. These were the:

- restoration to working order of historic computing machines for public display;
- provision of an organisational context for the expertise of computer designers and practitioners with unique knowledge of historic machines;
- capture, documentation and preservation of computing knowhow.

Computer restoration, public display, and the notion of a 'club' were essential features of the original conception. Preservation and social utility were inseparably joined from the start. This paper reviews nearly 25 years of activity in pursuit of these aims.

Keywords: Computer Conservation Society, Resurrection, computer restoration.

1 Introduction

This paper recounts briefly the founding of the Computer Conservation Society (CCS) and the activities that have developed over the quarter of a century since then. The paper lists the projects that the CCS has undertaken and a number of these are described in detail in other papers submitted to this book. The paper concludes by looking at the key factors in making the CCS the world's largest computer history society and the leading source of expertise in the restoration of historic computers and the construction of replicas.

2 Foundation

The Computer Conservation Society (CCS) was founded in 1989. To explain why the CCS came to be founded at that time there is no better source than a CCS promotional leaflet prepared by Chris Burton [1].

> *It was a time when the computer industry had existed for about half a century, and when many people had spent a professional lifetime in the industry. The industry had matured, but was still poised for ever greater technological and social changes as it had been from its beginnings in the 1940s. It was time to take stock and reflect on the extraordinary*

A. Tatnall, T. Blyth, and R. Johnson (Eds.): HC 2013, IFIP AICT 416, pp. 249–257, 2013.

developments to date, and in particular, to be concerned that many of the pioneering people and hardware and software were fast disappearing.

At the same time, many computer professionals were finding themselves retired or otherwise at the end of direct involvement in the industry, yet with energy to spare and interest in their earlier systems. Some had approached the Science Museum, for example, asking whether their abilities and interests could be harnessed to helping to preserve old systems. This coincided with a perception by the Museum that it had artefacts, but limited expertise to do other than prevent deterioration – in particular it was not able to present their technological and historical significance.

Thus the Society came into existence as a way of structuring and channelling these complementary interests.

The story of how it was founded is recorded in two early issues of *Resurrection* [2], the bulletin of the CCS. Nick Enticknap, the first Editor of Resurrection, recounts in the first issue of Resurrection that the CCS *"is the brainchild of Doron Swade, Curator of Computing at the Science Museum"* [3]. In Issue 7, Doron Swade himself recounts that:

The origins of the Society are within easy recall. As curator of computing I paid innumerable site visits in response to offers of obsolete equipment from potential donors faced with having to dispose of cherished machines. Visiting these doomed equipments and engaging with their minders made it evident that there was expertise, goodwill and enthusiasm that lacked organised expression. The Computer Conservation Society was conceived to provide a social and organisational focus for this community of isolated practitioners who wished to share, contribute, impart knowledge and skill, or simply participate in a continuing way in an activity that was meaningful to them. [4]

The two people he met at the British Computer Society were its Technical Vice-President, Roger Johnson, the author of this paper, and Tony Sale, the BCS' Technical Director. Tony Sale was an extraordinary "electronics polymath" but not a public personality at that time. He had served in the Royal Air Force working on radar, the UK security service MI5 specialising in wireless interception and run a computer bureau and software house. Roger Johnson was a computer science academic with a lifelong love of industrial archaeology. Tony Sale and the author were immediate converts to the cause and swiftly organised the establishment of the Computer Conservation Society as a Specialist Group (a special interest group) of the BCS. As a Specialist Group of the British Computer Society, it has benefited from BCS support, as well as from the status accorded by the Royal Charter. The association with the Science Museum provides access to the Museum's inventoried artefacts, as well as the generous provision of facilities for our meetings. In consequence, the CCS describes itself as being founded as a co-operative venture between the Science Museum and the BCS.

These formalities were quickly followed by the creation of an initial committee comprising Doron Swade, Tony Sale and the author together with two BCS Past

Presidents who were both computer pioneers. The first public meeting attracted 67 people. Most of the major threads of the CCS' activities were present almost from the beginning. At the first meeting five working parties were created each focussed on different pieces of computing equipment. A lecture programme was inaugurated and shortly afterwards the first issue of the CCS bulletin called *Resurrection* appeared.

From the beginning, the Society was fortunate in attracting a number of pioneers of the industry, many of whom subsequently served as officers, committee members or project team members. The total membership is presently about seven hundred, distributed all over the UK and the world, and of this number about 15% are active and attend meetings etc.

In 1993, in recognition of the important early work done in the Manchester and north-west Midlands area, the North West Group of the CCS was created, based in Manchester, and with a strong connection with the Manchester Museum of Science and Industry. This group has its own officers and committee and runs a thriving local series of meetings and other work.

3   Guiding Principles

Membership of the CCS has always been open to anyone who is interested in the history of computing whether or not they are a member of BCS [5]. There is no qualification required other than an expression of that interest! Furthermore, there is no membership fee, though members receive an annual invitation to make voluntary donations to the "rescue fund" which is used to support CCS projects when urgent expenditure has to be incurred, for example to safeguard an early computer. As mentioned, the Society benefits from support provided by the museums and the BCS. In addition, the CCS gratefully acknowledges that support, financial and in kind, for projects from a number of corporate bodies.

Another important policy that has emerged is that the CCS should not own any computers. A decision was made in the early days that the CCS would not acquire any computers or peripheral equipment. It was clear to the committee that computers should be owned by museums and the role of the CCS was to assist museums in restoring computers to a suitable condition for display or, when appropriate, for demonstration and constructing replicas. The rationale was based on several considerations. Firstly, the CCS was a group of volunteers with no legal status beyond that provided by the BCS and no long term guarantee of existence and hence no ability to own assets for the long term. Secondly the CCS wanted to work with any museum which had computing equipment and having our own equipment could potentially give rise to conflicts of interest. The one exception to the policy, for historic reasons, is the Bombe Rebuild which is formally owned by the BCS (as the CCS parent body) and is the subject of a long term agreement with Bletchley Park for its display there. Numerous minor issues over the years, such as securing public liability and other insurance, illustrate how many hours of volunteer time can be consumed on necessary but unrewarding matters. These are much better left to the professional staff of museums!

4   Bletchley Park

The CCS has always had strong links with Bletchley Park. Tony Sale led the early attempts to save it for the nation when it was threatened with demolition. The links continued as Tony built his replica of Colossus and John Harper and his team build the Bombe replica. As the governance of Bletchley Park evolved the links changed but the CCS remained firmly committed to ensuring that these two iconic replicas continue to be demonstrated as a tribute to the thousands who worked at Bletchley Park during the war.

Around these two projects various other projects sprang up. As the number of projects grew the work has been incorporated into The National Museum of Computing (TNMoC) [6]. This is a legally distinct body from the Bletchley Park Trust although they work closely together to provide an integrated attraction for visitors. TNMoC now has the largest collection of functional historic computers in Europe, many of which have been restored or built as CCS projects.

5   Other Achievements

Following his death in 2011, the CCS was very pleased to establish, with support from Google, the Tony Sale Award [7] to recognise singular engineering achievements in the area of computer conservation achievements in the growing area of computer conservation. The first Award was presented at a ceremony held October 2011. The winning project is the Ferranti Mark 1 LoveLetters, reconstruction of software for text generation submitted by Dr David Link from Cologne.

In 2012 four members of the CCS co-authored a book entitled *Turing and his Contemporaries* [8] as part of the celebrations of the centenary of Alan Turing's birth. All the proceeds from the book go to the CCS Rescue Fund and so far amount to around £4,000.

6   Working Parties

From its creation the most visible part of the CCS' work has been its support for the restoration of computers and their subsequent demonstration and its support for groups wishing to build replicas. Details of all the current Working Parties are listed on the CCS website at http://www.computerconservationsociety.org/wg.htm. Current projects are:

Manchester Baby	The project built, and now demonstrates and maintains a replica of the Small-Scale Experimental Machine (SSEM) - the world's first computer.	Museum of Science and Industry, Manchester
Pegasus	The Pegasus computer on display at the Science Museum was, for many years, the oldest extant working electronic computer in the world. Members of the CCS maintain and operate the Pegasus – and expect to resume regular fortnightly at the museum in the near future.	Science Museum, London

Bombe Rebuild	The rebuilt machine is now operational and can be seen at Bletchley Park.	Bletchley Park
ICT 1301	An original 1961 machine is being brought back to life. It has recently been moved into store with help from the CCS Rescue Fund from private premises in Kent.	National Museum of Computing, Bletchley Park (currently in store off-site)
Elliott 401	The CCS is restoring an Elliott 401 computer. This machine is not available to be seen by the general public at the moment.	Science Museum, London (currently in store)
Elliott	This team is responsible for a collection of Elliott 803, 903 and 905 computers. The TNMOC 803 and 903 machines can be seen working most weekends.	National Museum of Computing, Bletchley Park
DEC	The DEC project team is currently restoring a desktop 'straight' PDP8, the PDP11 Blacknest system, and demonstrates the last remaining PDP11 based air traffic control system from LATCC, West Drayton.	National Museum of Computing, Bletchley Park
Hartree Analyser	The project is restoring the pre-World War II differential analyser to demonstration condition.	Museum of Science and Industry, Manchester
Harwell Computer (also known as the WITCH computer)	This project team has successfully restored the original Harwell Computer to working order making it the world's oldest working computer. The team is now maintaining it for demonstration.	National Museum of Computing, Bletchley Park
ICL 2966	This project team is restoring an ICL 2966 mainframe to demonstration condition.	National Museum of Computing, Bletchley Park
EDSAC replica	This is latest project and is building a replica of the original Cambridge University EDSAC computer.	National Museum of Computing, Bletchley Park
Analytical Engine	This project aims to fulfil Charles Babbage's plans by constructing his Analytical Engine.	
Software Conservation	The mission is the preservation of historic software in machine readable form, ideally along with execution capability. The focus is on long-term preservation rather than special effects on a PC.	
Our Computer Heritage	This is a substantial online database which collects and disseminates information on all British manufactured computers, currently built up to 1965.	www.ourcomputerheritage.org

7   Lecture and Seminar Programme

Each year the CCS organises a series of monthly lectures from the autumn until early summer at the Science Museum. The lectures cover a wide range of topics covering hardware, systems software and applications. Every lecture has been recorded initially in audio and more recently on video.

There is a separate programme of lectures in the North West Group run at the Museum of Science and Industry in Manchester.

8   "Resurrection"

The CCS's quarterly bulletin sent free to all members funded from an annual BCS grant. It is a unique chronicle of the CCS' progress both of, and by, computer pioneers and practitioners providing members with news, articles, transcripts of lectures and other material in a 32-page A5 format. All issues of *Resurrection* are available online [9].

9   Two Key Challenges

9.1   Sustaining the Skills for the Future

Not surprisingly from the beginning, the CCS has repeatedly asked itself what it was doing and how it was doing it. In the first issue of *Resurrection,* Doron Swade wrote an article [10] discussing how the activities of the CCS and Science Museum "overlap, complement and extend". The close ties with the Science Museum have always ensured that CCS volunteers are well versed in curatorial standards before they are allowed to work on computers in the care of any museum. This has proved essential in building lasting relationships between the CCS and a range of museums.

One of the key drivers for the Science Museum was the realisation that museum staff faced a problem an order of magnitude greater in restoring a computer to demonstration condition compared to that of staff working on automotive or steam powered exhibits. Beginning in 1989 meant that for almost all the restored machines, volunteers could be found with experience of building or maintaining the computers. The CCS has concerned itself for some time about how to ensure that these skills are passed on to another generation of volunteers. Initial experience with students proved disappointing as the student population turns over quickly and once graduated most move away and take on major commitments. Consequently it appears likely that volunteers may be drawn from all age groups but that many, just because of having the time available, may be retired.

In reflecting on this in the specific context of and the demonstrations of the Science Museum Pegasus, discussions within the museum have identified three activities for volunteers, each of which requires different expertise and training. The three roles are, firstly, interpretation carried out by someone trained to explain the artefact to a group of visitors, secondly, demonstrators who have been trained to run demonstrations of the machine to accompany the interpreter's talk and finally a systems engineer who has the skills to maintain the computer including diagnosing and rectifying faults. While there is no reason why one person should not acquire the skills to fulfil all three roles, experience suggests that different personalities and backgrounds often lead to one role rather the others.

9.2   Connecting with Visitors

Although one of the first working parties was devoted to software preservation the awareness of the importance of this activity has steadily grown over the years. Naturally early work concentrated on restoring early computers to working condition. However old machines returned to running order and were placed on display the challenge arose of how to construct a meaningful narrative for the visitor. In a recent issue of *Resurrection,* Kevin Murrell discusses the issue of what software to run [11]. A computer is a complex artefact often running in a specialised application domain. Added to this must be added the differing interests of visitors from those who take a casual look, those who will stay for a short demo and finally those who are seeking an in depth explanation. This is a routine challenge for a museum but for many industrial archaeological artefacts the public have significant prior knowledge. However computers have three distinct aspects – hardware, systems software and an application domain. As Kevin notes in the paper, the opportunity to obtain a computer from a visually exciting and accessible application with its supporting software and data is likely to be very rare. However the air traffic control system on display at the National Museum of Computing ticks all the boxes. However it is clear that for the future compelling displays are important to providing visitors with a strong narrative.

It follows from Kevin's observations that many visitors seeing a visually attractive demonstration are primarily focussed on the output devices and the hardware and system software are largely invisible. Consequently it can be argued that many visitors are indifferent to whether the output is being produced by historic hardware, a replica or software emulation. Indeed one of the benefits of computing is that it is possible to write software today to demonstrate the capabilities of a historic computer. The blending of original, replica and emulated machines with original and modern software offers many creative challenges for the designers of future computing exhibits in our museums.

10   Factors for the CCS' Success

As it approaches its 25th anniversary, the CCS remains a cheerful, energetic and slightly renegade outfit. Its committees and working parties are populated by passionate volunteers dedicated to preserving computing history. So what are the key factors in its success?

    a. **IT Industry Legacy** – The UK had a multiplicity of hardware manufacturers for the first 20 years of the computer industry. This produced a range of computers around which to work. In turn this led to skilled engineers experienced in supporting these machines who were enthusiastic in later life to resume working with their early computers.

b. **Available artefacts** – Museums in the UK, supplemented by companies and individuals, retained numerous early computers and years later as opportunity offered were keen to see them displayed and when appropriate restored to demonstration condition. The museums became keen to have examples of computers on display and sometimes being demonstrated.

c. **Institutional support** – Restoring computers or building replicas needs a significant amount of secure space. Initially the Science Museum provided space to restore their Pegasus until it was placed on display. They also provide space today in their London store for work on the Elliott 401. Without such space the work would not be possible. CCS has also been grateful to both the University of Manchester for providing space for the building of the Manchester Baby replica and subsequently to the Museum of Science and Industry for displaying it prominently in their main entrance and also for supporting other restoration work in Manchester. Finally the emergence of the National Museum of Computing located at Bletchley Park provides substantial display space to display historic artefacts and also work space for current projects.

All these centres enable volunteers to support one another and to share expertise which is vital to sustaining volunteer communities. They foster a vital "club" spirit for the volunteers.

Finally the support of the BCS has been important funding in supporting its activities each year. The BCS provides a small operating grant and also meets the significant costs of producing and distributing *Resurrection*. They also provide free access to substantial administrative facilities including a membership database, use of their website and email facilities.

11   Future

Sir Maurice Wilkes remarked at an early meeting that he thought the CCS would last about two years and then run out of things to do. Happily Sir Maurice lived long enough to be able to enjoy reminding us of this comment and his pleasure at attending lectures on a growing range of new topics each year.

In many ways this is mirrored in the evolution of the CCS' published Aims. The original version from 1989 was to:

- promote the conservation of historic computers,
- develop awareness of the importance of historic computers, and
- encourage research on historic computers.

Today, while the first two aims remain essentially the same while the third aim has been supplemented and expanded reflecting the way the CCS' understanding of its role has evolved to:

- promote the conservation of historic computers and to identify existing computers which may need to be archived in the future,
- develop awareness of the importance of historic computers,
- develop expertise in the conservation and restoration of historic computers,
- represent the interests of Computer Conservation Society members with other bodies,
- promote the study of historic computers, their use and the history of the computer industry,
- publish information of relevance to these objectives for the information of Computer Conservation Society members and the wider public.

There are always more computers and their applications to display. Today's systems are tomorrow's history! The understanding which the CCS volunteers have developed in demonstrating working computer systems has highlighted the importance of identifying examples of contemporary systems for museums to acquire. This has to involve acquiring as much of the working environment, application software and peripherals as well as the core system, so as to provide accessible exhibits for museum visitors.

Public interest in the development of information technology continues to grow and the CCS is committed within its resources to responding to that interest by acquiring and disseminating information about information technology.

Through their work the CCS membership promotes awareness of the unique transformative power of IT upon civil society worldwide both as a tribute to those who have gone before and to fire the imaginations of those who will come after us.

Acknowledgments. I would like to thank colleagues in the BCS Computer Conservation Society for their help in preparing this paper. However, the opinions in this paper are those of the author and this is not an official CCS paper. Any errors are solely the fault of the author.

References

1. The Computer Conservation Society. Promotional leaflet prepared by Chris Burton, Private correspondence with author (2003)
2. Resurrection - all issues available online at,
   http://www.computerconservationsociety.org/resurrection.htm
3. Enticknap, N.: Computer Conservation Society – birth. Resurrection 1(1), 5 (1990)
4. Swade, D.: The CCS and the Science Museum – what now? Resurrection (7), 7 (1993)
5. CCS Membership,
   http://www.computerconservationsociety.org/Joining.htm
6. The National Museum of Computing, http://www.tnmoc.org/
7. Tony Sale Award, http://www.sale-award.org/
8. Lavington, S. (ed.): Turing and his contemporaries – Building the world's first computers. Published by BCS (2012) ISBN 978-1-906124-90-8
9. Resurrection,
   http://www.computerconservationsociety.org/resurrection.htm
10. Swade, D.: Computer Conservation and Curatorship. Resurrection 1(1), 8 (1990)
11. Murrell, K.: Demonstrating Restored and Replica Computers. Resurrection (60), 18–22

Museums – What They Can and Should Be Doing

Charles H. Lindsey

Museum of Science and Industry, Manchester (volunteer)
chl@clerew.man.ac.uk

Abstract. Museums have a duty, not only to preserve the Objects in their care, but also to preserve the skills and the mindsets of those who created them; furthermore, those concepts must somehow be conveyed to the visiting public. I shall give examples of how this can be achieved when illustrating how the early computers paved the way for the ubiquitous devices that we know today. These will include interactive gadgets to show the underlying principles, and videos of the objects in use.

Keywords: Museums, purpose, history, mindsets.

1 What Is the Purpose of a Museum?

I suggest there are four main objectives:

1. To inform and educate the visiting Public as to the nature and significance of the Objects on display.
2. To enable serious researchers, perhaps far in the future, to examine the Objects in order to discover their precise nature, history, capabilities and manner of use.

No great disagreement about those two, I would imagine.

3. To preserve the skills necessary for the maintenance and operation of the Objects. That one is not so obvious. Some Museums do it well. For example, the skills of operating cotton machinery are well preserved at MOSI[1], Styal Mill[2] and, most effectively, at Helmshore[3]. When it comes to computing, little happens except when pressurized by the CCS[4]. MOSI has the reconstructed "Baby" (a replica of the world's first stored-program computer) which is preserving the art of working with thermionic valves – and just in time given that the people with the necessary skills are dying off at an unseemly rate.

    Sometimes the pioneers have all died off, and then the skills have to be rediscovered by Trial and Error, as I am discovering myself with Hartree's Differential Analyser (where many times the Trial has indeed turned out to be an Error).

---

[1] The Museum of Science and Industry, Manchester.
[2] Quarry Bank Mill, Cheshire.
[3] Helmshore Mills Textile Museum, Lancashire.
[4] The Computer Conservation Society.

A. Tatnall, T. Blyth, and R. Johnson (Eds.): HC 2013, IFIP AICT 416, pp. 258–265, 2013.

TNMOC[5] is the shining example, expressly created for this purpose, but the Science Museum[6] has an ambivalent approach. It has the working Pegasus (as a result of CCS pressure, but beset with Health and Safety issues). Many years ago, it obtained a large piece of Hartree's Differential Analyser restored to (allegedly) working order, but after around 12 months it lost interest and it has lain idle ever since. It constructed a replica of Babbage's (never built) 2nd difference engine, and every day someone would come and crank the handle and show it in operation. Nowadays, that handle is only cranked when somebody especially requests it.

4. To preserve the "mindset" or "world-view" of the people who made the Objects.

And that one, I suspect, goes largely unrecognised, but it is the one I want to explore in this paper. It concerns what they thought they were trying to achieve. It concerns their view of the tools available for the purpose. It concerns the methods they used for going about their task – the problems they considered it important to address.

Now this "mindset" is what I want to convey to the Public. I do not expect the Public to be especially interested in the skills as such, though they may well appreciate seeing the results of exercising them. And note also that the "mindset" is a function of time, so it will have varied throughout History.

2   Historical Perspectives

2.1   When Did History Start?

Well the Romans had the abacus (a digital device) and they weighed things by sliding weights on a long lever (an analogue device).

But it was in the 19th Century when things really got going, with Babbage's ill-fated projects, and with the need for astronomical tables as the driving force. At the start of the 20th Century we had punched cards and mechanical calculators, such as the Brunsviga. Then came wheel-and-disc integrators, much used during the war for bomb sights and anti-aircraft control; and finally electronic devices and, above all, the Von Neumann model of the stored program computer.

2.2   When Should History End?

Initially, applications were purely arithmetical, whether for scientific or commercial purposes. Artificial intelligence was just a twinkle in the eye of Alan Turing and language translation in the eye of Andrew Booth; and that was it. Computers were large and bulky; you could look inside them and see how they were constructed, and they had lots of flashing lights and knobs to twiddle (a cartoonist's dream!) so you could see and control what was happening.

---

[5]   The National Museum of Computing, Bletchley Park.
[6]   The Science Museum, London.

And then, around 1980, two fundamental changes occurred (not entirely unrelated). The first was the Integrated Circuit – a computer on a chip. Now you cannot see what is inside. IC design is an esoteric art practised by Intel, ARM and a few others. I cannot foresee how, in 200 years' time, anyone will have preserved, or even be able to rediscover, that art. ICs are just not museum-friendly – right at the end of the gallery you may see a computer chip opened up, with a large magnifying glass (or even a microscope) in front of it, and that is about as much as you can do.

The second change was the WIMP interface, coupled with the ability to manipulate images and sounds and to transmit them over the internet. Computers are now mostly about Communication, and Communications are mostly performed by Computers. Alan Turing has met Claude Shannon, and you can hardly tell the difference between them.

Museums are meant to record history, but things are now changing so rapidly that they cannot possibly keep up. So I therefore propose that we should regard Computer History, and the involvement of Museums with it, as having ended when these changes arrived. Someday, when the dust has settled and the perspectives have become clearer, that situation can be reviewed. But it won't be regarded as "Computer" History anymore, even though it is clear that whatever it is would never have come about if real computers hadn't happened first.

3   Why We Need Working Machines

There is a well-known saying: *A Picture is worth a thousand Words*. I would add two corollaries to this:

1. *A Live Demonstration is worth a thousand Pictures*

2. *Hands-on experience is worth a thousand Live Demonstrations*

Clearly, a working machine fulfils our aim to preserve those skills. But even working machines cannot be demonstrated continuously, so their interpretation is still important. We can distinguish several situations:

3.1   Purely Static Objects

Early manufacturers took great pride in enclosing their computers in shiny cabinets so you could not see what was inside. So at least the doors should be left open, or the covers left off, if there is something to be seen within. If it is a chain printer, then you need to be able to see the chain. If it is a hard disc, then it needs to be sectioned so you can see how the heads moved. Indeed, for any Object in a Museum, there should be sufficient information provided to show the visitor, at least roughly, how it worked. These Objects may have worked once, but restoration is impractical, or impossibly expensive; but still they have a story to tell.

3.2   Once-in-a-Blue-Moon Objects

These are usually made of shining brass and are kept in glass cabinets where they cannot be sullied by dirty fingers. But this hardly helps the public to appreciate their significance. So, once every 50 years at least, they should be taken out and turned over by hand to show how they did whatever they were intended to do. *And then you make a video of the operation,* which can be seen on demand by the visiting Public and even sold for profit in the Museum shop. There are lots of Objects this could be done to, but I have my eye focussed on two of them in the Science Museum:

1.   The piece of Babbage's Difference Engine. "Sacrilege" I can hear the Curators saying. But I know this works, because I have done it before with the smaller piece of that machine kept in the Computer Laboratory at Cambridge; it worked just fine (no adjustments needed) and we used it to produce a small table of squares and cubes.
2.   Kelvin's Harmonic Analyser. By peering closely at it, I was able to work out what it did (which is not what I had expected it to do – Kelvin had a later machine for that). But it would be fascinating to watch it (or a video of it) in action, and it would be a brilliant tool for explaining what Fourier analysis is all about.

3.3   Replicas

Where the original machine no longer exists, but where its historical significance is sufficiently great, building a replica can be justified, though I am far from convinced this is so for machines which never existed physically (unless there is serious doubt as to whether they would actually have worked). The great advantage of a replica is that it is not an original to be preserved at all costs, and so you can experiment with it; moreover it still fulfils the objective of preserving the skills needed for its construction and use.

3.4   Restoring Original Machines

Museum curators can get somewhat paranoid about the destruction of valuable historical evidence, which is an inevitable accompaniment to restoration. For Hartree's differential analyser, we are keeping careful records of what we have done, and any part that is re-manufactured or otherwise not part of the original is painted blue. But where the Museum is prepared to allow it (and the simplest way to ensure that is for the donor to make it a condition) it has great advantages; for sure the skills are preserved, and the Public can see it in operation. But a word of warning here; the Public needs to see something worthwhile, to learn something new, to be impressed; a black box that simply dishes out correct results will not do. Ideally, the machine needs to be seen solving real (but perhaps small) problems of the type it was intended for. And don't forget to video the presentation for when demonstrations are not actually in progress.

And another word of warning: make sure that plans are in place to ensure demonstrations will continue for whatever is the expected lifetime of the restoration. Museums can be exceedingly fickle; priorities and visions of their "Grand Objective" can change as fast as new Directors get appointed. So each project must have a "Champion", and a fairly ruthless one at that. Fortunately, the CSS is well placed to provide and support such Champions, and to ensure their succession as time takes its toll.

3.5   Emulation

Is this not an alternative to restoration? To some extent Yes; it preserves some (but not all) of the skills, it is much cheaper, and people can download the emulation and play with it at home. But it is best regarded as an adjunct to rather than a substitute for the real thing.

4   Mindsets

These change over time – even within the period from c.1950 to c.1980 upon which we are concentrating. They concern the issues which the computer designers of that time had to contend with, the choices they had to make, the technologies available to them, the methodologies that they used. We need to give the Public some feel for them, because they see present day computers as communication and image manipulation/display gadgets with jazzy interfaces for which our issues do not seem immediately relevant. Evidently, within our time-frame, computing was much more related to Mathematics, and giving the Public some feel for Mathematics is, in this age, an important objective in itself.

So what are the tools available to us? Good written material (and handouts) associated with the Objects, demonstrations of working exhibits, videos (which can go beyond simple images of the demonstrations – animation can be used to explain the underlying principles), hands-on contact with small actual objects; but, above all, interactive gadgets to illustrate the principles concerned (though they have to be of robust construction so as to be small-child-proof). So here are some examples, and some suggestions as to how to put these ideas across.

4.1   Analog vs. Digital

Analog computing has been going in and out of fashion for many centuries, and I don't think we have seen the last of it yet. Slide rules are the best tool to get the basic idea across; they were the pocket calculators of their day, every Museum will have several examples on show, and I have built a large one at MOSI for people to play with (and it aims to show how they were actually used, rather than simply demonstrating that it can multiply 2 by 3 to get 6). Another device that should be on hand (or on video) is a planimeter.

To illustrate digital, you cannot beat a simple abacus (preferably a Russian *shoty* with ten beads per digit, although the ones in your glass cabinet are more likely to be Chinese or Japanese). It is an excellent tool to illustrate carry propagation (now there is an issue that caused much worry for the early computer designers); and you can then move up to a Brunsviga which again illustrates carry propagation, and then you go on to use it for multiplication, explaining that the same basic process must be occurring in every pocket calculator, computer and mobile telephone. Actually, the best way to show carry propagation in action is that video of Babbage's Difference Engine that I called for earlier, and if you could manage to get the hand cranked piece of his analytical engine working, that would illustrate anticipatory carry too.

4.2   Decimal vs. Binary

That certainly needs to be explained. MOSI has a nice interactive 4-bit binary adder/subtracter that gets well used.

4.3   Serial vs. Parallel

Nobody in his right mind would make a serial computer these days, but if they had never been made and seen to work at the start, nobody would have attempted to make a parallel one. The distinction is important if you want to illustrate delay-line storage.

4.4   Logic Diagrams

A topic not part of the usual Museum fare, but it is essential to tell how everything inside a computer is built out of a small number of basic logic elements – **and, or** and **not**. What is needed is an interactive mechanical model of an adder, clearly showing the individual gates and their interconnections. Make it however you will; steel balls rolling down grooves; mechanical representations of diodes (levers A and B pushing lever C down with a spring as a pull-up resistor makes an OR-gate – turn it upside down for an AND-gate). Let the kiddies set up two binary numbers, and then watch the carry propagating.

4.5   Packaging

Early computers were wired up just like wireless sets. Everything hard soldered in place, so if it broke, it took you hours to locate the fault, mend it, and get it running again. So they invented removable packages with simple gates on them. So examples of such packages should be on display (and that is why I suggested leaving the computer door open so they can be seen). If you can arrange a simple binary counter made out of packages and a scope to show it counting up, so much the better.

Now, of course, components are much more reliable, so everything is again hard soldered onto a motherboard (and if that breaks, you just throw it away and get another one – that is called "progress").

4.6   Order Codes

A lot of effort was made in the early days to get these right. Writing in machine code is unfashionable these days, but people need to realise that it is still there behind the scenes, whatever programming language is used. If you are running an emulator for something with a nice simple order code (e.g. the Baby or a Pegasus, ignoring all the drum stuff), then you should provide an opportunity for people to write their own small programs. Nothing complicated: "Squares and Cubes" or "Fibonacci Numbers" are quite sufficient to get the basic idea across.

4.7   Input/Output

Nobody these days has ever seen punched paper tape, let alone a teleprinter. So it needs to be on view. At MOSI, even though our Pegasus is not working, it is planned to commission the paper tape equipment and attach it to the emulator. This will make demonstrations much more interesting, because you can *see* things happening, which is an essential feature of any demonstration.

The same goes for punched cards, with the addition that they were in use long before computers came on the scene. Showing a full tabulator in operation is probably too much (leave that for the videos), but if you can lay your hands on a working card sorter, then that can make a most spectacular demonstration; moreover, it is easy to explain how it works, and it is fairly easy to maintain.

4.8   Memory

There is a progression – Williams tubes, through delay lines, core stores, and up to ICs – and a corresponding exponential growth in capacity. There should be exhibits to illustrate this progression. An interesting interactive would be a single core plane, with pushbuttons to select a row and column for current to flow through, a knob to determine the direction of the current (write or read), and a CRT, or at least a LED, to show whether a 1 or a 0 had been stored there.

4.9   External Storage

Tape decks should be in evidence (though having a working one might be a step too far). A drum would be fine, so long as you can see inside it. Exchangeable discs so people can gawk at how few megabytes they held, compared to their huge bulk. Floppy discs, and their drives (opened up). And of course a sectioned hard drive as already mentioned.

4.10   Software

This is a huge topic, and I am not sure that a Museum is the right place to exhibit it. But it does need to be preserved, and that is a whole new ballpark which I do not propose to enter here.

5   Videos

You will have noticed my frequent mention of these, and I am surprised that Museums do not already make greater use of them, and not just for computers. Every gallery should have one, with a well-structured menu so people can choose exactly what they would like to see. Clearly, they should illustrate the Objects on local display, but there is the opportunity to go further, showing Objects from other Museums, and exploring underlying concepts in more detail, perhaps with the aid of animations.

6   And Finally

There is a temptation for Museums to concentrate overmuch on the quality of their displays; but this can easily lead to a triumph of Form over Content. Museum Managers bear a responsibility to ensure their visitors come away knowing more than when they came in. At their best, they can provide brilliant solutions for bringing this about. But, sadly, sometimes they can also be a part of the problem.

Acknowledgements. Thanks are due to Peter Onion, who presented this paper to the Conference at excruciatingly short notice when I was unwell.

History, Nostalgia and Software

David Holdsworth

Computer Conservation Society and Leeds University, UK
ecldh@leeds.ac.uk

Abstract. The early history of computing is dominated by hardware development, but once we got non-trivial machines to work, the character of the machines was defined by their software not their hardware. Modern computers can be programmed to emulate computers of yesteryear, and then run original software. Sadly, much software from the past has been lost with cavalier disregard for its historic significance. However, we are having some success in resurrecting past systems, and can run such software as survives so well that past users of these old systems often react with nostalgic glee on first encountering one of these emulations. We can do this even where the software only survives in the form of printer listings. The challenge is to make such emulations relevant to people who never knew the original.

Keywords: software, preservation, emulation.

1 Introduction

As we preserve technology from the past, we seek to make it comprehensible, and even eye-catching, to current and future generations. We need to address a vast range of levels of historical interest from the school child on a museum trip to the serious historian working to learn more of the technology that is long past current usage. With regard to the visitor in a museum (real or virtual), the problems seem to be particularly acute with regard to computing, where the hardware had very little of visual interest, few moving parts, and rarely made interesting sounds. In the past, computers on film and TV usually appeared as images of spinning tape decks, but once disk drives became common place that opportunity was denied to film makers, although flashing lights stayed around for some time, especially on IBM 360/370.

Actually, the real nature of a computer is defined by its software at least as much as by its hardware. Around my desk are three active computers, two Intel and one ARM, plus an Android smart-phone which is also ARM. From a user perspective the software is what describes these machines. The one Win98 system is rather the odd-one-out (Intel CPU). The other three machines all run variants of GNU/Linux, and the two most similar machines are the Ubuntu [1] laptop with its Intel CPU and the Raspberry Pi [2] with its ARM CPU. The two Intel machines are not very much alike.

It is not really possible to demonstrate a preserved computer without running any of its software, whereas we can demonstrate the software without actually possessing the original hardware. We can go beyond demonstration and even do useful work [3].

A. Tatnall, T. Blyth, and R. Johnson (Eds.): HC 2013, IFIP AICT 416, pp. 266–273, 2013.

In the heydays of time-sharing systems many users of a computer sat at teletypes and never saw the actual hardware. What they saw was software — software which sadly has all too often been completely lost, or may survive only as tatty printer listings.

The goal of the Computer Conservation Society (CCS) activity in software is long-term preservation of historic software in digital form, along with emulation software that will allow realistic execution of the preserved software, and meaningful access to the source text. We have achieved this both for ICL's George3 [4] and for Whetstone Algol on the KDF9 [5]. We are aware of emulations of the BBC micro [6] [7], IBM mainframes [8], DEC machines [9], and SIMH [10].

We have had real success in producing systems that can be used by those who knew the original. The challenge is to go from this nostalgia to preservation with historical relevance, both to serious historians and to passing museum visitors and googlers. There is some encouragement in a post on DesignSpark [11] where the author has found our system for George 3 and got it to work quite independently. In an effort to investigate the scale of this challenge, I am currently working on resurrection of Leo III software. Before the project I had no non-trivial knowledge of the Leo III. So I am experiencing at first hand the problems of understanding the past when lacking personal nostalgia. The nostalgia of others is proving invaluable.

Software is key to the preservation of computer history, keeping the originals as objects of study, and writing tools (notably emulators) to enable that study.

2   Documentation

Just as Disraeli should have said "Lies, damned lies, statistics, — and spreadsheets", so our title should perhaps be expanded to "History, nostalgia, software, — and documentation". Software without documentation can be difficult to use or understand, but documentation without software can be a sterile read. Unfortunately, whereas documentation often survives in libraries, the software itself has not often survived. In making preserved software (and also hardware) meaningful for future generations, documentation will be vital, both the original stuff and newly written material. Moreover, it needs to be digital.

For today's systems, user documentation is on-line (or maybe CD), and searchable with today's software tools. The systems of the 1950s and 60s had user documentation that ran to a few volumes. We have scanned copies of some of this stuff, and the quantity is sufficiently small that the serious historian is not put off reading it in its entirety. Our own work in CCS has combined OCR with manual editing to produce searchable manuals whose on-line appearance resembles very much the original, and offers the prospect of enhancement with hyper-links. For a taster from our on-going Leo III project, look at [12]. We have used the same technique on system documentation for KDF9 [13].

When we come into the 1970s, documentation is still normally on paper, often produced by a traditional hot-metal process, but is now very voluminous — metres of shelf space of A4 sized manuals. However, the quality of printing is much better than that of earlier documentation, giving hope that the emerging generation of OCR software will get near-perfect recognition. A minority of documents already exist as searchable on-line documents such as IBM's *360 Principles of Operation* [14]. As well as such searchable access to the original documents for scholars of IT history, we need material which is much more compact for the customers in the Clapham computer shop. Back in the 1970s, several user institutions rightly concluded that this large quantity of manufacturers' documentation was going to be a hurdle to end-users, and wrote their own user documentation, such as Leeds University's description of George3 [15]. The manufacturers also got wind of this issue and produced handy pocket cards for use in an era when more computer staff wore jackets. IBMers were always well-known for their dress sense and IBM's green and yellow cards are rightly famous [16].

3   Nostalgia as an Asset

Although nostalgia can be a false friend in blinding implementers to the fact that their emulations are only meaningful to those who knew the original, it is becoming clear that it is also an indispensable asset.

Nostalgia is a great asset to the Leo III project. I have been lent User Manuals and software listings. The Leo Society has recruited a team of enthusiastic volunteers who are copy-typing the listings in duplicate using the techniques explored in the resurrection of Whetstone Algol [5]. Not only is nostalgia a great motivator of such a team, but it also teases out recollections of those parts of a system that never quite made it into the documentation. Quite early in the project it became clear that the surviving documentation and preserved software would not be sufficient to achieve a working system such as was produced for the ICL1900 or KDF9. The vocabulary of computing has changed since the Leo III manuals were written. It was not too difficult to see that a "compartment" in the Leo III store is a "word" in today's parlance, but it took several e-mails with the old Leo hands to tease out just what was meant by a "switch". It turns out to be rather like an Algol 60 switch, or perhaps more like FORTRAN's computed GOTO. The manual was obviously written by someone who expected the reader to know exactly what a switch was. As time progresses, we can expect that this vocabulary drift will render the earliest documentation more mysterious, and perhaps even misleading.

It seems likely that most old computers do not have their properties sufficiently accurately documented to enable emulators to be written which are accurate enough to run real software. Once written, such an emulator becomes a definitive description of the workings of the machine and deserves a place in the historical record. The fact of its successful execution of original software gives it that credo.

Nostalgia is, of course, a wasting asset as mortality takes its inevitable toll. There is an urgent need to collect old software from garages and probate sales, and get the stuff working while we still can.

4   Beyond Nostalgia

In seeking to put antediluvian software in a historic context, it is vital to provide facilities to enable a computer user of today to have some sense of the experience of using the computers of yesteryear. When we look back to the days when computers had operators, we see that the experiences of an operator were different from those of an end-user. Going back before the days of time-sharing or multi-access, programmers would write code by hand on coding sheets, and the code was then typed onto cards or paper tape by data-preparation staff.

Fig. 1. Dennis Ritchie and Ken Thompson and their PDP-11 (reprinted with permission of Alcatel-Lucent USA Inc.)

If we were to show this picture of Ritchie and Thompson (fig 1) to a person whose first experience of computers was a Windows PC or iPad, what would be their understanding of this scene? If we were to show this coding sheet from Leo III (fig 2) to a such a person would they have the first idea of how it was used?

If we are to give a feel for the computing activities pre-PC, we need to give access to the keys of that era, card punch, paper-tape punch or on-line teletype. Given that keeping

Serial No.	Action	Reference	Item	1
0				
1				
2				
3				
4				
5				
6				

Fig. 2. Coding sheet for Leo III

these machines working is rather difficult (especially teletypes), we need helpful software emulations. When searching on-line for emulators for teletypes or card punches, we find facilities that emulate the computer end, producing images of paper tape or cards. We need emulation of the user end, with sound effects, and operating at the real speed. We should also have videos of the actual hardware in operation, and put these on-line.

Those who never used such computer systems will not easily appreciate the effort required to get anything to work. I have thought only half seriously of offering a website that runs programs with an over-night turn-round.

5   Software as Part of History

In our preservation of George3, we were able to copy the actual system from a working installation. In particular, we made files that are images of the original magnetic tapes, in such a way that we can reproduce the effect of reading the tape. I do have a copy of MSDOS from 1988. We can (and should) keep this material indefinitely [17]. For the most part, the companies that produced the software of yesteryear have survived even less well than their software. IBM is a notable exception, and persistent exploration of their website, can eventually tease out historical activity such as SIMH [10]. Understandably, IBM's website is much more directed towards the present and to the future.

Older material has rarely survived in digital form, but nostalgically stored printer listings do turn up from time to time. We have encountered preserved source text in digital form, but equivalent binary code had not been preserved. Our own work [5] has shown that such relics can be brought back to life. It is fair to ask to what extent such a resurrection is only a replica. At the same time we should accept that in a digital world, where copies are perfect, the concept of the original object is no longer really valid. For all that, I suggest that we do the best service to historians of the future by retaining digital copies as close to the original bit stream as we can sensibly do [17].

Whatever form we choose for retention of digital materials, our criterion should be that it *"must allow the recreation of the significant properties of the original digital object, if one assumes that appropriate hardware technology is available"* [18]. On the assumption that an intelligent choice of "significant properties" is made, such a criterion ensures that someone studying the material in the future will not be hampered by a loss of information. Such ambitions point to keeping the original byte-streams in files that are copied onto current technology from time to time. This has the advantage of being a very low cost strategy.

6   Software as a Tool of History

It is only possible for historic software to play its part in history if alongside its preservation we implement software tools to make it accessible to users of current technology. A major weakness of the retention of printer listings of software as historical documents is the difficulty of appreciating just how the software actually operated, either by seeing it run, or by browsing the source text. For KDF9 software we have used software to generate HTML both to give the on-screen appearance that closely resembles the printout from KDF9 data-preparation equipment (viz, Flexowriter), and to provide hot-links that enable the following of subroutine calls in an assembly language program [19]. The technique is readily applicable to pretty well any programming language.

Whether studying software, or merely exercising a bit of healthy curiosity, there is nothing to beat actually being able to run the stuff. CCS activities in this area can be seen on our website (http://sw.ccs.bcs.org), where we have a variety of simulators as free-standing programs, mostly written in C or Ada. SIMH [10] offers facilities for simulation of a number of systems, running on different platforms.

Although the CPUs of early (and not so early) computers tended to be particular to the machine, peripheral equipment showed less variety. Quite early on we designed a data format for storing images of magnetic tapes in files that enables them to be read in a variety of emulation environments. It was the UNIX operating system that brought us the notion that any data stream could be considered as a file. Emulation of a disk drive by a file is trivially easy. For the most part emulations also use files for representation of decks of cards, reels of paper tape or printer listings, with text editors and browsers to give access to their contents. On-line teletypes can be emulated easily by the increasingly elusive *telnet* command connected to an emulator by TCP/IP. but this gives an overly sanitised view of 1960s on-line computing. I have so far searched the net in vain for a 10 characters-per-second teletype emulation complete with sound effects. Even better would be to have an image of a teletype head, like football results were once presented on UK TV.

In this world where the running of custom software on one's own hardware becomes rarer, we have looked at how best to offer a meaningful experience via a web browser. We have at the α-test stage a system for running KDF9 Algol [20] programs on a webserver. It takes the user's program typed into a window on a form, or uploaded from a file, converts it into KDF9 paper tape code and presents it to the genuine KDF9 Algol compiler running on an emulated KDF9. The Algol program is shown to the user as it would have appeared on a KDF9 Flexowriter (Rolls-Royce teletype), and the line printer output is also delivered to the web browser. All this running on a Raspberry Pi, little bigger than a credit card.

We have already alluded to the indigestibility of much of the documentation of the 1970s era, and to its existence only in paper form. Our use of OCR software in this area has been an invaluable aid, leading us to look forward to a time when its accuracy will eliminate the need for proof reading. Just as Google's PageRank software [21] has tamed what seemed like an amorphous sprawl in the early days of the World Wide Web, so we can hope that software will be developed that deals with the paper legacy from computing's earlier phases.

7   Long Term Preservation

Although digital material may seem somewhat ephemeral, its long term retention is actually much easier than for more tangible historical material. I have personally suffered the loss of historic listings as a library ran out of storage space. If our historic software and associated software tools are to persist into history, it is vital that we have a reliable strategy for their preservation in digital form. This is covered in reference [17], but here are some key points.

Despite the rapid development of digital technology there are aspects of IT that endure. The key to digital longevity lies in relying only on such enduring aspects. It would appear that the byte is here to stay, and that a sequence of bytes will be able to be preserved for a very long time — just plain files periodically copied onto current media, ideal for keeping the original software in a byte-stream whose contents never change. We have no faith on long-lived media. Even if the medium is indestructible, the device to read it is not. Technological evolution is tracked by maintenance of the access tools. It is important that these tools (e.g. emulators) are written with a view to longevity [22]. Reference [23] (cited in [22]) hints that a subset of C may be the best choice for writing emulators. There is so much important software written in C, that we can be confident that it will still work for many decades to come. A recent survey of emulators held by the CCS showed those written in C to be the most durable, slightly more so than those written in Ada. For documentation, we can confidently use HTML, and JPEG, which are non-proprietary open standards. Adobe have started hinting that PDF readers are reaching the end of the line. Long-term validity of proprietary data formats is rarely in the interests of their owners.

8   Conclusion

We need to pay more attention to software. Its importance to the history of computing has been underestimated for some time. We need to keep old software, both source and binary, and to write new software to enable our successors better to appreciate the systems of the past. As an illustration of the historical significance of software let us return to Fig 1. There is a lot of hardware visible in this picture, but the chances are that little of it survives today, and the company that made it certainly does not survive. Of the people in the picture Denis Ritchie died in 2011, but both he and Ken Thompson survive in Wikipedia. The software in this picture is invisible, but its legacy is ubiquitous today, and likely to remain so long into the future.

As well as keeping historic software as part of the historical record, we also need to have software tools which both enable the serious study of that historical record, and permit some understanding and appreciation by the casual visitor whether in a museum or on-line. Some of today's casual visitors can be turned into tomorrow's enthusiasts by appropriate software, both old software preserved on current hardware, and new software written to give access to the old. Much of the marshalling of this software relies upon the nostalgia of ageing veterans.

Acknowledgments. The rescue of software from printer listings has involved heroic efforts on the part of Brian Wichmann, Graham Toal, Roderick McLeod, Bill Findlay, Ray Smith, Geoff Cooper, Ken Kemp, Chuck Knowles, John Daines, Tony Jackson, Dave Jones.

References

1. ubuntu, http://www.ubuntu.com/ubuntu
2. Raspberry Pi, http://www.raspberrypi.org
3. Spoor, B.: Problem Solving with George 3 Today. Resurrection (36) (2005) ISSN 0958-7403, http://www.cs.man.ac.uk/CCS/res/res36.htm#e
4. Holdsworth, D.: George3 – Emulation of the ICL (1900), http://sw.ccs.bcs.org/CCs/g3/
5. Holdsworth, D.: Rescuing Software from Lineprinter Listings. Resurrection (57) (2012) ISSN 0958-7403, http://www.cs.man.ac.uk/CCS/res/res57.htm#e
6. B-EM, A Freeware BBC Micro Emulator for DOS, Windows and Mac OS X (2012), http://b-em.bbcmicro.com
7. Hedstrom, M., Wheatley, P.R., Sergeant, D.M., et al.: The CAMiLEON Project, http://www2.si.umich.edu/CAMILEON/

8. The Hercules System/370, ESA/390, and z/Architecture Emulator, http://www.hercules-390.eu
9. West, J.: pdp11 home page, http://www.pdp11.org
10. Jones, M.T.: Emulation and computing history (2011), http://www.ibm.com/developerworks/opensource/library/os-emulatehistory/
11. Black, A.: Running George 3 on a Raspberry Pi, Blog post on DesignSpark (2013), http://www.designspark.com/blog/running-george-3-on-a-raspberry-pi
12. Holdsworth, D.: Leo III Resurrection (2013), http://sw.ccs.bcs.org/leo/
13. English Electric.: KDF9 Director Manuals, http://sw.ccs.bcs.org/KDF9/directorManuals/manuals.htm
14. IBM: IBM 360 Principles of Operation, http://bitsavers.trailing-edge.com/pdf/ibm/360/princOps/A22-6821-0_360PrincOps.pdf
15. Hock, A.A.: Leeds University User Manual - section E (1976), http://sw.ccs.bcs.org/CCs/g3/LeedsDoc/sect-e.htm
16. Alcock, D.: Dave's Green Card Collection (2004), http://planetmvs.com/greencard/
17. Holdsworth, D.: Curation Reference Manual, Digital Curation Centre (2007), http://www.dcc.ac.uk/resources/curation-reference-manual/completed-chapters/preservation-strategies
18. Holdsworth, D., Sergeant, D.M.: A Blueprint for Representation Information in the OAIS Model. In: 8th NASA Goddard Conference on Mass Storage Systems and Technologies (2000), http://www.storageconference.org/2000/papers/D02PA.PDF
19. Holdsworth, D.: Whetstone Algol resurrection (2011), http://sw.ccs.bcs.org/CCs/KDF9/walgol.htm
20. English Electric: Algol Programming (c1963), http://www.findlayw.plus.com/KDF9/EE%20KDF9%20Algol%20Manual.pdf
21. Page, L., et al.: The PageRank citation ranking: Bringing order to the Web, Stanford (1998), http://ilpubs.stanford.edu:8090/422/1/1999-66.pdf
22. Holdsworth, D., Wheatley, P.R.: Emulation, Preservation and Abstraction. RLG DigiNews 5(4) (2001), http://worldcat.org/arcviewer/1/OCC/2007/08/08/0000070511/viewer/file3149.html
23. Holdsworth, D.: C-ing ahead for digital longevity (2001), http://www.leeds.ac.uk/CAMiLEON/dh/cingahd.html

The Teenage "Baby" on Show

Christopher P. Burton

The Computer Conservation Society
cpb@envex.demon.co.uk

Abstract. It is now fifteen years since the replica of the Manchester University Small-Scale Experimental Machine ("Baby") was handed over to MOSI, the Museum of Science and Industry in Manchester. This article summarises some of the experience of the exposure of the object to the public from the point of view of the volunteers who maintain and demonstrate it.

Keywords: SSEM, Small-Scale Experimental Machine, "Baby" computer, computer replica, MOSI, Museum of Science and Industry, Manchester computers.

1   The "Baby" Replica

The original Small-Scale Experimental Machine was built in the Electro-Technics department of the University of Manchester by Williams, Kilburn and Tootill in 1947 and 1948 [1]. It was a test-bed for the cathode ray tube storage system which they had been developing since before 1946 [2]. On 21st June 1948 it correctly ran a program to calculate the highest factor of an integer, thereby becoming the earliest stored-program computer to work. The machine was subsequently greatly enlarged and developed so as to become the prototype of the Manchester University Mark I computer in 1949.

In late 1994 the Computer Conservation Society (CCS) instigated construction of a replica of the computer as it existed in June 1948 [3]. The goal was to run that first program again on 21st June 1998 to celebrate 50 years of stored-program computing. The project was sponsored by the computer systems company ICL and the assembly took place in Manchester Computing Centre in the Computer Science building at the University of Manchester. The work was done by a small team of volunteers, most of whom were members of the CCS. The workshop team in ICL's West Gorton R&D centre manufactured parts, but construction and wiring of sub-assemblies was done by volunteers in their homes. These electronic units and mechanical items were then brought to the university for assembling into the complete system.

The replica was complete and working by February 1998, whereupon it was dismantled and transported to MOSI. Here it was re-assembled and the next few months were devoted to tidying, shaking-out remaining errors and generally preparing for the anniversary celebrations. Highlight of the celebrations was running the first program again by the same men who achieved it 50 years earlier, and then the formal handing-over of the machine into the care of MOSI [4].

A. Tatnall, T. Blyth, and R. Johnson (Eds.): HC 2013, IFIP AICT 416, pp. 274–284, 2013.

The museum is itself located on an historic site, with numerous large and important buildings dating from the mid-1800s and earlier. These buildings are of intrinsic interest themselves, as well as housing and displaying the museum collections. Focus is on Manchester-oriented inventions and history, so collections cover textile manufacture, steam engines, railways, city infrastructure, the factory system and so on. Very good interactive galleries for children are present, indeed there is a strong learning environment for parties from schools.

One large four-storey building is "The 1830 Warehouse", the world's first railway goods warehouse. This is largely intact from Victorian times – brick-built, wooden floors, timber and cast iron pillars, large windows and hydraulic hoists, all still present. In 1998, the top floor was empty but planned to become the "Futures Gallery" to show communications, from writing to railways, and telegraph to television. It was felt that this would be a suitable background to display the "Baby", and plans were made to move it there.

Fig. 1. The 1830 Warehouse (Image ©MOSI)

2   A Luggable Computer

The original machine was experimental and most interconnecting wires between units were made to screw terminals. The replica echoes this construction so to move it conveniently it is divided into nine separate racks of equipment by disconnecting about 200 carefully labelled wires. A team of four men can then carry each rack onto appropriate transport. This requires care because the electronic components are not protected in any way and so are vulnerable to accidental damage.

2.1   Move 1 – University to Top Floor of 1830 Warehouse

The racks of the machine were moved the few miles from the university to the 1830 Warehouse on Tuesday 24th February 1998. Two days later the machine had been connected up together again and worked after fixing a few small faults. This quick return to working order was a great tribute to the care with which the ICL operatives transported the machine.

As already mentioned, the installation was handed over to MOSI a few months later, and there it could be shown to the public in a spacious and authentic-looking setting. There was no "passing trade" – museum visitors had to find out from signage and enquiry where the "Baby" was, and then make the effort to ascend to the top floor to find it. Nevertheless there was a steady stream of visitors and probably very few days with no visitors. There were sufficient volunteers available to respond to visitors on Tuesdays from 10:00 to 16:00 with a pattern of scheduled demonstrations at 12:00 and 14:00. On other days a 'visitor present' detector triggered a voice commentary with synchronised spotlights to enliven the exhibit and educate the visitor.

Fig. 2. "Futures Gallery" – Top Floor of 1830 Warehouse – 1998 to 2005 (Image ©MOSI)

Computers are notoriously boring to look at unless there is something moving or animated. For "Baby" the interesting thing to watch is the monitor cathode ray tube, 6 inches diameter, showing the pattern of 0s and 1s in the store, and where the results of computations are displayed. For safety, the public is kept 2 meters away from the machine by a barrier and the monitor screen is too distant to see clearly. We therefore embedded two slave monitor screens in protected housings within the barrier for close inspection by visitors. However we eventually found that we could not maintain adequate brightness from these tubes at affordable cost, and the technique was later abandoned and a bright oscilloscope placed near the computer as a substitute

The replica remained in place for almost seven years and was demonstrated to visitors once a week. The museum plans now called for re-allocation of space on the Top Floor. So in April 2005 the machine was dismantled once again to move to a new location.

2.2   Move 2 – Top Floor to Second Floor of 1830 Warehouse

Preparations, transporting the machine and re-assembly took a few days by museum staff. Connecting and re-commissioning took a couple of weeks' part time work by volunteers, whereupon the pattern of displaying and demonstrating the "Baby" re-started. It was now somewhat easier for visitors to find the machine, and visitor numbers were increasing. A number of VIPs including the Prime Minister at the time were escorted up to see the machine in operation as it was becoming recognised as an important representative of Manchester's scientific and industrial history. The site was somewhat gloomy, although quite in keeping with the original university laboratory. However, after two years, in mid-2007, yet more upheaval was anticipated as the whole area on the second floor was earmarked for an important new gallery sponsored by British Telecom called "Connected Earth". We were on the move again. By this time MOSI had much more ambitious plans for "Baby".

Fig. 3. Second floor of the 1830 Warehouse – 2005 to 2007

2.3   Move 3 – To Ground Floor of Main Building

The Grand Plan was that the Main Building, also known as the Great Western Warehouse, another historic building on the site, was to be transformed internally. On the ground floor is the primary visitor entrance area, with substantial galleries and services on the three floors above. A major ground-to-roof reconstruction would provide a very large visitor orientation area on the ground floor and prestige galleries and conference facilities on the floors above. "Baby" would be part of this scheme. This was the plan but it was some way off for implementation, and meanwhile "Baby" would be on display on the ground floor, not far from where visitors currently arrived, and right on the route visitors took to other parts of the museum. In the public eye indeed!

Once again, the machine was un-wired and disassembled, to vacate the space needed by Connected Earth. It took some time to prepare the new site in the Main Building which was a little smaller than we were used to, and care had to be taken to ensure the safety of visitors. So the machine was in limbo for a couple of months before the volunteer team could get access to re-assemble and re-wire. Once power was available on-site, it took a day to confirm the computer was in good order and ready to display and demonstrate to the public.

Fig. 4. Ground floor of Main Building – 2007 to 2009

The new location meant that there were many more visitors looking at "Baby" even on non-demonstration days. Audio-visual aids in the barrier surrounding the machine helped tell people what they were looking at. A recruiting drive had yielded several extra volunteers able to talk about the machine and the history of the original, so there was non-stop activity all day on Tuesdays, and occasional demonstrations on other days and weekends, for example at school holiday times. Evening demonstrations for conference delegates were also very popular, sometimes accompanied by more formal lectures.

But our months in that location were numbered, as planned from the beginning. After just two years, the system had to be moved into storage so that the huge refurbishment task in the building could start. In November 2009 everything was transported to a secluded storage area further along and higher up in the building, where nominally no construction work was to take place. How little we knew!

2.4   Move 4 – Ground Floor to Storage Area of Main Building

The expectation was that the "Baby" would be safe in storage together with the large quantity of spare valves (vacuum tubes) and other components and associated test equipment and documents. There was insufficient availability of power to be able to operate the whole machine for testing purposes while in storage, though there was the prospect of applying power to separate parts of the system.

Fig. 5. The spacious Revolution Manchester Gallery – "Baby" in far corner (Image ©MOSI)

At some stage in early 2010, the building contractors broke through the partition barrier and stored quantities of drywall gypsum plaster-board in the area. This was not discovered for several weeks, when the volunteers were astounded to find that the place had also been used as a workshop for cutting-up the drywall, and everything was coated in a thick layer of powder. Not the most appropriate way to look after a museum object! When the builders had been ousted, the team spent several weeks during June and July with brushes and vacuum cleaner attempting to restore the situation. Repairs were made to the chassis which had been damaged and where possible a limited amount of testing carried out.

Meanwhile a splendid new spacious visitor orientation area, the 'Revolution Manchester Gallery' was being completed, and preparations made there for a site for "Baby", to be highlighted as an 'Icon of Manchester Science'. Once again the barrier separating the public from the machine would be exploited, with embedded iPads and other interactive material for use by visitors. In mid-November 2010 the racks were yet again carried to the new site, placed in position and the machine covered in dust sheets pending completion of the gallery. The machine had been out of the public's gaze for a little over a year, had endured two moves and there was evident physical damage to many of the fragile valves.

2.5   Move 5 – Storage Area to Revolution Manchester Gallery

Fig. 6. - Visitors interested in "An Icon of Manchester Science"

A week before Christmas 2010 a power feed was available on the new site and the work of re-commissioning could begin. Visual checks showed that at least 50 of the little glass diodes had bent pins or cracks in the glass, not always fatal, but a cause for concern. This was due to suffering in the "builders' workshop" and insufficient recognition of the vulnerabilities by staff moving the machine. After weeding out defective diodes, and locating and repairing various broken or disconnected wires, the machine was running programs again in January 2011. The volunteers achieved this success in only eight work days, despite the intervening holiday, but assisted by the piecemeal testing that had been possible after cleaning while in storage.

In the past two years on the new site, the "Baby" has settled into a pattern of more regular attendance by volunteers able to talk about the object to the public, so that usually three days per week are staffed. The size of the volunteer team has doubled, taking a load off those volunteers who are able to repair the machine. The machine is by no means very reliable – areas of concern are residual problems due to past damage to valves, severe problems due to ageing of resistors, especially in the sensitive analogue arithmetic units, and problems maintaining the CRT stores. In many cases the machine can be kept working by artifice and backup facilities, but in any case visitors seem to enjoy watching volunteer engineers, equipped with oscilloscope and test meter, attempting to fix faults.

3   Some Reliability Data during 15 Years on Show

The volunteer team maintains a maintenance log book to record faults, repairs and notes to communicate with other volunteers. Discipline in filling-in the log is usually quite good, but inevitably varies with individual consciences and the degree of mental concentration in different circumstances. Frequently, an adjustment of a control for example will not be recorded. Similarly, in the heat of the moment, replacement of a valve might not get recorded. Nevertheless, assuming omissions are random, and inclusions are of faults which take most time to clear, some sort of comparison of faults over time can be seen in Table 1 below. The figures belie the amount of time spent just trying to figure-out that a fault is present and what is causing it. The data includes re-commissioning after a move as well as in normal demonstrations, hence the unexpectedly high number of connection faults.

Apart from the large number of valve faults in 2010 due to physical damage, it is surprising how few faults of this type have appeared over the years. The original machine was said to have required several valve replacements per week. The difference may be attributed to a couple of reasons – a) the replica is only switched on for a few hours per week and b) the valves we have used were new but old stock, probably made in the 1950s when manufacturers were forced to pay attention to reliability. The pioneers had to make do with items made in the frenzy of wartime.

Table 1. Categorised definite faults

Year	Faulty valve or CRT	Connection	Other small component	Power system	Other	TOTAL
1998	1	2	3			6
1999	2	3	2	4	3	14
2000	2	3	4	2	1	12
2001	1			2		3
2002	1	1	1	4		7
2003	6	2	2	1	3	14
2004	1	1	2.	1	1	6
2005	2	6	3	2	3	16
2006	1	3	3			7
2007	2	8			4	14
2008	5	2			2	9
2009	1		2	1	1	5
2010	19	2				21
2011	5	4	5		2	16
2012	3	1	3	2		9
2013	6		1			7

4   The Volunteer Team

For the first year of operation, the team of volunteers who had built the replica performed demonstrations and talked to the public. As the years passed so these individuals dropped-out and fresh enthusiasts joined-in, and inevitably there was change in expertise in repair skills. On the other hand newer volunteers tended to be more self-selecting to be good at interacting with visitors. Recently the classification of volunteers has been systematised to provide a "volunteer career path" and a contribution to improving Health and Safety issues [5]. Level 1 people are explainers but are not qualified to operate or even to switch-on the "Baby". Level 2 embraces Level 1 and additionally the volunteer may operate the machine to run defined programs. Level 3 qualifies to run test programs and make diagnoses, and perform fallback procedures to maximise demonstrability of the machine. Finally, Level 4 volunteers are those able to do all the previous tasks and carry out detailed diagnosis and repair of the machine. This grading scheme is in line with similar schemes being set up at the London Science Museum and at The National Museum of Computing.

The enthusiasm, skill and dedication of the team of volunteers are major factors contributing to the success of the "Baby" as a museum object. They are helped by the Museum's policy of encouraging and supporting volunteers. There is a "Friends" organisation with accommodation on site, which has been in existence for decades, and which formally represents volunteers' views. From time to time MOSI will provide a script for volunteers to use to succinctly tell the story within a visitor's span of attention. This is a good basis, but inevitably the explainer will embellish with his own thoughts, depending on the degree of knowledge or interest shown by the visitor. As one of the key volunteers tellingly said,

I find the following always gets a positive reaction and immediate understanding by the public of where we have come from. We hold up a Cathode Ray Tube and say, "This was what a flash drive looked like in 1948, long before we invented USB, and it holds less than a millionth of a gigabyte!"

This dependence on volunteers to bring otherwise boring hardware to life is reinforced by the following statement [6] by John Beckerson, Senior Curator at MOSI. The author is grateful to him for permission to pass on his comments.

'That's cool!' a teenage visitor remarked upon encountering parts of Baby when it was last moved across site by a sweating team of curators and volunteers.

You'd think that 1940s technology would be far from 'cool'. Yet today's teenagers and digital creatives find the Baby a fascinating example of early electronics because their lives are so deeply reliant upon electronic devices descended from its principles. The Baby has more appeal now than it had 20 years ago; because as we move to an increasingly digital world, public curiosity about the origins of that world is thriving. People far beyond the walls of academia have become familiar with illustrious names such as Turing and the Manchester Baby has put the names of Williams, Kilburn and Tootill on that list.

For the Museum, the Baby has been one of our great success stories. It is a compelling visitor attraction. When the Museum produced its newest gallery, Revolution Manchester, it was no surprise that the Baby found pride of place as one of the iconic objects in our collection. Not only does it stand as a signpost to the digital future, it also helps today's citizens understand a part of our scientific and industrial past which is just as important as the glorious steam engines which are so popular in the adjacent Power Hall.

Part of the reason the Baby is so popular is the thousands of hours of volunteer time which go into maintaining and explaining it. Thanks to the storytelling expertise of the volunteers, what might otherwise be a curious but also mysterious and incomprehensible object becomes a living tale about discovery, the men who made it happen, and the impact of their research. The huge value that our volunteers bring enables them to speak at different levels. They interpret the Baby in different ways to suit each visitor. One person might simply require a brief summary: whilst another could be an engineer desiring deep technical detail. No fixed exhibition could ever provide this level of flexibility. It is the winning combination of the machine and the men and women who run it - and tell its story every time they come on duty - that makes the Baby one of MOSI's best-loved exhibits.

5   Conclusions

During the fifteen years of its display in the museum, the "Baby" has endured a surprising amount of movement and disruption. This is uncommon for a large object which is complex, operational and requires dismantling and re-assembly every time it moves. Nevertheless, it is always repairable and can be brought back to life by the enthusiastic volunteers. That enthusiasm is manifest when they explain the history and functionality of the machine to visitors. In its current location as an Icon of Manchester Science, it is more popular than ever with visitors, providing an unusual and spectacular attraction. The author is grateful to curatorial staff at MOSI for help in preparation of this paper, and especially to the volunteer team who are proud to feel that is "their baby".

References

1. Williams, F.C., Kilburn, T., Tootill, G.C.: Universal high-speed digital computers: a small-scale experimental machine. Proc. IEE 2(pt. 2, 61), 13–28 (1951), Also located at `ftp://ftp.cs.man.ac.uk/pub/CCS-Archive/misc/iee1.pdf`
2. Williams, F.C., Kilburn, T.: A storage system for use with binary-digital computing machines. Proc. IEE 96(pt. 2, 30), 183–200 (1949)
3. Burton, C.P.: Replicating the Manchester Baby: Motives, Methods and Messages from the Past. IEEE Annals of the History of Computing 27(3), 23–33 (2005)
4. Overviews of the original and replica SSEM are located at `http://www.computer50.org`, `http://www.digital60.org`
5. Current volunteers' news located at `http://www.cs.man.ac.uk/CCS/SSEM/volunteers/`
6. Beckerson, J.: Email to the author (June 11, 2013)

Part IX

Reconstruction Stories

Reconstruction of Konrad Zuse's Z3

Horst Zuse

Schaperstraße 21, 10719 Berlin, Germany
horst.zuse@t-online.de

Abstract. This paper describes the reconstruction of Konrad Zuse's Machine Z3 by the author Horst Zuse from 2008. Konrad Zuse built the Z3 machine between 1939 and 1941 with some friends and a small amount of support by the government. The main idea for reconstructing the Z3 was to learn how this machine works and how much effort is necessary to build such a machine. Another main topic was to show this machine to the public.

Keywords: Z3, Zuse, computer, freely programmable, reconstruction of the Z3, memory, binary system, floating point numbers.

1   Introduction

In this paper we describe the reconstruction of Konrad Zuse's Machine Z3 by the author Horst Zuse from 2008.

Today, in the whole world Konrad Zuse almost unanimously is accepted as the creator / inventor of the first free programmable computer with a binary floating point and switching system, which really worked. This machine - called Z3 - was completed in his small workshop in Berlin (Kreuzberg) in 1941. Zuse's first thoughts about the logical and technical principles go back to 1934. Konrad Zuse, also created the first programming language (1942-1945) in the world, called the Plankalkül. In 1949 he founded the computer company Zuse KG in Neukirchen (close to Fulda) and built till 1964 more than 250 computers for universities and companies. Konrad Zuse was born on June 22, 1910 in Berlin and died on December 18, 1995 in Hünfeld.

2   Konrad Zuse's First Ideas on Computing

In 1934 Konrad Zuse formulated the first ideas on computing. The reason was the expensive calculations as a civil engineer. His idea was that such stupid calculations should be done by machines and not by human beings. The first question, which Konrad Zuse discussed in 1934 was: *What mathematical problems should a computing machine solve?* His answer was the following definition of computing (1936): *To build new specifications from given specifications by a prescription.* In the year 1943 he extended the definition to: *Computing is the deviation of result specifications to any specifications by a prescription.*

A. Tatnall, T. Blyth, and R. Johnson (Eds.): HC 2013, IFIP AICT 416, pp. 287–296, 2013.
© IFIP International Federation for Information Processing 2013

From these definitions Konrad Zuse defined the logical architecture of his computers Z1 (1936-38), Z2 (1938), Z3 (1939-41) and Z4 (1941-45). From the beginning, it was clear for him, that his computers should be freely programmable. This means that they should read an arbitrary meaningful sequence of instructions from a punch tape and the machines should work in the binary digit system, because Konrad Zuse wanted to construct his computers with binary switching elements. Not only should the numbers be represented in a binary form, but the whole logic of the machine should work in a binary switching mechanism (0-1-principle). He planned a high performance binary floating point unit, which allowed calculating very small and very big numbers with sufficient precision. He implemented a high performance adder with a one-step carry-ahead and precise arithmetic exceptions handling. He developed a memory where each cell could be addressed by the punch tape and could store arbitrary data. Finally, he constructed a control unit, which controlled the whole machine, and implemented input- and output devices from the binary to the decimal number system and vice versa. Let us make a closer look at his machines.

2.1   Konrad Zuse's First Computers Z1 and Z3

In 1936 the logical plan for the first computer V1 (later he changed the name to Z1 in order to avoid a connection with the rocket V1), which he wanted to build, was finished. He had studied almost all the available mechanical calculating machines using the decimal number system of this time. He never had the plan to build a modified or extended decimal machine. He wanted to build a new machine for universal scientific applications.

2.2.1   Computer Z1

His first machine Z1, which worked on these principles, was constructed from 1936-1938. It was a machine with a 64 cell (words) memory of 22-bits and the components

 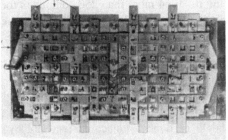

Fig. 1. Left: The computer Z1 in the living room of his parents in 1938. Right: Building blocks (thin metal sheets) of the Z1.

as discussed above. The Z1 consisted completely of thin metal sheets, which friends and he produced with a jigsaw. The clock frequency was around one Hertz. The Z1 was the first freely programmable machine, based on a binary principle, of the world.

The Z1 was in many ways a remarkable machine. Konrad Zuse used thin metal sheets in order to construct this machine. There were no relays in it. The only one electrical unit was an electrical engine in order to give the clock frequency of one Hertz to the machine. The Z1 was freely programmable via a punch tape and a punch tape reader. There was a clear separation of the punch tape reader, the control unit for supervising the whole machine and the execution of the instructions, the arithmetic unit with the two Registers R1 and R2, the memory with 64 words of 22-bits and the input and output devices.

2.2.2   Computer Z3

Konrad Zuse built the machine Z3 from 1939 to 1941 in the Methfesselstraße 7 in Berlin-Kreuzberg with some friends and a small amount of support by the government.

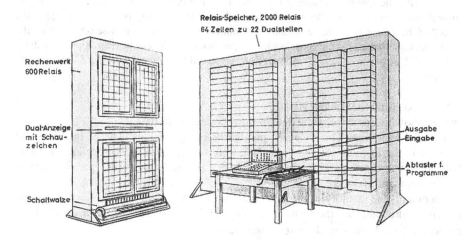

Fig. 2. A drawing of the Z3 by Konrad Zuse (the exactly date of this drawing is unclear). The height of the machine is around 2,20m, the width of one cupboard is 1,20m. On the left side is the arithmetic unit; on the right are both the memory cupboards. In the front the input- and output device and the punch tape reader. 800 relays in the arithmetic unit and 2000 in the memories.

With the Z3 Konrad Zuse wanted to show, that it is possible to build a reliable working machine for very complicated arithmetic calculations, which is freely programmable and is based on a binary floating point number and switching system. For reliability reasons he used relays for the entire machine.

Fig. 3. Left: The rebuilt computer Z3 in 1964 with Konrad Zuse. The machine is from the cubical expansion much smaller than the original one. The memory is on the left side (- the logo Z of the Zuse KG can be seen) and the arithmetic unit with the stepwise relays are on the right side. Left on the front the console with the punch tape reader can be seen. Right: The diary of Konrad Zuse at May 12, 1941: Konrad Zuse presented the original working Z3 to scientists in Berlin.

2.2.3   Architecture of the Z3
We are showing some technical data of the architecture of the Z3.

Parallel Machine: The Z3 was a parallel working machine. The 22-bits from the memory to the Register R1 and vice versa were moved in one step (cycle). The same holds for the binary arithmetic unit, where, among others, two parallel adders (exponent, mantissa) were used.

Memory: The memory of the Z3 consisted of 64 words of 22-bits. Each word was directly addressable by the instructions Pr z or Ps z, where z is the address in the range: $64 \leq z \leq 1$. For each bit a relay was needed.

Floating Point Numbers: Konrad Zuse used floating point numbers.

Instructions: The Z3 disposed of the nine instructions.

Arithmetic Unit and Carry Ahead: The arithmetic unit of the Z3 is Konrad Zuse's masterstroke. He reduced all the arithmetic operations to addition or subtraction. For the realization of the addition (subtraction is an addition of the complement of one number and the number) Konrad Zuse implemented a special switch because he wanted to avoid too many cycles for the addition of two binary floating point numbers. Using the special switch, he could reduce the addition from at least 14 cycles with a serial addition down to three cycles with a parallel addition. Although there were only five instructions (Ls1, Ls2, Lm, Li, and Lw) for arithmetic operations, some more operations were implemented which could be called from the input device. He also simplified the execution of the arithmetic operations with micro-sequences controlled by stepwise relays.

Fig. 4. Left: Stepwise relay for the control in order to make, among others, the multiplication by repeated addition. Right: A relay of the Z3.

Konrad Zuse used a self-developed *carry look-ahead* circuit of relays for the addition of floating point numbers. With this concept he could add two floating point numbers in three cycles independent of number of bits.

Arithmetic Exception Handling: The Z3 disposed of an arithmetic exception handling.

The undefined state was shown on the output device on the left side with small lights. For the numbers 0 and ∞ Konrad Zuse used special bit codes in the exponent. An exponent of –64 is the decimal 0. An exponent of –63 or +63 represents ±∞. The Z3 calculates always correctly, if an argument is 0 or ∞ and the other argument is in the allowed range.

Fig. 5. Left: The input- and output devices of the Z3. At the front the numbers could be put in by buttons. There were four buttons for the mantissa and 17 buttons for the exponent (from -8 to +8). The results were shown by lamps. Right: The output device of the Z3 with the lamps for the decimal numbers (right) and the arithmetic exception handling on the left side.

The binary floating point numbers were converted to decimal floating numbers. For these conversions he needed between 9 and 41 cycles depending on the exponent. The mantissa consisted of four decimal digits (five digits for the 1) and the exponent was between –8 and +8. The biggest decimal number which could be shown was $19999E10^8$.

Clock Driven Machine / Clock Frequency: The Z3 is a clock driven machine. Konrad Zuse used this principle to synchronize the different components of the machine. In order to do this he implemented a special impulse generator with a drum.

Fig. 6. The impulse generator for the Z3. The speed of the capstan could be controlled in steps (5 Hertz). It is an electric motor which drives a shaft, upon which are attached a number of arms (or protruding levers), where each arm is used to close a switch, and the angular separation between the arms caused different switches to be closed at different times, thereby allowing the system to control the flow of data between the various units.

We now describe the reconstruction of the new Z3.

3   The Construction of the New Z3 by the Author

The reconstruction of the new Z3 (called Z3r) begun in 2008 by the author. The author planned the whole conception of the new Z3 and the whole wiring was done by the author. The main idea to reconstruct the machine Z3 was to learn how this machine works and how much effort is necessary to build such a machine. Another main topic was to show this machine Z3 to the public.

The ideas to rebuild the Z3 were the following:

- In 2010, June 22 was the 100th anniversary of the birth Konrad Zuse.
- The cubical expansion of the reconstruction should be the original one, see above. The 1961 reconstruction is much smaller and there exists only one memory cupboard.
- The Machine Z3 is very qualified in order to explain to interested people the question: What is a computer? This is a very simple question but the answer is not easy and we think that such an explanation is not possible with a PC
- The most important components of the Z3 should be demonstrated separately. This is not possible with the reconstruction from 1961.
- The clock frequency generator should by shown to the visitors. It is a basic element of a computer and most people have of no idea about it.
- The arithmetic units with mantissa and exponent should be shown separately.
- The shifter for the mantissa to make multiplications and divisions with the arithmetic unit. It should be shown separately.
- The conversion of decimal numbers to binary numbers and vice versa.
- The punch reader for the freely programming component.
- The input- and output device for floating point numbers.

- The two memory cupboards. The design is changed from the original one in order to see the multiplexer, implemented as a fir tree.
- Control unit for the interpretation of programs und the arithmetic operations, like, addition, subtraction, multiplication, division and the square root.

Around 2500 modern relays of the company FINDER in Germany were used to reconstruct the Z3. Additionally we used ca. 50 time relays. The functionality is the same as with the relays in the forties.

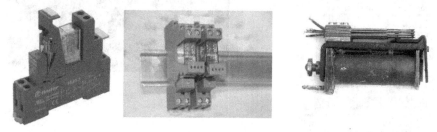

Fig. 7. Left: Modern relays with LEDs of the company FINDER in Germany close to Rüsselsheim. Right: A relay from 1941.

There are two or four switches in a relay. In 2008 we did start the reconstruction of the new Z3 (Z3r) in the working room of our apartment in Berlin Wilmersdorf.

Fig. 8. The working room of the author in Berlin the fifth floor without an elevator. It is the arithmetic unit.

Fig. 9. Left: The design of one memory cupboard. Right: The author building the memory.

Each blue coloured relay is one-bit in the notation of today. There are 768 relays, meaning 768-bits. There is a multiplexer in order to control the addresses of the memory. The green coloured relays on the top show the multiplexer. It looks like a fir tree and was designed by the author. There are five rows to address the 32 memory cells (controlled by the punch tape).

Fig. 10. Left: The punch tape reader. Right: The hidden safe implemented in the input-device. With 60 buttons it is possible to control all the components of the new separately. It did not exist in the original Z3.

3.1   Problems Reconstructing the New Z3

There were a lot of problems reconstructing the new Z3, although there are existing circuits of the Z3 in the patent application Z391 of 1941 /Rojas98/. Konrad Zuse never got this patent; it was rejected in 1967 because of lack of amount of invention. However, it was necessary to modify many circuits. The reasons were among others the following:

- The clock frequency of the new Z3 is realized with special frequency relays of FINDER. The original Z3 had an impulse generator with a drum.
- The control unit of the new Z3 is realized with time relays. It was not possible to get enough stepwise relays.
- Electronic stepwise relays were used instead of mechanical ones.

The next image shows the new Z3 in 2011 in the Heinz Nixdorf Museum Forum in Paderborn.

Fig. 11. The new Z3 in the year 2011

The left and right cupboards are the memories. On the top is the multiplexer for determining the addresses in the memory. It looks like a fir tree with five rows of relays and was designed by the author. In both memories 32 words of 22-bits can be stored. The cupboard in the middle is the arithmetic unit for the exponent und the mantissa. In the front is the input and output device.

Finally the new Z3 will be located in the Konrad-Zuse.Museum in Hünfeld. Till the end of 2013 the Z3 is located in the Deutsche Technik Museum in Berlin.

4   Who Supported the Reconstruction of the Z3

The reconstruction of the new Z3 was very complex. It was much more work than the author and the supporters believed, it was really a hard job. The work was very often interrupted by presentations by the author about history of computing from 2008 till today. The sponsors and supporters of the project came from the area of Hünfeld close to Fulda. Supporters were a lot of companies in Germany.

Sponsors
- Förderung Stiftung der Sparkasse Fulda.
- Zuschuss Land Hessen: Hessisches Ministerium f. Wissenschaft und Kunst.
- Dr. Tim Olbricht aus Hünfeld.
- Eigenanteil Stiftung Stadt- und Kreisgeschichtliches: Museum Hünfeld mit Konrad-Zuse-Museum.

Supporters of the Projekt
- Fa. Dux Elektrokontakt GmbH, 04303 Leipzig: Switches.
- Fa. Eltec Engineering GmbH, 10587 Berlin: Mechanical planning.
- Fa. Finder GmbH, 65468 Trebur-Astheim: Relays.
- Fa. Erwin Krug & Söhne GmbH Co KG, 14199 Berlin: Cupboards
- Fa. Harting Deutschland GmbH Co KG, 32381 Minden: Connections.
- Fa. Wago Kontakttechnik GmbH & Co KG, 32385 Minden: Connexions.
- Kanzlei Hübner & Dr. Körting, 10623 Berlin: Protection of registered design.
- Fa. ELSAME GmbH - Forckenbeckstrasse 9-13, 14199 Berlin: Location of the Z3 in 2011 for further developments.

Literature

/ROJA98/   Rojas Raul (Editor): Die Rechenmaschinen von Konrad Zuse, Springer Verlag, 1998.

This is a detailed analysis of a Konrad Zuse's machines Z1 and Z3 with many new details, also the drawing in the patent application from 1941 are shown. It also contains the report of the fight of Konrad Zuse for his patents from 1938 till 1967. Konrad Zuse lost this fight in 1967 because of lack of amount of invention.

EDSAC Replica Project

Andrew Herbert and David Hartley

The National Museum of Computing, UK
david.hartley@tnmoc.org

Abstract. EDSAC (The Electronic Delay Storage Automatic Calculator) was the world's first practical stored program electronic computer. The goal of the EDSAC Replica Project is to build a *functional replica* of the University of Cambridge EDSAC Computer as it was in 1949, and for the replica to be a working demonstration at the UK National Museum of Computing.

Keywords: EDSAC, replica, functional.

1   EDSAC Background

The Electronic Delay Storage Automatic Calculator (EDSAC) was the world's first practical stored program electronic computer. Running its first program on 6th May 1949 EDSAC provided a scientific computing service to Cambridge University ahead of any similar provision elsewhere. To its users EDSAC represented a thousand fold increment in computing power over the mechanical calculators that preceded it and contributed to three Cambridge Nobel Prizes by enabling faster and larger scale computations than had hitherto been practical.

EDSAC was designed by Maurice Wilkes (later Professor Sir Maurice Wilkes) of the Cambridge University Mathematical Laboratory in 1947. At the instigation of Professor Douglas Hartree, an eminent Cambridge mathematician, Wilkes attended the famous Moore School Lectures at the University of Pennsylvania in the summer of 1946 at which the American computer pioneers presented experience with machines such as the ENIAC and perhaps more importantly, Von Neumann presented a paper on the design of the EDVAC that first crystallised the principles of operation for modern stored program computers. Greatly influenced by EDVAC, Wilkes sketched a design for EDSAC while travelling home on the *Queen Mary* and on arrival back in Cambridge in September 1946 he assembled a team of engineers led by W. Renwick to start construction of a machine.

Events moved quickly after the first successful program ran on 6th May 1949: the machine was completed and a conference took place the following month by which time the computer was already in regular service. EDSAC continued in use for nearly 10 years until replaced by its successor, EDSAC 2. Throughout its life EDSAC underwent continual improvement and by the end of its life, the size of the store had doubled from 512 to 1024 18 bit words, and additional instructions, an index register and magnetic tape storage facilities had been added.

A. Tatnall, T. Blyth, and R. Johnson (Eds.): HC 2013, IFIP AICT 416, pp. 297–308, 2013.
© IFIP International Federation for Information Processing 2013

Fig. 1. EDSAC, May 1949

By the standards of the time, EDSAC ran reliably throughout its life, typically delivering 35 hours of computation a week. Outside of normal hours it often ran unattended by engineers, under the control of authorized users. This can be attributed to the conservative nature of Wilkes' design. The central clock ran at 500KHz, allowing generous margins for internal synchronisation and the architecture was serial, reducing the number of circuits to be constructed from large and expensive thermionic valves.

EDSAC was fondly remembered by its users, many of whom attended a 50th anniversary conference at Cambridge in 1999. Sadly little of the machine survives in physical form and the documentary record in the Cambridge University library is fragmentary. Over the last decade, with the death of Wilkes and most of those who worked with him, knowledge of this important machine in the history of computing is rapidly fading away.

2   Project Aims

The goal of the EDSAC Replica Project is to build a *functional replica* of EDSAC as it was in 1949. By *functional replica* we are expressing the intention to build a machine that runs programs as EDSAC would have done in 1949, which appears physically as similar as possible to the appearance of EDSAC in photographs, is consistent with the surviving documentation and where we have to re-invent parts of the machine, we do so using appropriate historical circuit designs and assembly techniques. We plan to exhibit the EDSAC replica at the UK National Museum of Computing at Bletchley Park.

Our aims for the replica project are that it should:

- Provide a tangible demonstration of the achievements of the Cambridge pioneers.
- Celebrate the achievements of British scientific and technological contributions to the early development of computing.
- Assemble archive material relating to this historic machine and capture the knowledge of the few remaining pioneers who developed and used it.
- Build as authentic a replica as possible taking into account the availability of components and materials and modern safety standards.
- Undertake the work within the spirit of the designers and technology of the time.
- Produce a working artefact of exceptional educational value to students and the general public.
- Be an exemplar of British engineering and encourage new students to take up computing and engineering.
- Demonstrate the working machine to the public as often as is practical once it is built and commissioned at The National Museum of Computing.
- Be constructed and equipped with sufficient spares to enable the machine to run for the next 25 years.
- Train a new generation of volunteers, unfamiliar with 1940s valve technology, to build, run, demonstrate and maintain the replica for the foreseeable future.

3   Project Organization

The second author of this paper (David Hartley) with the encouragement of Dr Hermann Hauser, a well-known Cambridge technology entrepreneur originally conceived the project. Led by Hartley, the University of Cambridge, the British Computer Society and the Hauser-Raspe Foundation jointly set up The EDSAC Replica Project as a registered UK charity. Initial funding came from The Hauser-Raspe Foundation, Google and a private individual who have, at the time of writing, generously contributed half of the estimated project cost of £250,000.

Volunteers are undertaking much of the construction of the replica with some work contracted out to commercial suppliers. The first author (Andrew Herbert) is the Project Manager. Equally important in the leadership of the project is the role of Chris Burton as Chief Designer. Chris brings to the project experience of the restoration of a Ferranti Pegasus computer at the London Science Museum and the construction of a functional replica of the University of Manchester Small Scale Experimental Machine ("Baby") for the Manchester Museum of Science and Industry. The target date for completion is mid to late 2015.

Wilkes was unsentimental about the machines he designed: when EDSAC 2 was ready for use, EDSAC was unceremoniously scrapped to make room for it. Just a few pieces were sent to museums: 3 examples of the most common type of EDSAC chassis and 3 short mercury delay line tubes.

A number of accessories such as hand punches for correcting paper tape also survive but that is all. Fortunately there is a reasonably good photographic record: Wilkes had official photographs made from glass-plate negatives and these remain in the Cambridge University Library. His own personal photograph album has been donated by his family to the Cambridge University Computer Laboratory to put alongside other personal photographs collected at the time of the EDSAC'99 conference. Importantly a 1951 16mm colour film made in the Mathematical Laboratory (the former name of the present Computer Laboratory) showing the operation of the machine survives. However most of the images are undated and it can be seen that significant changes were made to the machine throughout its life and therefore care has to be taken in using them to settle questions about EDSAC's appearance in 1949.

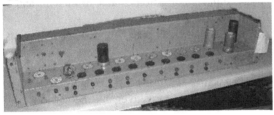

Fig. 2. Surviving EDSAC Chassis

The documentary record is on the surface rather more complete. A key document is *The EDSAC Report* deposited by Wilkes in the University Library. This gives a good overview of the architecture of the machine and its logical design. There are hints at some of the circuit elements used but no description of the physical layout. Moreover it is unclear whether the EDSAC Report is a design specification or a write-up of the completed machine, or perhaps something in between, so it too must be used with caution.

We then have academic papers written about EDSAC. Mostly these are at the architectural level and focus on how EDSAC was programmed – another of the EDSAC innovations was the simplicity and convenience of its programming system. A few papers give more detailed engineering information, particularly about the mercury delay lines used for the main store.

Then there are Wilkes' memoirs and his speeches on EDSAC to various historical societies and computer associations, but these

Fig. 3. Chassis Underside

tend to speak more to the context in which EDSAC was conceived and used than in giving technical detail.

Finally we have some surviving notebooks from the project team and "EDSAC Operating Memoranda" and "EDSAC Programming Bulletins" issued to users of EDSAC that shed some light on technical detail. Early documents on the Lyons LEO I computer have also proved useful: the design of LEO was based on EDSAC and comments in LEO papers about "improvements" relative to EDSAC help us to reverse engineer the original design.

In summary, the project has enough information to know the principles of how EDSAC worked and was used, but lacks most of the detail required to construct an exact replica. The essential project task is to bridge this gap.

4   EDSAC Physical Design

Physically EDSAC consisted of three rows of open racks, each row comprising four, three and five racks respectively and each rack holding up to 14 shelves containing electronics. (Wilkes called the shelves "panels", and in the project we follow more modern terminology and call them "chassis"; our mechanical engineering subcontractor calls them "shelves"). The total footprint of the racks is about 5m^2 and they are approximately 2.5m high. In total there are 142 chassis.

In addition to the racks, further floor space was taken up by wooden "coffins" containing the mercury delay line tanks used for the main store and registers. The coffins provided a level of temperature stability and were approximately 2m long. The store was later moved to a thermostatically controlled oven.

The operator controlled the machine from a simple panel with a Reset and Start button mounted on one of the racks: a paper tape reader for input and teleprinter for output were placed on a wooden table. A separate engineer's desk accommodated a three-oscilloscope unit that allowed the contents of selected memory tubes to be inspected. (Later in the life of EDSAC all these elements moved to a single operator's desk).

EDSAC was powered from a motor generator unit in a separate room: the electrical consumption is estimated at 15KW.

In terms of building a replica, the racks and chassis are relatively straightforward to reconstruct as we have a sample chassis and several photographs from which we can estimate leading dimensions. Working with a local engineering company in Cambridge (Teversham Engineering Ltd) we have CAD models for chassis and racks. In contrast to the original, where making a chassis would probably have taken an engineer most of a day in the Mathematical Laboratory's workshops, using their Computer Aided manufacturing systems, Teversham Engineering can cut, punch, drill and fold chassis in a matter of minutes.

The chassis model is a generic template as different chassis had different punching depending upon the circuits it contained. This is where difficulties arise – we do not have a photograph of every chassis and over the lifetime of EDSAC some chassis were moved, or changed and new functions introduced. To further frustrate us, we know each chassis had an identifying engraved label, and while we can see these on the photographs, the resolution is insufficient to read them, even with modern image enhancement techniques.

Fig. 4. Illegible Chassis Label

We therefore have had to co-design the physical structure of the machine with the logical design and the circuit design. From logical design we can predict which circuit elements might have been used, and from those likely physical layouts of valves and test points on chassis: these can then be matched to photographs. We can further reasonably assume that chassis implementing related parts of the same set of logical functions (e.g., arithmetic, computer control, store addressing etc.) are grouped close together and from that make a well-informed guess as to where those chassis might have been placed in the racks if not fully visible.

In making the physical racks and chassis we have followed original dimensions but for convenience substituted modern metric fixings for the frames. On the chassis we have retained the BA fixings used on the original.

Surprisingly while the valves we need have been relatively easy to obtain from dealers, valve holders have been more difficult and top clips impossible. It is possible to get valve holders made in quantity but they are expensive: they can also be imported from the Far East but the quality is unsatisfactory. In the case of International Octal sockets we have located slightly oversize items and turned them down to standard size to fit the chassis.

Similarly we have been able to get tag strips for connecting components manufactured in bulk, a great convenience as we need at least two for every chassis. Customised tag strips are required for the connections between chassis: these are being hand made as each chassis type has a unique design. Fortunately a suitable punch, tags and blank paxolin strips could be obtained from the same source as the manufactured strips.

Another area requiring custom manufacture has been the provision of electromagnetic delay line inductances. These consist of wound coils on a Tufnol former wired to capacitors on a thick wire frame. Through the British Vintage Wireless Society we have been able to get the coils wound to our specification. The manufacture of formers and wiring up is being undertaken by project volunteers.

An area in which we have chosen to compromise is with passive components such as resistors and capacitors. Modern components are generally much smaller than their equivalents from the 1940s and painted differently. While old components can be found, they have often drifted away from their nominal value and the potential for them failing in use is high. We have therefore decided to use modern components for reasons of reliability. Where possible we look for modern components of a suitably large size (for example by choosing resistors of a higher power rating than necessary) so that the visual appearance is suitable. Further, through our relationship with the British Vintage Wireless Society we have located some suppliers of modern components to old designs. Given the scale of EDSAC we have decided against following some of the society's practices for hand building lookalike versions of old components. To a significant degree this compromise will not impact the appearance of the replica as most of the passive components lie underneath the chassis, and the valves, for which we are using genuine parts, are the most visible and characteristic aspect. We may choose to build one or two representative chassis with correct vintage components for illustrative purposes and to emphasise that the use of more modern ones elsewhere has not compromised the integrity of the replica machine.

5   EDSAC Logical Design

Recovery of the logical design of EDSAC was a key first achievement of the project. Fortunately, from the EDSAC Report and early papers about EDSAC there is a wealth of detail about the functional units within the machine and the data paths between them. The EDSAC Report also contains a number of timing diagrams showing how signals are delayed as they pass through parts of the machine. From this information Bill Purvis has constructed an EDSAC logic simulator called ELSIE that reads in a description of the machine and simulates execution of a program. By stepwise refinement Bill was able to arrive at a design that correctly executes EDSAC programs and was consistent with the functions for which we have descriptions. A number of areas such as paper tape input, teleprinter output and initial instruction loading have been left as black-box subsystems, but most of the rest of the machine has been analysed to a sufficient level of detail to allow circuit design to start.

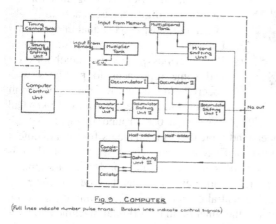

Fig. 5. A Logic Diagram from the EDSAC Report

In early versions of ELSIE signals were represented as rectangular pulses in units of clock pulse intervals. As understanding of the logic developed and circuit elements were designed, the signal model was refined to better represent actual pulse shapes and delays to help the circuit designers determine where pulse resynchronisation and reshaping was required. In the same vein considerations of the timing of signal propagation have helped decide how close the various logical units might have been to one another.

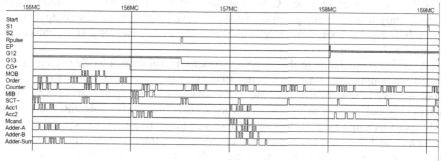

Fig. 6. Typical ELSIE Output

6   EDSAC Electronic Design

Fig. 7. EDSAC Digit Pulse Generator

Electronic design was the area where we had least to start with: the EDSAC Report shows a circuit for a flip-flop, but without any component values stated: we had some hand-drawn diagrams for the clock and digit pulse generating sub-system and just one original chassis from the storage regeneration sub-system. From various papers and notebooks we had some references to problems with specific circuits and the names of circuit elements used. We also know Wilkes had a wartime background in radar and we can look to period textbooks to understand typical circuit elements from that context that might have been used or adapted for EDSAC. From these sketchy foundations Chris Burton has established a library of standard circuits for logic gates, pulse amplifiers and flip-flops for other project volunteers to use as they design complete circuits for logical functions such as the central clocking, arithmetic unit and so forth. Where we know the physical location of the function in the original machine and have a suitable photograph we can check the physical valve layout against the electronic design, and if necessary revise the electronic design to match the physical layout. Circuit design has been further complicated by the fact EDSAC is a serial machine and A.C. coupled making circuit principles unfamiliar to those who have grown up in the transistor age with parallel data paths and D.C. coupled circuits.

From the surviving original chassis and a few close-up photographs of chassis from the early days, Chris has also been able to lay down constructional principles for how individual components should be wired together, standard values chosen for components such as stopper resistors and so forth.

It is sobering to modern eyes to realise that a simple AND gate for EDSAC takes 3 pentode and two double diode thermionic valves, so with a maximum capacity on a shelf of about 18-20 valves, each chassis is limited to 3-4 gates only. With a total of 3,000 valves therefore EDSAC is equivalent to less than 600 gates (and indeed significantly less than this given the need for valve amplifiers to drive output signals etc.). It is easy to appreciate why Wilkes and his team went for a serial rather than parallel architecture.

A recurrent challenge in the on-going work to design replica EDSAC circuits is to avoid the temptation to design a better EDSAC. The temptation comes from several sources. We know from surviving notebooks that some parts of EDSAC were temperamental: the pioneers found workarounds for such problems rather than wholesale redesign as their driving purpose was to get to a fully working machine as soon as possible. Some circuits were later replaced by improved designs. but these are outside the scope of our goal to replicate EDSAC as it was in 1949. For example we have access to more modern components, e.g., plugs and sockets for interconnecting chassis rather than soldering wires between tag strips that would be more convenient and safer. We have been ruthless to avoid such temptations with two exceptions.

First we are putting a 0V (zero volt) rail on each chassis to help with electrical safety: on the original 0V rail was the chassis itself and chassis were tied together and thence to ground. This is a reversible "improvement" – we can chose to connect each such rail to chassis if we change our minds. Second, while we continue with the principle of using wiring between tag strips to interconnect chassis, we are using modern grip fasteners ("fastons") that clip tightly to the tags.

A related concern is the distribution of power and high voltage DC around the machine. The original machine had a motor generator delivering power to each rack that was distributed by soldering wires between short tag strips. We are exploring the possibility of using smaller modern power supplies on a per rack basis and modern connectors to feed power to each chassis for the obvious safety reasons. We also plan to use modern RCCBs for earth leakage and electric shock prevention. In these respects we will be thoroughly in the modern world, and in that spirit our working practices when commissioning and operating the machine will be subject to appropriate levels of health and safety management – something clearly not on the minds of the pioneers judging by some of the hazards visible in the early photographs!

For archival purposes, all of our circuit designs have been captured digitally using "DesignSpark", a circuit design and PCB layout program available from one of the major suppliers of electronic components (RSComponents). We also have a formal system of "Hardware Notes" for capturing key design decisions and principles and investigations into prototype circuits etc.

7   EDSAC Memory

Fig. 8. Wilkes and Mercury Delay Lines

The main store of EDSAC and its internal registers were constructed using mercury delay lines. This was a technology familiar to Wilkes from his wartime radar work, and through a colleague, Tommy Gold, he had the expertise needed to make mercury delay lines for EDSAC. These delay lines present a significant challenge to the replica project. Mercury is expensive and has to be handled as a dangerous substance. The precision engineering required to manufacture the required tubes and end plates is demanding. In service, the delay lines were temperature sensitive and a source of unreliability. Moreover the mercury attacked the seals in the units that had to be replaced and the mercury itself "cleaned" every couple of years.

All these considerations make replicating a mercury delay line store impractical. During the commissioning stage we plan to build an interim store using a modern microcontroller so that, in addition to simulating delay lines, we can provide facilities to preload and inspect store. We will arrange that the interim store has the same electric signal input and output as the original mercury delay lines so that the store access and regeneration circuits will be as in the original, and the option to build a mercury delay line store in the future remains open.

One project member, Peter Linington, has been investigating "nickel delay lines" as an alternative to mercury delay lines. Nickel delay lines were a popular storage technology in the 1950s, bridging the gap between mercury delay lines and ferrite core store. The current plan is to use these to replace the interim microcontroller store. They are a close physical analogue to mercury delay lines in that both use a mechanical transducer to send an acoustic pulse through a medium to "store" it. Conveniently they are also of similar dimensions. While there are surviving example nickel delay lines that can be inspected and technical papers on the physics of the medium, the means of constructing them has

Fig. 9. Nickel Delay Line Prototype Transducer

essentially been lost. Peter has been investigating techniques for annealing the wires, welding the fingers that actuate them and suitable materials to support the wires and to dampen out echoes etc. At the time of writing, he has a sample short delay line, suitable for uses as a register, which operates reliably with an error rate of 1 in 10^{11}, i.e., roughly one bit error per day of operation. Current developments are focussed on building a long delay line suitable for use in the main store. To fit an EDSAC store "coffin" the wire needs to be coiled or folded in half. Techniques to do this are under investigation.

As a long-term ambition we are giving consideration to replicating a short delay line tank (or possibly re-commissioning one of the surviving originals) as a standalone demonstration of how mercury delay lines work.

8   EDSAC Input-Output

Fig. 10. EDSAC tape reader and teleprinter

The original EDSAC took input from 5-hole paper tape, read by an electro-mechanical reader constructed in the Mathematical Laboratory. From Wilkes' personal photographs we have good views of the internal mechanism and John Deane has been sketching a design for manufacturing a replica. We have from the original the sprocket wheel required to pull the tape through. Holes in the tape were mechanically sensed and relays used to capture each row of data and signal it electrically to the computer.

Output was to a teleprinter and again we

have some photographs of the original. Bill Purvis is investigating how a Creed teleprinter from the 1950s could be adapted to meet our needs.

Two related items of "input-output" are the means for loading the initial orders when the Reset button is pressed and the "3-oscilloscope unit" on the engineer's desk. We know from the documentation that the initial orders were wired on a bank of telephony uniselectors and injected into the main store. We also have a photograph of the unit in the original machine. Fortunately uniselectors are still obtainable, and Andrew Brown is in the early stages of designing the initial orders loading sub-system. The 3-oscilloscope unit allowed the operator to select a bank of words in the store and see a visible representation of their content on one of the scopes and the current instruction and its address on the other two: with an execution speed of around 650 instructions per second it was relatively easy to monitor program execution in this way. Currently little work has been put into understanding how this unit was connected or designed internally, but is clearly a critical part of the original that needs to be re-created.

For the initial commissioning phase of the project, and as an operating convenience thereafter, we plan to use a modern PC as a substitute for tape reader and teleprinter (and as mentioned earlier for store also). The details are yet to be worked out but our aim would be to achieve plug compatibility at the lowest level so we can easily switch out the PC and run with real peripherals.

By setting the goal that the replica match EDSAC as it was in 1949, the project team set a challenge to those interested in programming the machine. The first programs ran using "initial orders 1" but in September of that year these had been replaced by David Wheeler's "initial orders 2" which introduced facilities for subroutine linkage and relocation, making it practical to write large programs using a library of standard functions. To run the iconic first programs (table of squares, list of prime numbers) we need initial orders 1. We knew that Wheeler had written a so-called set of "coordinating orders" that allowed initial orders 2 programs to be loaded under initial orders 1 with the coordinating orders as a prelude on their tapes. Unfortunately no description of the coordinating orders survives, and knowing of Wheeler's reputation as a masterful machine code programmer the software team doubted these could be replicated. Somewhat as an experiment we tried using initial orders 1 to load initial orders 2 to the top of store and then copy them down to the bottom end. Much to our delight this worked and so the secret of Wheeler's coordinating orders has been successfully penetrated!

9   Current Status

At the time of writing volunteers are wiring up chassis as follows:
1. The central Clock Pulse Generator – Peter Lawrence
2. The bank of Digit Pulse Generators – John Sanderson
3. The half adder (at the core of the "arithmetic unit") – Nigel Bennée
4. The storage access logic (tank address decoding) – John Pratt.

We have a prototype nickel delay line short tank for register memory – Peter Linington.

Design is underway for the tape reader – John Deane, teleprinter – Bill Purvis and initial instruction loading – Andrew Brown.

Fig. 11. Replica Chassis under Construction

In addition to the named designers above working with Chris Burton our Chief Designer, we have a further 6 or so volunteers helping with construction and most importantly, Alan Clarke who is our storekeeper and seeks out sources for all the parts required.

The aim is to have a first fully operating version of the replica at TNMOC with interim store and I/O by late summer 2015. As a first working exhibit we hope to have a rack on display with clock pulses and counting (i.e., adding) on display this summer (2013).

10   Summary

The goal of the EDSAC Replica Project is to build a functional replica of The University of Cambridge EDSAC Computer as it was when first operating in 1949 and for the replica to be a working demonstration at the UK National Museum of Computing. Little of the original EDSAC survives, but working from photographs and a fragmented documentary record, the project team have resolved many questions of physical, logical and electronic design and are, at the time of writing, constructing the first set of functional EDSAC chassis. The replica will use nickel delay lines for the main store in place of the mercury tanks of the original, but in all other respects the replica will be as close as possible to the original. The target date for project completion is 2015.

Fig. 12.

The Harwell Dekatron Computer

Kevin Murrell

Computer Conservation Society and The National Museum of Computing, UK
Kevin.murrell@tnmoc.org

Abstract. The Harwell Dekatron Computer is a very early digital computer designed and built by the British Atomic Energy Research Establishment in 1952. The computer used British Post Office relays for control and sequencing, and Dekatron counting tubes for storage. After several years' service, it was passed to a college where it was used to teach computer programming, before being lost to various storage centres. In 2008 the machine was re-discovered and the decision was made to restore the computer to working order. This paper describes the machine and the choices and decisions made during the restoration process.

Keywords: Harwell Dekatron Computer, restoration, WITCH, National Museum of Computing, Dekatrons.

1 Introduction: Restoring the Harwell Dekatron Computer

Design of the computer began in 1949 using techniques that were generally well understood, and used components that were available to the Harwell engineers at the time. There seem to have been remarkably few problems with the design when it came to commissioning the machine and running the first few tests, and the computer was completed and first made to work properly in April 1951 using just two of the store units. This was sufficient to prove the machine was functioning correctly, and to allow simple programs to be written to test the machine more fully. By 1952, the team had added the remaining Dekatron store units and handed the computer over to the theoretical physics division for proper use.

The very conservative design of the computer was quite deliberate as it led to a reliable workhorse that could be left unattended to plough through a long series of calculations. Harwell kept precise records of the work done by the computer, and in a paper published in 1953 it was reported that in its first year with the division, from May 1952 to February 1953, the machine ran on average 92½ hours each week or for 55% of the total available time. Typically any lost time was when the machine had finished its allotted tasks and was waiting for its operators to arrive the next morning!

By 1957, the mathematicians at Harwell were making little use of the Dekatron Computer, but did not wish to see the machine broken up, so an imaginative competition was devised to make further use of the computer and give it a new home in education.

On the 25th February 1957, Wolverhampton and Staffordshire College of Technology announced to the world they had won the competition and would soon receive the computer from Harwell. The official commissioning day in

A. Tatnall, T. Blyth, and R. Johnson (Eds.): HC 2013, IFIP AICT 416, pp. 309–313, 2013.

Wolverhampton was Wednesday, 4th December 1957, and at this point the machine was re-christened 'WITCH' – the 'Wolverhampton Instrument for Teaching Computation from Harwell'.

The college quickly established both a full time degree and a Diploma in Technology, and ran regular courses, many in the evening, to introduce computing to local colleges and schools. Computing moves at a frenetic space, and this was especially so during the 1960s and 1970s. The college made full use of the computer until 1973 when it was formally switched off and given to a local museum.

The computer was displayed in the museum for some time, but was eventually dismantled and put into long-term storage. In 2008, the author, by then the secretary of the Computer Conservation Society and a founder trustee of The National Museum of Computing in the UK, discovered a few parts of the machine and set about tracking down the remains of the computer. Quite quickly we discovered the bulk of the computer, albeit broken down into many pieces.

By now, there was a feeling of genuine excitement that this machine could be restored to working order and presented again for the public to see and appreciate. The work on collecting information about the machine continued in earnest, and again fate intervened when at an unrelated BCS (British Computer Society) meeting, we were given the contact details for Ted Cooke-Yarborough who was living near Abingdon – not far from Harwell. Ted was able to contact Dick Barnes, and very soon a meeting was arranged to tell them of our re-discovery of the machine and our plans for its restoration. The project team travelled to Abingdon in March 2009 to meet the two engineers to show them the results of our investigations and discuss our hopes to restore the machine to full working order. Barnes had kept a scrapbook of newspaper cuttings that proved very useful in understanding the history of the machine.

In April 2009 the project team wrote a formal restoration project plan to define what we hoped to achieve, what we needed to complete the project, and to detail any risks along the way. This plan was presented to the Computer Conservation Society (CCS) in May 2009 and was accepted as a new CCS Working Party. The CCS also kindly offered funds towards the initial costs of the project.

Some of the considerations we discussed were:

- Might we simply re-assemble the machine back to its original condition?
- Is enough of the original system available to consider its restoration to working order?
- Do we have the necessary tools and documentation?
- Do we have the sufficient spare parts that might be needed?
- How do we decide what might be replaced?
- Is original software available or accessible?
- Do we have the funds and the space to do this?

In September 2009, the machine was moved to its new home - the Large Systems Gallery at the National Museum of Computing. Even before any restoration work commenced, it was already attracting the curiosity of visitors, many of whom had never seen a computer looking anything like this machine with its rows of Dekatrons, valves and trigger tubes, and mysterious grey canisters filled with relays.

Our objective therefore was to restore the machine to a state where it could be reliably and safely operated for demonstration to the public and the many educational and corporate groups who visit the museum.

In common with all our restoration work, the philosophy is to change as little as possible, particularly external appearance. Although it may be tempting to re-spray a rusty old machine, as one might routinely do when restoring a classic car, we feel this alters the character of the machine – we want our historic exhibits to look their age! In general we confine our activities to cleaning and conservation to prevent further degradation. On the Harwell machine we used electrolysis to treat the areas worst affected by rust.

This computer has had a uniquely long working life, during which it was extensively modified and repaired. We decided early on that we would not attempt to return it to an 'original' condition, and indeed, as work progressed, it became clear that establishing the exact details of the original design would be rather difficult in some areas.

Particularly in the power supplies, it was necessary to replace failed elderly components that are no longer available, some of these being quite prominently visible. In those cases the original components have been left in place, with the much smaller modern replacement components hidden from view. This helps to ensure the machine retains its unique character.

Restoration work fell into three main categories: relays, mechanical, and electronics. The machine came with full circuit diagrams, and an excellent detailed technical description written by Dick Barnes at Harwell. There was also a reasonable quantity of spare components.

Once work had begun in earnest we quickly discovered that the machine deviated from the diagrams in a number of areas, and furthermore that modifications had been made for which documentation hasn't survived. This has made the work more challenging than it might otherwise have been, and efforts are still on-going to fully document the machine in its current state.

2   Relays

The machine was built using Post Office 3000 type relays, which were at the time a mature and well understood technology. They were designed to operate for decades in the harsh environment of a telephone exchange, and consequently were extremely well made. A number of relays were discovered with bent contacts, and one concern was they may have been deliberately set out of normal adjustment to compensate for some timing problem within the design of the machine. In the event we have discovered very few areas that depend critically on relative relay timings.

The long and tedious job of relay adjustment has been rewarded by relatively trouble free operation of the complex relay logic of the machine, which at the time of writing has been working for over two years. During this period the machine has been regularly demonstrated to museum visitors by means of a simple program that reads from two tape readers alternately using block search and transfer control instructions. We anticipate an on-going need for periodic cleaning and adjustment of the relay sets.

3   Mechanical

The output equipment consists of a Creed 7B printer, a Creed 75 tele-printer and a Creed 7TR re-perforator. All of these were specially modified at Harwell to operate with this machine. The printer and re-perforator date from the early 1940s, and so pre-date the rest of the machine by quite a few years.

The standard Creed models used serial I/O – a more primitive version of the RS-232 serial port which until recently could be found on every modern PC. By contrast this machine uses parallel 5-wire I/O. There are standard 5-bit character codes, but in common with many other early computers this machine used a custom character set. One reason for this was to simplify the logic required to assure correct operation – thus the numbers 0-9 that form the instruction code are all represented by combinations of two holes, and the block marking codes used to delineate program or data sections by combinations of three holes. This meant relatively simple logic could detect when an unexpected code was encountered and halt operation.

Restoration of these machines involved nothing more than a good clean and some adjustments – they really were built to last! Again we are fortunate to have experts in this technology at the museum who were able to carry out the work.

4   Electronics

Sequence control is entirely relay based, but arithmetic is all electronic, built using valves, trigger tubes and Dekatrons. There are also two high voltage power supply units – the rectifier unit converts the AC mains into several high DC voltages, and the stabiliser unit generates about a dozen precise DC voltages for use in the various circuits.

The rectifier unit has been extensively modified during the operational life of the machine, and now sports a variety of rectification technologies dating from the 1950s (copper oxide) to the present day (silicon diodes). We had to replace some of the original copper oxide rectifiers with modern components, but others had already been replaced during the machine's time at Wolverhampton. The other major problem in this unit was a leaking oil-filled transformer, eventually solved by copious use of Araldite. All the transformers in the machine were tested to ensure the insulation was still in good condition.

Once the power supplies were operating reliably we turned our attention to the pulse generator, which is one of the most complex parts of the machine. Its main job is to generate various sequences of pulses to step the Dekatrons, but it also has a hand in starting arithmetic operations, deciding when they are complete, and controlling the transfer and carry units which perform the actual addition and subtraction operations. Some of the subtler (and undocumented) aspects of its operation only became clear when it was back on the racks and interacting with the rest of the machine.

The majority of the work was done with the pulse generator on the bench, with a few switches connected up to provide control inputs. We found around half a dozen failed components – mainly diodes and capacitors. The other major issue has proven to be the high-speed trigger tubes which start and stop the Dekatron used in the pulse generator to count out ten pulses. We had a large supply of spare tubes that came with the machine, but the majority turned out not to work. We were lucky to find a supplier who allowed us to test their entire stock of several hundred, but this only yielded a small number of working ones, and some of these no longer work at the time of writing. The most likely explanation is the gas has escaped around where the pins enter the base – this is surprising since the problem of making valves reliably gas tight had been largely solved by the early 1950s. Keeping the machine running long term will eventually require a modification of these circuits to use a more reliable type of trigger tube.

The remainder of the units in the arithmetic rack were repaired one at a time on the bench with the help of the pulse generator and power supplies. These consist of the two halves of the accumulator, which also contain plug-in transfer and carry modules, and the translator unit that converts between 5-wire code and Dekatron compatible pulse trains. The translator is used both when reading numbers from tape into store and when printing out from store. No major issues were found with any of these units bar a handful of failed components.

With the arithmetic rack completed we turned our attention to the stores. The only major problem that Dekatrons suffer from is contamination of adjacent electrodes due to the glow being left on one cathode for a long period of time. This results in 'sticky' operation – either the glow won't reliably step past a particular cathode, or jumps straight over it. Both of these problems cause an incorrect answer. Luckily the process can be reversed by simply allowing the Dekatron to 'spin' for a long enough period.

No detailed operational log of the machine survives, but it's likely some of these faults have been present for many years and were probably partly responsible for the unreliability which we know the machine developed in its later life. These circuits must only just have worked when the machine was new, and hence even small component value changes caused a problem.

The goal of the restoration was to have the machine fully working and as reliable as it was when new. At the time of writing this has largely been achieved, with only a few reliability issues left to solve. The machine is once again able to run the original programs written for it in the 1950s.

The museum plans to produce teachers and students information packs about the machine that can be downloaded in advance of their visit. The packs will include detailed instructions on how the machine is programmed, example programs and potential programming challenges. We also hope to include a software emulation of the computer so that students can prepare programs prior to their visit, and then on the day actually run them on the live machine.

Very little remains of the history of computing in the UK from the late 1940s and early 1950s, and we are very lucky that this machine has led such as charmed life and managed to 'avoid the chop' on several occasions. Its important early role in pioneering nuclear technology, its long second life in education, and its third life as a museum exhibit enthusing young people, can now continue as an active machine enthusing and helping train a new generation of engineers and programmers.

Capturing, Restoring, and Presenting, the Independent Radar Investigation System (IRIS)

Benjamin Trethowan

The National Museum of Computing, Block H, Bletchley Park, Milton Keynes,
Buckinghamshire, United Kingdom
ben.trethowan@tnmoc.org

Abstract. This paper describes a recent project at The National Museum of Computing (TNMoC) to capture, restore to working order, and present to the public, an early air traffic control system. It discusses the importance of capturing an extensive range of information, relating to the system, at the point of donation, the value of this information within the restoration process, the techniques used within the restoration itself, and the value of expressing the social impact of the system in order to convey its relevance to the public.

Keywords: ANSP, ASTERIX, ATS, BEG, CAA, CCC, DEC, DEG, IRIS, LATCC, NATS, NERC, PDP, PRDS, RARE, RBEG, RDI, RDP, TNMoC.

1   Introduction

The Independent Radar Investigation System (IRIS) is an isolated Radar Data Processing (RDP) system, originally used for the investigation of air traffic incidents. It allowed recorded radar and voice (i.e. radiotelephony) data to be replayed together, in synchronisation, for investigative purposes. It was designed and built in the early 1970s at the London Area and Terminal Control Centre (LATCC) in West Drayton, Middlesex, on behalf of National Air Traffic Services (NATS); the UK's Air Navigation Service Provider (ANSP) for all en-route, and a large proportion of terminal, Air Traffic Services (ATS).

The IRIS was in use until the LATCC facility was finally decommissioned in January 2008, when air traffic operations transferred to the New En-Route Centre (NERC) facility in Swanwick, Hampshire. During its operational lifetime, the LATCC facility handled over 48 million aircraft movements.

Prior to the decommissioning of the LATCC facility, NATS had approached The National Museum of Computing (TNMoC) in order to donate the IRIS. It was felt that the IRIS represented a key element of the history of the UK's transport infrastructure, as well as an excellent example of early British computer engineering. TNMoC accepted the IRIS into its collection in April 2008, following its disassembly; packaging, and transport from the LATCC site in March 2008. Both organisations were keen that TNMoC should restore the IRIS to full working order, such that the system could be demonstrated for the enjoyment of the visiting public.

A. Tatnall, T. Blyth, and R. Johnson (Eds.): HC 2013, IFIP AICT 416, pp. 314–319, 2013.
© IFIP International Federation for Information Processing 2013

Between May and September 2008, a small team of volunteers at TNMoC carefully reassembled and restored the IRIS. Restoration activity was completed in October 2008, when the IRIS completed its first successful playback after departing the LATCC facility.

2   Background

The IRIS system is itself a small, standalone installation of a much larger RDP system, the Processed Radar Display Subsystem (PRDS). The operational requirement of PRDS was to "*accept radar plot and label data, flight plan data, etc. and to process and display this data.*"[1] In short, the PRDS provided air traffic controllers with their operational situation display, indicating the current position of all aircraft within the selected radar range and system coverage.

The PRDS was not the primary means of radar data processing, but provided a bypass function "*intended to provide an alternative radar display service when the Central Computer Complex (CCC) is unavailable.*"[1] In short, the PRDS accepted processed radar data, from a primary source, and displayed this to an air traffic controller during normal operations. However it also provided an alternative means of processing radar data, known as 'bypass', should the primary source fail for whatever reason.

The IRIS is composed of a small subset of the PRDS subsystems, representing the smallest / simplest collection of subsystems necessary to generate an operational situation display from recorded radar data. The IRIS is capable of processing a maximum of three radar data channels simultaneously, and displaying a maximum of two of these channels, on an operational situation display, at any one time.

The PRDS system architecture, and hence the IRIS system architecture, is based upon the use of the Digital Equipment Corporation (DEC) Programmed Data Processor (PDP) – 11 range. The IRIS uses four such PDP-11 processors, as follows; two PDP-11/34 processors for the Display Equipment Groups (DEGs), used to render vector graphics onto two operational situation displays, one PDP-11/84 processor for the Bypass Equipment Group (BEG), used to process two radar data channels, and one PDP-11/84 processor for the Redundant Bypass Equipment Group (RBEG), used to process one radar data channel and control / monitor all other systems.

To achieve playback within the IRIS; recorded radar data is fed into the RBEG and BEG systems for processing, the processed radar data is then passed onto the DEG systems for rendering, with the vector graphics commands then being passed onto the operational situation display (also known as the Sector Equipment Group (SEG)) for drawing onto the screen.

Both the RBEG and BEG systems continually process incoming radar data, regardless of the channel; range, or other selection made at the operational situation display. The DEG systems react to input from the operational situation displays, and are responsible for rendering the display in accordance with the selected channel; dual-channel, range, map overlay, and other user-selectable settings.

3   Capture

At the time of the original donation, both NATS and TNMoC were keen to ensure that as much supporting material / additional artefacts, relating to the IRIS, were captured as soon as possible. The LATCC site was due to be demolished shortly after the facility was vacated, so the only opportunity to accept and preserve this supporting material would have to be taken at the earliest possible stage. The exploitation of this opportunity, and the broadness of the material captured, later proved to be a vital element in achieving the successful restoration of the IRIS.

One of the first issues experienced during the restoration, which was only resolved as a result of the original broad capture, was that of bespoke system design. Despite the fact that the IRIS subsystems utilised a popular computing platform of the period (DEC PDP-11), it transpired that a large amount of the hardware within these platforms was either of a bespoke design, or had been modified. One such example concerned the Radar Data Interface (RDI) hardware contained within the RBEG and BEG systems. Whilst the RDI hardware was modeled on a familiar full-size UNIBUS card, for obvious reasons, the microelectronics upon the card were developed specifically for the PRDS by the systems' original supplier, Plessey. Initial problems with the RDI hardware, relating to component failure, were only resolved during the restoration process due to the availability of the original Plessey schematics, which had been captured alongside the IRIS at the point of donation. Had this information not been captured when it was, it would have long since been lost; given that the demolition of the LATCC site would have progressed several months by this stage. Considering also that the PRDS implementation was unique, there would have been no alternative source for this information.

A similar issue experienced during the restoration, resolved again by the availability of supporting material, was that of legacy proprietary data communication protocols. The UK Civil Aviation Authority (CAA) had developed a proprietary protocol for the exchange of radar data, based upon a synchronous serial method of communication. The IRIS subsystems were designed to accept radar data only in this format, and were not able to process more recent radar data formats such as the All Purpose Structured Eurocontrol Surveillance Information Exchange (ASTERIX) format. The need to monitor, test, and generate, radar data for the IRIS RDP subsystems, spawned a further need to first understand the CAA radar data format itself. Luckily, the original specification for this radar data format, issued by the CAA, had also been captured alongside IRIS at the point of donation.

In addition to the engineering issues mentioned previously, the successful restoration was also dependent upon gaining an acceptable appreciation of the complex operational context within which the IRIS system originally operated. The PRDS subsystems, from which IRIS is built, originally interfaced with a multitude of additional operational systems, performing functions such as aeronautical messaging; code / callsign conversion, meteorological data communication, and flight plan processing, etc. It was therefore necessary to understand how the IRIS subsystems should operate without the support of these additional systems, and how that might affect the behaviour that the IRIS would exhibit in its initial stages of operation, following restoration. Again, the initial capture had managed to preserve complete PRDS schematics, including training course material on how the PRDS operated with the additional LATCC systems. Without the availability of this sort of documentation, the successful restoration of the IRIS almost certainly would not have been possible.

4   Restoration

As well as reaping the benefits of a broad capture at the point of donation, the restoration team also utilised a number of other techniques to combat additional challenges and ensure success.

Unfortunately, it is almost never possible to capture absolutely everything that might be required to facilitate a successful restoration. Setting aside the common issues of storage capacity, transport costs, and underfunding, it is often the case that some supporting artefacts have already been lost; prior to the initial offer of donation being made.

For example, the technical documentation associated with a radar data recording and replay system, supplied alongside the IRIS, had already been lost; prior to the removal of the IRIS and its associated artefacts in April 2008. This recording and replay system, known as RARE, would later prove to be an essential element in achieving the successful restoration of the IRIS, by acting as a source of the CAA format radar data necessary to achieve playback. A number of issues were initially encountered during the restoration of the RARE system, many associated with the total lack of documentation and / or understanding of how the system should respond in certain situations, or when given certain stimuli. In an attempt to combat these issues, the restoration team contacted the original donor, NATS; made a number of external enquiries, and conducted a small amount of research, in order to trace a technical contact for the RARE system that might be able to provide the necessary information. After a number of weeks, an individual who had not only worked for the original manufacturer of the RARE system, but who had also been personally involved in its design, contacted TNMoC to offer his assistance. The information that this individual was able to provide, either in hard copy form, or through technical interchange meetings, led to the successful restoration of the RARE system, and subsequently the IRIS.

A similar situation was encountered in relation to the IRIS subsystems themselves. In this case, the issue was not that the supporting material had not been captured, or lost, but that it simply did not exist. A recurring issue, observed within the power supply units of some of the IRIS subsystems, did not appear to have been documented within any of the material available to the restoration team. After extensive investigations, the restoration team contacted the original donor, NATS, in order to ascertain whether any similar issues had been observed whilst the system was in service at the LATCC facility. Following discussions with NATS, it transpired that the issue we were observing was, in fact, a known one; and was the result of incorrect technical documentation. Whilst many of the existing NATS engineers were aware of this issue, and its cause, this information was not passed on to TNMoC at the point of donation as it had, quite simply, been forgotten about. The support of the original donor, and existing third-party suppliers, proved to be vital in these circumstances.

5   Challenges

Whilst many of the challenges encountered during the restoration process were resolved through the use of supporting material, or through contact with the original donor and its third-party suppliers, some could only be resolved through the successful application of engineering best practice.

One such challenge was that of degraded magnetic tape media, a common feature of many computer restoration projects. An additional radar data recording and replay system, known as the SE7000, had been supplied alongside the IRIS and accompanied by a number of radar data recordings on multi-track magnetic tape. The SE7000 is, quite simply, a multi-track magnetic tape deck, with multiple read / write heads that are used to record / replay multiple radar channels simultaneously. When inspecting the magnetic media that we had been given, it became apparent that the media was suffering from the common problem of oxide separation. The restoration team was fortunate enough to have been given some additional media however, which did not exhibit the separation issue. Thankfully, this has meant that we have been able to stop short of attempting to restore the degraded media, using a potentially hazardous process, for the time being.

Similar degradation issues were found to have affected the drive mechanism itself, with numerous rubber capstans and drive belts, etc. having perished. Contemporary replacement parts were found to resolve these issues however, allowing us to operate the SE7000 unit temporarily, in order to capture the radar data from any operable media onto a more suitable modern format.

Interestingly, the more recent RARE system suffered from similar issues, despite its use of closed tape cartridges (Exabyte) instead of open tape reels. A series of recurring issues were encountered with the Exabyte drive mechanisms, which had not been maintained since their withdrawal from service many years before the point of donation. A lack of suitable spares further exacerbated this problem, and led to the decision to immediately retire the RARE unit; following the successful capture of radar data from any operable media onto a more suitable modern format.

6   Social Impact

After defeating the many challenges of restoration, and successfully demonstrating the IRIS in full working order since October 2008, it is perhaps worth considering some of the motivations behind this project.

The IRIS offers us a unique opportunity to convey the impact that computing technology has had upon society, demonstrating why the history and development of computing is relevant to our visiting public. Our visitors have the opportunity to both study and interact with something that was a vital component of the UK's transport infrastructure for over 25 years, something that they can immediately identify with if they have ever flown away on holiday, or to a business meeting, etc.

It also delivers a significant visual impact as an operational exhibit; its size, and 'retro' appearance, provide a visually captivating display, far removed from the so-called 'beige boxes' that many of our visitors expect to see.

And finally, it presents us with an additional educational opportunity to captivate the many young people that visit our museum, and explain just how the development of computing technology has kept, and continues to keep, us safe in the sky.

Reference

1. National Air Traffic Services: Processed Radar Display Sub-system for the Civil Aviation Authority, vol. 1, RSL 1631, CRSS/A1/01 (April 1975)

Author Index

Printed in the United States
By Bookmasters